510.092 Ham O'Do   221700
O'Donnell.
William Rowan Hamilton.

The Lorette Wilmot Library
Nazareth College of Rochester

William Rowan Hamilton

Portrait of a Prodigy

Profiles of Genius Series
ISSN O332-3218

Volume 1: William Rowan Hamilton: Portrait of a Prodigy
by Seán O'Donnell (1983)
ISBN 0-906783-06-2 Hardback

Volume 2: George Boole: His Life and Work
by Desmond MacHale (1984)
ISBN 0-906783-05-4 Hardback

Further titles to be announced

William Rowan Hamilton

Portrait of a Prodigy

Seán O'Donnell

WITHDRAWN

BOOLE PRESS DUBLIN

LORETTE WILMOT LIBRARY
NAZARETH COLLEGE

*All rights reserved. No part of this publication
may be reproduced, stored in a retrieval system or
transmitted in any form or by any means, electronic,
electrostatic, magnetic tape, mechanical, photocopying,
recording or otherwise, without prior permission in
writing from the publishers.*

Boole Press Limited
P.O. Box 5, 51 Sandycove Road,
Dún Laoghaire, Co. Dublin, Ireland.

Copyright © Boole Press Limited
First Edition 1983

Volume 1 'Profiles of Genius'   ISBN 0332-3218
Hardback ISBN 0-906783-06-2

221700

British Library CIP Data
O'Donnell, Seán
    William Rowan Hamilton. — (Profiles of Genius, ISSN 0332-3218; v. 1)
    1. Hamilton, *Sir* William Rowan   2. Mathematicians — Ireland —Biography
    I. Title   II. Series
    510'.92'4   QA29.H2
ISBN 0-906783-06-2
ISBN 0-906783-15-1 Pbk

Computer-generated and typeset in 11 pt. Plantin by Printset and Design Ltd., Dublin
Printed in Ireland by Mount Salus Press Limited, Dublin
Cover Design by Frances Boland

510.092
Ham
O'Do

Contents

PART II: MATURITY

PART III: DECLINE

LIST OF ILLUSTRATIONS

CHRONOLOGY

1800, July 3:	Archibald Hamilton marries Sarah Hutton in Dublin.
1805, Aug. 4:	Their fourth child, William Rowan Hamilton, born.
1808:	Sent to be educated by Uncle James at Trim.
1813, May 1:	Pronounced master of three languages.
1815:	Learning Sanskrit and oriental languages.
1817, May 10:	Mother Sarah dies.
1818:	First meeting with Zerah Colburn.
1819, Dec. 10:	Father Archibald dies.
1820, Nov. 22:	Starts Newton's *Principia*.
1822, July 11:	Solves a problem defeating his future tutor.
Sept. 23:	Mentions 'some curious discoveries' in mathematics.
1823, July 7:	First place in Trinity College Entrance Examination.
1824, Aug. 17:	Meets Catherine Disney.
Dec. 13:	Submits unsuccessful paper *On Caustics* to Royal Irish Academy (RIA).
1825, May 5:	Catherine Disney marries.
1827, April 23:	Submits successful paper on *Systems of Rays*.
June 16:	Appointed Professor of Astronomy at Dunsink.
Sept. 15:	First meeting with Wordsworth.
1829, Aug:	Wordsworth visits Dunsink.
1830, Feb. 10:	Adare arrives to study.
1831, Sept. 1:	Meets Ellen de Vere.
Dec. 7:	Rejected by her.
1832, March:	Visits Coleridge in London.
Oct. 22:	Predicts existence of conical refraction.
1833, April 9:	Marries Helen Bayly.
	Publishes *Third Supplement* to *Systems of Rays*.
1834, April 10:	Submits papers on *General Methods in Dynamics*.
1835, June 1:	Presents idea of *Algebra as Science of Pure Time*.
Aug. 15:	Knighted at Dublin meeting of British Association for Advancement of Science.
1837, Dec. 12:	Elected President of RIA.
1840, March:	Wife Helen leaves him for two years.
1843, March:	Board requests annual public report on Dunsink.
May 25:	Awarded pension from Civil List.

Oct. 16:	Discovers quaternions.
1844, Aug:	Starts series of eighteen papers on quaternions.
1845, April:	Catherine Disney/Barlow visits Observatory.
1846, Feb. 11:	Incapacitated at meeting of Geological Society.
March 16:	Resigns as President of RIA.
Dec. 14:	Reports discovery of hodograph.
1847, Oct. 24:	Suicide of MacCullagh.
1848, June:	Starts writing *Lectures on Quaternions*.
Sept:	Gives up attempt at abstinence.
1851, April:	Becomes churchwarden at Castleknock.
May 14:	Poetess sister Eliza dies.
Nov. 15:	Aubrey de Vere becomes a Catholic.
1853:	*Lectures on Quaternions* published.
Oct:	Catherine Disney dies.
1856, Aug:	Invents Icosian calculus.
1858:	Starts writing *Elements of Quaternions*.
Aug:	Tait introduced as disciple of quaternions.
1863, July:	Helps to save RIA from loss of independence.
1865, Jan. 9:	Elected first among Foreign Associates by American National Academy of Sciences.
May 13:	Falls ill with gout.
Sept. 2:	Dies at Dunsink.
1866:	*Elements of Quaternions* published.
1882 — 1891:	Biography, by Robert Graves, published in three volumes.
1889, March 3:	Sister Sydney dies in New Zealand.
1926:	Hamilton's treatment applied to quantum mechanics.
1931 — 1967:	Collected mathematical papers appear in three volumes.
1980:	Second biography published, by Thomas Hankins.

Sir William Rowan Hamilton

Formal Portrait, Courtesy Royal Irish Academy
Painted by Sarah Purser, from a photograph

FOREWORD

by A. J. McConnell

Joint Editor of the Hamilton Mathematical Papers

Mathematicians usually lead quiet unobtrusive lives, in which the general public are not interested since their work is in any case intelligible only to other mathematicians. However William Rowan Hamilton, the greatest Irish mathematician and one of the great mathematicians of all time, is an exception to this rule.

His life was relatively quiet but it was certainly not unobtrusive. As a child, he was widely recognised as a prodigy; he became Astronomer Royal of Ireland at the age of 22 while still an undergraduate at the university; he was knighted at 30 for the scientific work he had already achieved and, even at the beginning of his career, was regarded by many as a future second Newton. His mathematical work, important as it was regarded immediately after publication, became even more important half a century after his death when it was found to be essential for the development of the revolutionary new theories of physics in the present century. Hamilton also discovered an algebra of so-called imaginary numbers, called quaternions, which opened up a vast new field of mathematics and curiously enough started for a time an esoteric cult for many people who, in fact, had not the foggiest idea of what a quaternion actually was.

More important still for our knowledge of the man himself, Hamilton was an incorrigible letter-writer and he left an enormous mass of correspondence which put on record his everyday activities, his innermost thoughts and emotions. We have therefore the sources for a biography that can be fascinating even for those who understand very little of his scientific work.

Dr. Séan O'Donnell has done an excellent job in writing such a book in which he gives us a vivid account of Hamilton's unique education, his poetry, his social life (he loved meeting people), his lonely and isolated years at Dunsink, his triumphs and his failures, his unhappy marriage and even his romantic and unfulfilled love-affair which tormented him all his life. It is a tale well told and above all, it is the story of a very human person.

AUTHOR'S PREFACE

Genius originally referred to the Roman god of productivity, who was a tutelary divinity directly related to the guardian angel of later Christian times. Each state and city was deemed to be watched over by its own particular genius and so too was every individual. In this way, genius came to be regarded as a sort of higher and better self from which protection and also inspiration was derived.

From such origins the modern idea of genius has gradually evolved. Now it denotes superior intellectual or artistic ability or understanding, particularly if accompanied by unusual creativity. In this way, the topic is of interest to psychologists and educators, to historians and indeed to all who are interested in the general development of human affairs.

The origins and characteristics of genius are however still very poorly described and even less understood. Too little is known of individual case histories to make it possible to generalise with confidence. That genius should be almost synonymous with high intelligence seems no more than obvious; yet all too often, this high intellectual ability is not displayed consistently. Neither does unusual intellect necessarily guarantee a high level of creativity, any more than lack of intelligence denotes a total absence of inventiveness. In short the aetiology of genius, the science of its causes and origins, can scarcely yet be said to have begun.[1]

It is with a view to making some contribution to this notable lacuna in our understanding that the present work is written. Our subject, William Rowan Hamilton, was a famed child prodigy whose youthful attainments have not been accurately assessed before. He grew up to become one of the greatest mathematicians of the 19th century and was indeed widely recognised as such during his own lifetime. Yet Hamilton's main contribution to modern mathematics could not be utilised or even recognised until a full sixty years after his death. He has therefore been aptly described as an 18th-century figure who happened to live in the 19th, while still mainly speaking for our own times.[2]

Like many inventors and innovators, Hamilton was thus often out of step with his contemporaries. To compound the irony, he died engrossed in a mistaken bid for immortality and obviously quite unaware of the most important source on which his future reputation would grow.

Hamilton was also a fascinating personality, embodying in many ways the layman's stock image of the absent-minded scientist. His study resembled an intellectual pigsty, awash with papers, and yet he could always tell if anyone had disturbed its order even fractionally. He was typically late for appointments, inclined to great surges of work when the creative urge seized him and blessed with the happy delusion that he could always explain himself to the average listener.

In addition Hamilton was poet, philosopher and even occasional astronomer. His many observations on the connections between creativity and poetry, and between mathematics and beauty, still seem surprisingly relevant. He also perceived it as his conscientious duty to leave on record as much as possible concerning his intellectual habits. Such records go back to early childhood, so enabling the biographer to trace his intellectual development through its various stages in great detail.

Hamilton is therefore an especially appropriate subject for a descriptive study of the development of genius in a highly creative individual. Two very adequate biographies already exist. The first by his friend, Robert P. Graves, appeared in the 1880s and to its author we are indebted for preserving many personal papers and anecdotes. Graves was all-embracing to the point of exhaustion for the modern reader and his book exhibits a certain lack of perspective because of the inclusion of so much detail. His work is nevertheless much more than the conventional Victorian hagiography and all scholars of Hamilton must remain deeply in his debt.[3]

The second major biography has appeared only recently, almost exactly a century after the first. Thomas L. Hankins is an historian of science who has, with scholarship and precision, clarified Hamilton's significant role in the world of mathematics. His researches have also unearthed and reassembled many personal details which Victorian propriety obliged Graves to conceal. He has clearly produced the definitive biography of Hamilton in the context of the history of mathematics.[4]

The present work has a different purpose. It is an attempt to come to grips with Hamilton's formidable personality rather than his achievements, to further an understanding of the individual rather than of what he did. These aims are again most readily attained through the historical treatment of personal development, so that in this manner therefore the pyschological portrait also comes to resemble biography.

As a consequence of this approach, even the most recondite achievements thereby appear less mysterious because ordinary mortals are enabled to form a better appreciation of how they came to be. In this manner, our aim of striving towards a better understanding of genius in general is hopefully enhanced.

While furthering such objectives, various new findings and also possibilities for further research have been unearthed in the present work.

We can now for example reassess the previously unclear role of Hamilton's early tutor, Uncle James. The fable of young William's thirteen languages, generally accepted uncritically by most reference works, is likewise scrutinised. Furthermore, there is the hitherto overlooked but very obvious evolution from his youthful speculations on the origins of Euclid, to his own later ideas on the possible connection between algebra and time.

There is also a possible new solution to the longstanding legend of physical paternal connection between our subject and the Irish patriot Archibald Hamilton Rowan.

Every researcher on Hamilton must ultimately turn to his large legacy of letters and work-books, most of which are now lodged in the archives of Trinity College, Dublin. There are approximately six thousand letters concerning Hamilton and about two hundred and fifty notebooks; their combined total probably runs to the order of ten million words. This estimate is quite distinct from the equally vast body of purely mathematical writing interspersed and often intermingled with the manuscripts.

At first glance one might think that Hamilton had never left his pen down, so extensive is his literary legacy. Calculation however suggests that an hour or two of regular writing daily would have been more than adequate. The total number of letters which have survived, for example, would merely average one missive in and out weekly over a lifetime of sixty years.

Hamilton may then have been notable more for the manner in which he preserved his correspondence, including numerous drafts, rather than for the total of non-mathematical material he wrote. Taking another scientist for obvious comparison, it is salutary to note that Einstein left about six times as many documents.[5]

For permission to use these manuscripts, I am indebted to the Board of Trinity College, Dublin. I am equally grateful to Keeper of the Manuscripts, William O'Sullivan and to Stuart Ó Seanóir for their unfailing courtesy and help at various points. I am likewise indebted to Professor Patrick Wayman, Director of Dunsink Observatory, and to Mrs. Dolan of the Royal Irish Academy.

I owe further thanks to Mr. Johnston of the Dublin Civic Museum for sharing with me his great knowledge of the capital a century and a half ago. The same applies to Mr. William Stuart for aid unstintingly given during his parallel research into the history of Irish horology. Gary Tee of Auckland University, New Zealand, researched the details of Hamilton's last sister Sydney, during her final years. And it was my wife Eileen who helped with the typescript at a crucial stage.

Finally, I am indebted to Trevor West and W.T. Coffey, both of Trinity College, Dublin, along with Diarmuid O'Mathuna of Boston. They were immensely helpful in highlighting various errors of background and interpretation; any remaining faults in expression do not of course derive from them.

Seán O'Donnell

PART I

GROWTH

1 ANCESTORS AND ORIGINS

"We ... claim to be Scotch of the time of James I, but believe that our pedigree can be traced back beyond the Norman Conquest to certain Earls of France."

Hamilton to de Morgan, July 26, 1852

William Rowan Hamilton was, by any measure, the greatest scientist that Ireland has yet produced. Born in a fashionable Dublin suburb in 1805, he has several times stated that his ancestors came over from Scotland two hundred years before. He also thought that they might be traced back even earlier to the knights of Normandy.[1] Since these origins are both interesting and relevant, it is of importance to indicate the various stages through which they may have transpired.

Hamble was an old English word meaning 'crooked' and there were various rivers in Yorkshire and elsewhere of that name. *Dún* or *done* likewise meant a 'treeless hill', so that the roots of the fairly common mediaeval place-name *Hambledun* or *Hameldone* seem clear.[2]

When the Normans conquered England after 1066, they often adopted surnames associated with their new territories. And as they advanced further north into Scotland, these territorial surnames naturally spread too. About 1315 we therefore find the ancient Gaelic territory of Cadzow being allocated to a follower of Robert the Bruce called Walter Fitz Gilbert *de Hameldone*. This land lay twelve miles southeast of modern Glasgow and in due course its owners were granted noble title as the Dukes of Hamilton.[3]

In later years, the Hamilton family also conferred their title on the local township which now goes by that name. From the same locality in succeeding centuries, emigrant descendants spread worldwide, establishing new settlements having the ancestral place-name in places as diverse as New Zealand, Canada, Australia and Bermuda.

The Irish Hamiltons

Some of these pioneering Hamiltons naturally also came to Ireland. There however, the Norman Conquest had never been anywhere near as complete or successful as in the neighbouring isle. So it is not altogether surprising to find that the first Hamilton of importance to set foot in Ireland did so as a

3

spy. When 28-year-old James Hamilton from Ayrshire landed in Dublin in 1587, he was on a secret mission for his monarch King James VI. To mask his purpose he opened a Latin school in Great Ship Street and one of his first pupils there was the future Biblical chronologist, Archbishop Ussher.[4]

At any rate Hamilton's cover was evidently very effective for by 1592 we find him appointed as one of the first fellows in nearby Trinity College. The College had just been established by Queen Elizabeth as part of the University of Dublin the year before.[5]

James Hamilton was duly rewarded for his enterprise when his Scottish monarch succeeded Elizabeth to the combined thrones of England and Scotland in 1603. He was awarded large estates confiscated from the older Gaelic race of Catholic Irish noblemen, much as his predecessor Walter Fitz Gilbert had been enriched in Scotland three centuries before. James built a great castle at Killyleagh in County Down to dominate his new possessions. Other relatives also joined him in the great Scottish takeover of land from the Irish natives, part of the mass migration known to historians as the Plantation of Ulster.

Two hundred years later, there were many distantly related Hamiltons scattered throughout the upper echelons of Irish society as landowners, soldiers, prominent professional or business men. Less influential members often served as curates in the Established Church. The Church of Ireland at that time was a sort of repository of intellect, because a very high proportion of the most academically able spent some time in Holy Orders. All of these clergymen were an integral part of the Ascendancy; they formed the dominant class who, combined with other denominations like Methodism or Presbyterianism, formed in toto some one million Protestants. These kept about four times that number of the earlier native or Catholic class effectively subdued.

In keeping with their Norman origins, nearly all Protestants declared at least partial allegiance to England. Catholics on the other hand mostly wanted more freedom and greater independence from the Crown. Indeed the continuing struggle between these two great polarising forces in Irish society is not yet fully resolved and it forms an ever-present part of the background throughout our subject's life and times.

A brief consideration of some earlier intellectual Hamiltons may illustrate the general social climate into which young William Rowan Hamilton was born. There was for example an earlier scientist called William Hamilton (1755-1797), no near relation as far as can be ascertained. He was a mineralogist and meteorologist in an era when these sciences had scarcely begun. He also helped to found a discussion group called the Palaeosophers, a learned society which soon merged with the rival Neosophers to form the Royal Irish Academy in about 1785. Later, William became a Church of Ireland rector and also local magistrate at Fanad in County Donegal. There, he succeeded in making himself so unpopular with the local inhabitants that they eventually murdered him.[6]

Another intellectual was the Rev. James A. Hamilton who enjoyed a more serene career. He had his own private observatory at Cookstown in County Tyrone. Astronomy at that time was much in favour with the clerical establishment, largely because it was confidently expected that following Newton's discoveries, it would in due course provide further proof of the Creator's wisdom. In 1791, James Hamilton was appointed director of the major new observatory which Primate Rokeby had just established at Armagh. There he remained until his death twenty-four years later, supported by tithes from several parishes while writing papers on astronomy.[7]

At least two Hamiltons also distinguished themselves in very different literary fields. Elizabeth Hamilton (1758-1816), a Belfast novelist and writer on education, was one of the earliest women active in this sphere.[8] Her career was quite different from that of Dublin-born James Hamilton (1769-1829), a businessman who launched internationally his own novel method of rapid language learning. His Hamiltonian system, which anticipated modern practice, stressed meaning instead of grammar; it was a revolutionary innovation and was demonstrated successfully in American centres like Hartford, Harvard, Princeton and Yale.[9]

Finally, there was Archibald Hamilton Rowan, a rebel aristocrat destined to succeed to the original lands and title of Killyleagh. A rake and a spendthrift in early life, Archibald was to mature into a genuine liberal. He took the second surname Rowan at the age of sixteen so as to gain an inheritance from his maternal grandfather. Well known as a befriender of the underprivileged, he became involved with the United Irishmen who were then actively conspiring against English rule. For these activities, he was imprisoned for a time in Dublin, but then succeeded in escaping and fleeing into exile in 1795.[10]

During these latter escapades, Archibald H. Rowan was greatly aided by a much younger legal friend who had been associated with the family from early days — one Archibald Hamilton from Dublin. And since he was to become the father of our subject, it is at this point that the story of William Rowan Hamilton specifically begins ...

The Two Archibalds

The exact and somewhat curious relationship between the two Archibalds is of some consequence, directly affecting one of the more durable legends concerning our subject. This was the opinion, widely held in Dublin, that Archibald H. Rowan was in fact William Rowan Hamilton's real father!

Three arguments have traditionally been advanced to support this view. First there is the striking continuity of the Rowan title, bestowed as a first name on the younger man. Then there is the fact that our subject was packed off more or less permanently to the country by his family at the age of three. Finally there is the striking similarity in physical appearance between the two, a resemblance clearly obvious if one compares the older

Archibald Hamilton Rowan in old age   *(after Drummond's 'Life')*

portraits of our subject in later chapters with that of Hamilton Rowan, reproduced here.

More detailed consideration however soon indicates that the possibility of Archibald H. Rowan being William Rowan Hamilton's natural father is very difficult to sustain. The older man was under very strict legal banishment in London at the crucial time.[11] And since he was a very tall and imposing figure, well-known in Dublin, it would have been uncommonly imprudent for him to venture back there while the State was considering a full pardon. The choice of Rowan as a middle name for the youngster does seem a bit more leading but if so, the reasons for it were likely rather different from those previously surmised. Finally, the fact that the young boy was despatched to his uncle in the country most likely had nothing at all to do with the questions of paternity; its origins rather lay in financial and educational considerations which we will examine in due course.

This still requires the highly striking resemblance between the two to be explained. Ordinary experience would suggest that there must have been some close physical connection here. Concerning this question, my own research suggests very strongly how such might readily have transpired. It indicates that A. H. Rowan may very well have been our subject's grandfather rather than his father!

To examine this possibility in proper context, we must go back as far as 1763. Archibald H. Rowan was then just twelve years old and his mother, Mrs. Gawen Hamilton, had recently adopted a young Scottish girl aged about fifteen. She was Grace McFerrand from the parish of Kirkmaiden on the Scottish coast opposite Killyleagh and she would have spent most of her time with her patroness at the town houses in London and Dublin.[12] There too or nearby would have lived Archibald and also his much younger sister with the curiously masculine name, Sydney.

In 1773 however, Archibald suddenly left London under mysterious circumstances to live on the Continent for several years. His biographer and descendant, Harold Nicolson, finds this move quite inexplicable and "can only imagine that some unfortunate love affair drove him from his home". Archibald did however return from time to time to stay with his mother; other sources reveal that he made several secret visits to Ireland during these years. Finally he married another ward of the household in 1781.[13]

It was also during these same years that Grace McFerrand married one William Hamilton in Dublin. He was an apothecary and contemporary street directories first reveal him in business at Anglesea Street in 1774. A year later he had moved to 30 Jervis Street and there the family would remain for nearly thirty years.[14]

No date has yet emerged for the marriage of William and Grace McFerrand, but it was very likely around the time he changed houses in 1774. We can surmise this because the parish records of their local church (St. Mary's in Jervis Street) record a son, Arthur Rowan, born to the couple on July 6, 1775. Indeed the change of residence may have been facilitated by the dowry of £500 which his new bride brought him, a sum hardly over-generous in view of the fact that Mrs. Gawen Hamilton's income would then have been about £8,000 per year.[15]

Three other surviving children were born to Grace McFerrand in subsequent years, all of them destined to shape the life of our subject during the next century. James who lived to become his formative mentor was born in 1776, according to Hamilton's first biographer, Robert Graves. Jane Sydney who played an equally important role in his childhood was born in 1779, according to the same source. And finally there was Archibald, a child whose name if not leading must seem alternatively a little unwise. He was to be our subject's future father and Graves assigns him the birth-date 1778 from entries in an old family bible.[16]

There is something clearly mysterious about these datings. For one thing, the parish records of St. Mary's do not record in any form the births of either James or Sydney — as if perhaps they were not born in this locality. The Hamilton shop however remained at 30 Jervis Street for almost thirty years, from 1775 onwards. Then Archibald is registered as having been born on March 15, 1779!

The manner of Archibald's birth registration is also curious and indeed requires some comment. Written in a different hand from all others nearby, it appears as a late entry inserted on the top of a column at some unspecified time afterwards. And it records the infant as the "son of — and Grace Hamilton of 30 Jervis St."!

Now the matter of paternal omission here seems so indicative and striking that it is obviously worth considering some more. One finds that registers of the period in Dublin sometimes omitted the name of the father in this way. A check on the concurrent register of St. Patrick's Cathedral suggests that this happened about one time in sixty on average.[17] It may have occurred occasionally that the registrar could not remember a parent's first name when he eventually got round to entering his records. William Hamilton however was a prominent apothecary who lived within shouting distance of St. Mary's, so that forgetfulness by the registrar is a theory which can hardly be sustained in this case.

Given our new knowledge that Archibald Hamilton had an unusual and most curious birth registration, Graves presents just enough apparent clues in circumspect Victorian fashion to intrigue us. He notes that Archibald was called by his "Christian name after A. H. Rowan, from which trifling circumstance, added to his personal attachment to the latter, many supposed an affinity existed where no intermixture of blood ever circulated." Graves continues his account as follows:

> Mrs. Gawen Hamilton took a special interest in this child of her young friend, had him constantly in her house, controlled his school education, used his services as an amanuensis, offered to bear the charge of his passing through the University in preparation for the Bar and to secure a provision for him in her will. (But) his mother and the boy declined this offer, thereby losing the favour of Mrs. Hamilton, and earning expressions of gratitude from her son and other members of the family.

While there is obviously scope for further investigation of these questions, on balance there does seem a strong case for postulating that Archibald Hamilton was the natural son of A. H. Rowan and Grace McFerrand who grew up in the same house together. It may have been that when the girl was found to be pregnant, she was speedily married off to the relatively poor William Hamilton of Dublin — a common stratagem to maintain respectability. Alternatively the affair may even have been carried on after Grace's marriage, an interpretation suggested by Rowan's several secret visits to Ireland and her apparent absence from the matrimonial household during these years.

Disguised family memories of these goings-on may also lie behind later uncertainty about our subject's exact ancestral origins. There is for example the contention by his early biographer P. G. Tait that "(Hamilton's) grandfather came over from Scotland to Dublin with two young sons ... Archibald (and) James."[17a]

In any case the manner and even the date of Archibald's birth are far from clear. But the existence of some connection may be construed from the continuing attention paid to him by the Killyleagh clan. The available evidence suggests either of the following interpretations: (a) that A. Hamilton Rowan fathered the son of Grace McFerrand in London and she returned to Dublin where the birth was registered five years later; or (b) that the child was conceived during a visit to Dublin from the Continent by A. Hamilton Rowan. And if my reconstruction of these happenings is correct, there is no need to seek further for the remarkable physical resemblance between A. H. Rowan and our subject who was Archibald Hamilton's son.

The Dublin Hamiltons

Whatever the real course of his matrimonial life, William who was Grace's husband did not survive long at the new apothecary's shop in 30 Jervis Street. He died of a chill caught while drilling with the independence-seeking Irish Volunteers in May 1783. Again street directories reveal that the business was run awhile by other male Hamiltons, being finally converted into a haberdashery for Grace in 1792. For a middle-aged woman to run a shop while bringing up three teenage children was evidently a struggle, so that Grace sank into financial difficulties from which her sons were able to rescue her in about 1803.

Of Grace's three surviving children, James entered Trinity College in 1792. There he gained honours in most subjects, duly graduating within four years. Soon afterwards, he reappears as curate of the Established Church at Trim, some thirty miles to the northwest, and there his mother went to spend her final days. James was also Diocesan Schoolmaster for the Trim locality and it is in this important role that we will meet with him again.

Sydney Hamilton was the daughter of the family; her curiously masculine name, derived from the Killyleagh clan, would eventually pass down to a future niece. She too went to live with James at his Trim household; she was aged about twenty-four when her mother joined them in 1803. She was a well-educated young woman, conversant with the classics and Hebrew: the lack of a dowry through family poverty possibly diminished her chances of marriage in an age when such considerations were paramount. But biographers now owe Sydney a debt of some magnitude, for she was the first person to leave accurate reports on the childhood attainments of the future William Rowan Hamilton.

Finally of course there was Archibald, long-term intimate of Killyleagh and at least associate of A. H. Rowan. Apprenticed in youth to an attorney, Archibald first set up in business on his own account at his mother's house in 30 Jervis Street in 1797. According to his parish birth entry, he would have been just eighteen years of age by then, a fact which only adds to the mystery! At any rate he evidently prospered, moving to separate offices at No. 43 in the same street within three years. Archibald did well enough in legal circles to be considered for important commercial posts. He could for example apply to become secretary to the flourishing Grand Canal

Combined Family Trees of the Hamiltons   *(after Graves and Nicholson)*

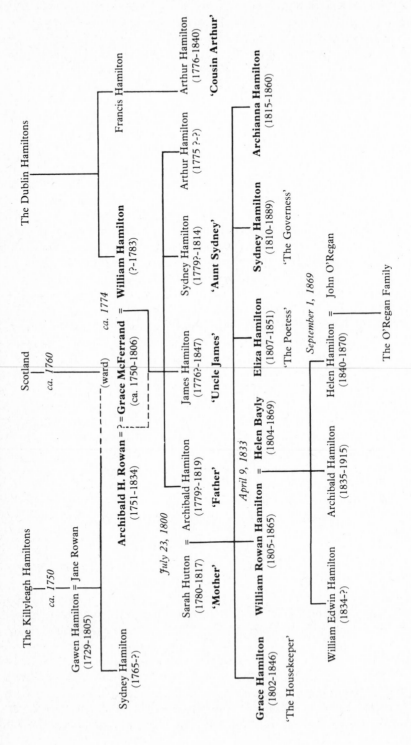

Company and later he became solicitor to the Incorporated Association for the Suppression of Vice, a state-supported proselytising organisation.

In these legal enterprises Archibald was often aided by his cousin Arthur, a barrister-at-law of similar age. Arthur worked for the excise authorities (and also for the Dublin Metropolitan Police) and often toured the country on circuit.[18] He had his own house at 18 South Cumberland Street. And even though he never married, he was to play a major role as substitute father to our subject and to his orphan sisters in later years.

Meanwhile Archibald Hamilton was assiduous in attending to the interests of the banished rebel aristocrat, A. H. Rowan. When the latter's wife left Ireland to join her husband in exile in 1800, Archibald became official agent for their considerable Irish holdings. One of his duties in this role was to secure the succession of Killyleagh on the imminent death of his client's father. Indeed he was engaged on this very business on the night when our subject, William Rowan Hamilton, was born.

Five years earlier, in 1800, Archibald had married Sarah Hutton, a 20-year-old local girl from a prosperous coach-building family. The Huttons were well established in middle-class Dublin society and lived at 113 Summerhill on the northern fringe of the city. Sarah's mother was a French lady named Guignard, but contrary to what has been stated there does not seem to be any evidence of unusual intellectual brilliance on this side of the family.[19]

It may however be worth considering the somewhat international genetic mixture in Sarah's and Archibald's future family. This is a matter of some importance because of the typically Victorian controversy over whether our subject might be classified as of Irish or Scottish descent. Perhaps the most revealing aspect in this controversy is that ultimately none of the participants got the facts correct![20]

Obviously in such matters much depends on just how far back one decides to go. But if we revert to the second generation of ancestors only, the genes of William Rowan Hamilton derive from three different nationalities. He was one-fourth Scottish (Grace McFerrand), one-fourth French (Madamoiselle Guignard) and two-fourths Irish (the Huttons and the Hamiltons).

The newlyweds went to live at 29 Dominick Street and Archibald also transferred his office there. This is now a tenement area, but was then a fine new terrace of Georgian houses on the select northern fringes of the capital. Whether or not No. 29 had any connection with the house owned by A. H. Rowan in the same street remains unclear. At any rate, it was within easy walking distance of the old parish church of St. Mary's and also near most of the relatives on both sides of the family.[21] It remains a curious fact that the older branches of the Dublin Hamiltons never strayed far from their origins on the north side of the city and the same was also true of their descendants in later years.

Children arrived with almost yearly regularity in accordance with the manner of the times. There were nine births altogether between 1801 and

1815, and Graves has detailed each of them with his customary thoroughness. Four girls survived to adulthood unmarried, each of whom was to play a special role in their famous brother's future life. There were also four boys, of whom only William Rowan survived and he was born at the dividing moment between August 3 and 4, 1805. Like Christ and Newton, our subject arrived at the traditionally auspicious stroke of midnight and to this striking demonstration of first precision may be related his unusual consciousness of timing and coincidence in later years.[22]

2 THE GIFTED CHILD

"Willy is indeed an original, for he will not (if he can help it) do anything like any other."

Aunt Sydney to mother, 1811

The family into which young William Rowan Hamilton had now arrived was luckily one with great interest in, and respect for, matters intellectual and was evidently also conscious of their son's early promise. Somebody therefore appears to have taken a deliberate decision to preserve such family letters as related to the future prodigy and because of this, we can observe his progress with unusual precision from his earliest days.

The first such report comes from his mother when her new baby was less than a month old, both of them evidently having just returned from a visit to her in-laws at Trim:

> *Sarah Hamilton to her husband, August 31, 1805:* We are all as full as possible of the hives. They are so itchy even William has some, but he seems blessed with such a felicity of temper as not easily to be discomposed. I hope it may continue as he grows up.[1]

One year later, Archibald was again evidently absent somewhere on legal business and his wife continues to report on the household:

> *July 23, 1806:* The dear children are well. William is growing very fat and walks quite stoutly now ...[2]

Following this, there is an hiatus of almost two years until the boy reappears domiciled in the care of his Uncle James at Trim. This was the period when the returned A. H. Rowan had just resumed charge of the family estates at Killyleagh and elsewhere. These undertakings had previously been in the hands of his agent, Archibald. Now the transfer of responsibility was marked by a monumental row between the two, a legal quarrel which eventually ended up in the courts.

Graves attributes the blame almost entirely to A. H. Rowan in this quarrel, specifically because he failed to reimburse Archibald for his years of dedicated service during the rebel aristocrat's exile. This account however may be suspect due to the writer's general lack of sympathy with nationalist ideals. Nicolson, in contrast, states that A. H. Rowan had always offered to pay the sum of £1,500 eventually awarded by the courts;[3] this version seems more in keeping with his normally generous character. It is also possible that Archibald had been engaged in bill-broking on his own account.[4]

Archibald seems therefore to have been at least partially responsible for the misfortune of bankruptcy which befell him in 1809. So worsening family finances were probably one factor in the decision to send young William to Trim about a year before. But equally there must have been a desire to provide the boy with proper education in an age when there were very few teachers or tutors as well qualified as Uncle James in Trim. A third factor also emerges when we realise that the Hamiltons were always very much what sociologists now term 'an extended family'. There were constant comings and goings between aunts, cousins, in-laws and the various households, so that transfer of an infant from one family to another was probably quite commonplace.

Archibald himself never had the benefit of a university education and its absence shows in many of his surviving letters. These are often lengthy screeds without the hint of a paragraph, effusive, divergent and almost wild at times. Whether it be an account of his travels or a tract defending the heretical Seceders,[5] his letters often exhibit a certain degree of exaggerated self-importance and hyperbole. Archibald's letters nevertheless also give evidence of vast intellectual energy, however misapplied, and in this sense resemble some of the vast outpourings of his son much later in very different spheres.

Early bankruptcy also meant that Archibald was forced to seek temporary employment in England, while his Dublin office continued to remain open. This employment he seems to have obtained without much difficulty, working for the London Fishmonger's Company in connection with the Irish estates which they had gained during the plantations sanctioned by James I. Archibald therefore returned to his old role as a landlord's agent, which involved much travel. Once he took his son on what seems to have been an expense-account trip to Derry during which they travelled in a luxurious post-chaise, scattering bawbees to the poor folk as they swept along.[6]

Archibald however never grew wealthy, 'though not for the want of trying' as he himself somewhat ruefully admits. At no stage was he ever the rich businessman which some accounts erroneously claim.[7] But he was undoubtedly affable, sociable and what we would now call an enlightened liberal. A fervent advocate of general education for the majority, he looked forward to the time when better government would give Ireland a more dignified place in the international community.

These were of course somewhat radical ideas for his social circle and era. They must also have clashed uneasily with Archibald's interest in the highly Calvinist Moravian Church. He may have formed this interest through his wife Sarah, whose sister Susan had married a Moravian minister, the Rev. John Willey in County Down. Archibald's daughters were educated at the Moravian Settlement at Fairfield near Manchester during their early years. And the family attended the Moravian Church of St. Mary's in nearby

Bethesda Place, while also retaining the connection with the original St. Mary's near 30 Jervis Street.

Archibald's Calvinist daughter, Eliza, could hardly approve of his liberal and outgoing tendencies. But she still succeeded in summing up his character very well: "My father had too much of the nature, character and disposition of the poet Burns, of whose writings I remember he was a passionate advocate, not to be marked out for misfortune in this world."[8]

The Milieu of Trim

There were then several excellent reasons for a promising child to be sent away by the Hamilton household for education elsewhere: indeed there were even better ones for their choice of the school at Trim. Archibald's brother, James, occupied the curacy, with a young wife and a large spacious house; there too lived his sister Sydney, now 29 and probably past marrying age. The house they inhabited had been a fortified manor; it now housed the Meath Diocesan School, over which James ruled.

James' predecessor in this post had been the Rev. Mark Wainwright, an incumbent who ingratiated himself with the government by sending reports on local rebels during the Insurrection of 1798.[9] He had been appointed by the Bishop ". . . to instruct the children in the said school in the Latin tongue and in all other tongues in which you are skilled." This was a task for which his successor was certainly well equipped and that to a highly unusual degree.

Young Rev. James Hamilton was an honours graduate in Classics of Trinity College; that he had a detailed knowledge of related oriental languages is clear from one of his sermons that has survived.[10] In addition, he had a wide general interest in subjects such as hypnotism, music and antiquities. Finally, he had his own ideas on education and the possibility of deliberately creating genius, a matter we will examine further in the following chapter.

Such a paragon must have seemed the ideal tutor for educating an infant nephew with apparent promise, a role which James in fact filled with diligence and efficiency. All those intellectual habits and practices which would characterise his nephew in later years can very readily be traced back to the early days at Trim.

Youngsters in that era however did not begin formal schooling in the modern manner until perhaps the age of ten. Before that, there was often little systematic instruction corresponding to what we would now call the primary school stage. Mothers or private tutors frequently took the place of the modern teacher; Sydney, James' sister, seems to have played this role at Trim. She was obviously an alert, observant and well-educated young woman; her observations are remarkably informative as she charts the progress of her nephew over the first nine years.

If the boy was fortunate in being placed in such a vital and stimulating

King John's Castle on the Boyne at Trim *(Engraving by E. Roberts after a drawing by Geo. Petrie. Courtesy Irish Architectural Archive)*

atmosphere throughout his childhood, he was equally lucky in his adopted town. Trim was then a sleepy village of perhaps two thousand people, but few places in Ireland possessed more historic ruins. Just fifty yards from Hamilton's front door stood the Yellow Steeple, an ancient abbey tower where two hundred refugees were said to have been burnt alive centuries before. On the other side of the house was a terraced garden sloping down to its own landing place on the historic River Boyne. And directly opposite across this river stood the spectacular remains of King John's Castle, then and now the largest such ruin in Ireland.

Other ruins and historic associations abounded in the vicinity, such as the former monastic settlement at Bective Abbey and the great prehistoric tumuli of Newgrange. Indeed the entire Boyne Valley for about 20 miles around Trim is archaeologically the richest location in the country. There is ample evidence that young Hamilton was conscious of this fact from an early age. We can assume that the stimulation afforded by the area to a young mind thirsting for knowledge of all kinds must have been intense indeed.[11]

Whether or not such contacts and local atmosphere exercise any direct effect on a budding genius is obviously an arguable point. There were for example many hundreds of other children reared in Trim who grew up into perfectly ordinary individuals. However, it does seem clear that young William was to profit considerably from his new environment; his later habits reflect the training of his childhood with remarkable fidelity. Had he been born with similar genetic endowment into some remote jungle — or even into a less fortunate Dublin family — his future achievements could hardly have been realised as effortlessly.

Young Hamilton was therefore doubly fortunate, in the quality of his youthful upbringing and in his genetic endowment. This is certainly one of the most important conclusions which can be drawn from his career and as such, a theme to which we will return again.

Aunt Sydney's Letters

It is now time to consider the detailed progress of our subject from about 1808 until 1816, the time from his arrival in Trim until he seems to have started on formal or secondary school. Over this period, we can follow William through the medium of Aunt Sydney's reports, a collection of about two dozen letters written to his mother Sarah. Sydney was obviously an enthusiastic reporter as well as being a keen observer, so that the entire series constitutes a study in the development of a gifted child. Nowadays she would have made a good educational psychologist:

> *Circa 1808:* Willy is, thank God, very well, and as impudent as ever; if he goes on every three years in the same way, he will be a very hopeful blade. I believe it is a General he is to be, for if he gets a stick it is a gun and anything that makes noise is a drum, and you would laugh to hear him singing and trying to beat time; when he is marching head and all goes. This must be nature, for where has he seen it?[12]

Here Sydney notes young William's development of a sense of timing and rhythm, and also his capacity for imaginative but ordinary play. Indeed this inclination to normal childhood pastimes never deserted Hamilton despite his rapidly expanding erudition, a fact which begins to emerge more clearly in the next report:

> *September 18, 1808:* Your dear little Willy is very well and improving very fast; indeed James pays unremitting attention to him, and Willy is a very apt scholar, and yet how he picks up everything I know not, for he never stops playing and jumping about; I sometimes threaten to tie his legs when he comes to say his lessons.
>
> When the boys are reading the Bible, James calls him in to read, principally to shame some boys who are double his age who do not read near so well, and you would laugh to hear the consequential manner in which he reads.

Like so many gifted children, young William was obviously highly energetic and not averse to showing off. But even though he was as yet just a three-year-old, James had obviously recognised his learning potential:

> *October 17, 1808:* I will give you an account of the plan that has been pursued with him. He has never yet spelled a lesson in a book, and though he can read and spell the most difficult words, he is not yet out of monosyllables.
>
> James printed on cards every word he has yet spelled; he began with

every monosyllable in which 'A' was the principal letter and so on alphabetically, never beginning a new set until he could spell them off book and on book ... James is now preparing words of two syllables (and) attributes his so soon reading well to this plan.

He plays, 'till teatime, when maps cut out in different ways are brought forward, then arithmetic as far as ten, is gone through in addition, subtraction and multiplication; he has only got as far as ten yet.

His uncle is teaching him to leap, and he can clear his hat with his feet close together...

James was obviously taking care that his pupil should grow up into a well-balanced individual, one competent in athletics as well as academic matters. Obviously young William's mathematics were still at a very elementary stage, but his approach to spelling was entirely systematic and thorough. To this first example of systematic research through the dictionaries can then be related the similar attitudes with which the later mathematician approached his own pioneering projects in the years to come.

William nevertheless remained an otherwise normal and well-adjusted child despite his unusual learning achievements:

1809: He is a most sensible little creature, but at the same time has a great deal of roguery about him. James does not let him out much, for fear of being spoiled by praise, for he says he thinks that is the reason so few children grow up clever.

That James was careful to maintain due balance between ordinary childhood and rapid learning is also evident from another letter soon afterwards:

February 20, 1810: Willy is going well, but James is not pushing him on; he is however, I think, increasing daily in knowledge. This severe weather has kept him from visiting, at which I am very glad, for he was beginning to have a great share of self-complacency, but is now, I am happy to say, returned to his little, careless innocent ways.

The boy was now obviously beginning to realise that he was different from most other children, but was also apparently wise enough to adjust his thinking as appropriate:

May 1810: Willy began in a very high-flown style when he went into the boat, but very soon found he was rather too high for his company; he therefore very cleverly adapted himself to them for the rest of the way, by talking as much folly as he could, and they declared they had never met a more sensible boy!

It is also around this time that we first hear of his rapidly growing competence in grammar and languages:

August 14, 1810: Willy is as fond as usual of using his Hebrew or Latin on any occasion that strikes his imagination. You would be amazed to hear him translating the first chapters of Genesis and very anxious to get to the account of the flood.

Already however he was beginning to experience that difficulty in communicating with lesser intellects which was so seriously to diminish his effectiveness in later years:

1810: Willy, despairing of success in teaching Rose Hebrew, is now trying to instruct her in the different figures of speech. You would have been amused had you heard him the other day giving her examples of simile ...

Rose was a serving-maid in the household and failure to instruct her obviously did not dampen the boy's originality:

> *Circa 1810:* He is a most curious genius. He came the day before yesterday to tell me his east side was itching, and last night when I bid him sit down to his tea he said he must sit at the west side![13]

And this originality was rapidly becoming more obvious:

> *January 4, 1811:* Willy is as great an original as ever: 'Pray can you find out any similitude between a participle and a mule?' (he enquired); he says that as a mule is between an ass and a horse, so a participle is between a noun and a verb; this discovery he made yesterday morning while saying his Hebrew grammar.

> *January 11, 1811*: The children are playing busily in the school room, as the day is too bad for them to go out. But Willy is indeed an original, for he will not (if he can help it) do anything like any other. You would find it difficult to puzzle him in addition or multiplication, but even there he must go some strange way unless he is fought with.[14]

Curiously enough however the boy was evidently not very accomplished in writing at this stage. Some of Sydney's letters around this time are defaced with childish scrawls and elementary attempts at printing capital characters, attempts obviously destructive of her writing implements:

> *April 10, 1811*: If you cannot read this letter, you may thank your son, who has spoiled every pen he could lay his hands upon. He is as great an original as ever. (But) I really cannot write any more with these pens and so must conclude.[15]

The Emergent Prodigy

By now, the people of Trim and the neighbourhood were beginning to realise that a very unusual prodigy had arrived in their midst. Prodigies were then the subject of much interest in academic circles and so young Hamilton found himself the centre of attention from the local intelligentsia. Prominent among these adulators was the Rev. Elliot, Vicar of Trim, and consequently Uncle James' clerical superior. Aunt Sydney reports:

> *November 6, 1809:* Willy was the subject of conversation most of the evening. Mr. Elliot declared that such a child he had never seen and that he was certain there was not another such in Ireland, that he not only read well, but was made to understand what he read. Every place I went I was told that Mr. Elliot had been talking about Willy and that he could talk of nothing else; but if he knew half the things Willy knows, he would indeed be astonished.

The vicar evidently continued to promulgate the prowess of his local prodigy at every opportunity:

> *1810:* Mr. Elliot took him the other day to visit a Mr. Winter, who lives about two miles off, and educates both his boys and girls at home; he

was very much astonished and James said he never saw Willy behave so well. He repeated Dryden's and Collins's Ode inimitably, read both English and Greek, and repeated his Hebrew, for Mr. Elliot insisted on his giving them a little of everything.

1810: There was a Mr. Montgomery with the Elliots the other day; he is a curate and takes a certain number of boys. They had been talking a great deal of Willy to him; however he looked on it all as nonsense,'till after tea Mr. Elliot got a Greek Homer and desired Mr. Montgomery to examine him ... To his amazement Willy went on with the greatest ease.

Mr. Montgomery dropped the book and paced the room; but every now and then he would come and stare at Willy, and when he went away, he told Mr. and Mrs. Elliot that such a thing he had never heard of and that he really was seized with a degree of awe that made him almost afraid to look at Willy.

He would not, he said, have thought so much of it had he been a grave, quiet child; but to see him the whole evening acting in the most infantile manner and then reading all these things astonished him more than he could express.

The vicar's wife was also evidently seized with the same amazement and enthusiasm:

January 25, 1810: Mrs. Elliot declares she will take him to the Bishop. James says he must not go for some time, but she tells him he shall, so she has written a longer account of him to Mrs. Gratton. She says she would give a great deal to be able to show him to Mr. Gratton.[16]

Evidently this visit to the Bishop materialised about four months later, but unfortunately we have no record of what his Lordship had to say. Soon afterwards, we hear of young William's play activities and of his fantasies which were already largely cast in a strongly classic mould:

1812: His favourite play at present is the Trojan War and which he makes Grace assist in; it is laughable enough to hear them, for they perform the parts both of mortals and immortals, (though) Jove at times is rather overbearing. They do better in the field, as the war is forgot in the chase after the sheep.

I found him the other day in the garden at the stump of an old tree, with some bit of old iron; he told me not to disturb him, for he was Vulcan and very busy. His spirits are very great.

William was still as concerned as ever with classical playacting the following year:

1813: He found an old hinge today in the garden, which he assures me is an antient spur, formerly used in battle; and he brought forward so many reasons to convince me that I was obliged to appear perfectly satisfied.

Throughout this time, William's acquaintance with Hebrew was evidently being furthered to ever-higher levels of competence:

June 17, 1814: James is very glad you are trying to get the new edition of

the Hebrew testament . . . the one corrected from the version published
by Dr. Hutter at Nuremberg, 1600.

Mr. Gresham was much astonished at William, who is now at my
elbow: he was swimming with his uncle this morning.

Unfortunately, this is the latest extant letter of those which Aunt Sydney
wrote. With perspicacity and enthusiasm, she has left us a unique record of a
gifted child in the course of development. It is entirely due to her that we
can follow Hamilton through his early years. She was obviously a person of
high intelligence and versatility so that it grieves us to discover she died of
cancer in Dublin at the age of 35. This was just four months after her last
letter quoted here was penned.

Sydney was probably a substitute mother-figure as well as mentor to
young William; her death must have been a grievous loss to him at the
tender age of nine. Taken in conjunction with that other earlier instance of
maternal separation six years previously (when his family despatched him to
the countryside), the two losses collectively do much to explain his striking
incompetence in relating to the opposite sex in later years.

But Aunt Sydney's letters and young William's occasional visits to
Dublin had drawn his own absent family into the general enthusiasm for
their astonishing prodigy. Witness for example this early letter from his
mother to her unmarried sister, Mary Hutton:

1810: I had William in town and he took up my whole thoughts: he is
one of the most surprising children you can imagine: it is scarcely
credible; he not only reads well, but with such nice judgement and
point, that it would shame many who have finished their education. His
reciting is astonishing and his clear and accurate knowledge of
geography beyond belief; but you will think this nothing when I tell you
that he reads Latin, Greek and Hebrew!

It is truly funny to see the faces some of the Wise Heads put on after
examining him: they first look incredulous — they stare; then say that it
is wrong to let his mind be so over-stocked. They cannot suppose that
all this is learned by him as play and that he could no more speak or play
as children in general do, than he could fly. Everything he must have a
reason for.

And from the same source three years later, we get a more precise report:

May 1, 1813: We had a most pleasing letter from James Hamilton
today, saying that he could now say that William was master of three
languages and that he prepares his business without any assistance and
that it is always correct. He also says that he finds so little difficulty in
learning French and Italian that he wishes to read Homer in French.
He is enraptured with the *Iliad* and carries it about with him, spouting
from it whatever particularly pleases him. This will give you pleasure to
hear and was very gratifying to us.

Apart from affording us precise knowledge of William's competence in
Latin, Greek and Hebrew, this letter is noteworthy in another respect. It is
our first report of what was to become one of Hamilton's most characteristic
personality traits in later years — his habit of carrying his favourite books

everywhere and opening them for perusal quite regardless of surroundings or company.

Characteristically also, Hamilton was never loath to exhibit his superior learning and this latter trait too can be discerned even at this early stage. So much emerges from the following diary entry of his cousin, Hannah Hutton:

> *September 1813:* As we passed through the Scalp, William amused us by all at once expressing with animation his feelings in Latin. I was greatly surprised to find, on further questioning him, that the composition was his own; for although I knew that he was a child of extraordinary genius, I could hardly think it possible for a boy of his years to have such enlarged ideas.
>
> His subject was an address to Nature and to Art, delivered in a bold and manly style; he concluded it by asking pardon of the latter for preferring the former greatly before her. Each face expressed satisfaction while listening to the little orator.

Twenty years later William would still deliver lectures along similar lines, but now on a vastly extended scale. Then his audience would consist of the Dublin intellectuals who flocked to Trinity College to hear his Introductory Lectures on Astronomy or of his fellow scientists at the various annual meetings of the British Association. These listeners too would pronounce themselves impressed and uplifted by Hamilton's scientific oratory. And yet, there seems a very clear line of development from the little boy accustomed to eliciting praise from his elders by gratuitous displays of learned thought!

William's Dublin family were equally proud as their Trim relatives of their unusual prodigy. So now they also joined in promoting his education in various ways. His father Archibald was frequently in England, prosecuting his legal business, where he was able to purchase books which were unobtainable in Trim. So much is evident from a letter written to his wife from England:

> *September 29, 1814:* I told you of the Arabic Bible for William. I hope he may persevere and may retain his proper regard for money as well as learning. I can manage anything but my own money concerns. I hope he will be wiser.

In fact, events much later would prove Archibald's foreboding about William's financial acumen to be only too soundly based. In any case, the father now seems worried about the possibility of his own early demise, leaving a young family quite unprovided for. He may also have been depressed by the death of his sister Sydney, which occurred about this time. His daughters, Grace and Eliza (then aged 13 and 6 respectively), were now at the Moravian Settlement near Manchester; their father's letter to them is markedly gloomy in tone:

> *January 30, 1815:* William is not satisfied until he learns the mother tongue of the Oriental languages, the Sanskrit, and I have written for the necessary books. Providence is very gracious in giving me such a son and you such a brother. Now my dear children, as life is uncertain and I may be called away, value as you ought such a brother and prove

yourselves by your industry and attention deserving of his support and countenance. I doubt not but you will do so.

Perhaps the Brethren may suggest a mode of getting the Oriental translations or original grammars, etc. for William. I would spare no expense. Any of the Brethren's original vocabularies, grammars, etc. of any country William would be glad to get at.

It should perhaps be explained here that Archibald's current employment (with the Fishmongers' Company in London while dealing with their Irish estates) seems to have suggested the possibility of a similar career for his son. In this field, however, the much larger East India Company undoubtedly offered far greater scope for talent and hard work. Hence Archibald's interest at this stage in the boy acquiring as many Eastern languages as possible.

How Many Languages?

It was also about this time however that Archibald's high pride in his son's linguistic attainments evidently got the better of his veracity. A scant five months after his last letter seeking Oriental grammars from the Moravian Brethren, we find him boasting far more expansively in a letter to his friend Dr. Bielby:

May 18, 1815: William continues his even course of commanding and persevering talent. What he may turn out in maturer years is hard to say; but there is every reason for a well-founded hope that he will be at least a very learned man and, I trust, also a very worthy character.

His thirst for the Oriental languages is unabated. He is now master of most, indeed of all except the minor and comparatively provincial ones.

The Hebrew, Persian, and Arabic are about to be confirmed by the superior and intimate acquaintance with the Sanskrit, in which he is already a proficient.

The Chaldee and Syriac he is grounded in, and the Hindostanee, Malay, Mahratta, Bengali and others.

He is about to commence the Chinese, but the difficulty of procuring books is very great. It cost me a large sum to supply him from London, but I hope the money was well expended.[17]

Now this letter seems to be the ultimate source, alone and entirely uncorroborated, of the many later exaggerations concerning Hamilton's linguistic abilities. It is therefore worth considering in more detail. Graves, for example, quotes Archibald in this letter without comment but, significantly, with no approbation; he does not include the more esoteric tongues in the listing of Hamilton's achievements about this time.[18] Hankins similarly follows Graves here and does not comment further on this issue.[19]

However, others have accepted Archibald's letter at its face value. Various short biographies therefore state that young William was acquainted with thirteen languages by the time he was thirteen.[20] In *Men of Mathematics*, E.T. Bell first mistakenly attributes Archibald's letter to James and then proceeds to berate the latter for having turned out "one of the most shocking examples of a linguistic monstrosity in history".[21] Bell is however mistaken on so many elementary facts that his account is at best unreliable; the legend of thirteen languages by the age of thirteen is nevertheless now firmly entrenched in most of the standard encyclopaediae and reference works.[22]

It is therefore important to take a somewhat more critical look at Hamilton's linguistic abilities in the light of what can be substantiated from other sources. Almost certainly, the boasts of Archibald are then seen to be untrue. At the very best they are a highly exaggerated version of his son's abilities. To be acquainted with a language normally implies at least some ability to speak or read or write it. And to imagine that young William ever attained such levels in Far Eastern tongues like Hindostanee or Chinese simply strains all credibility. For in fact there exists no other evidence —beyond this single letter of his father — that any such competence was ever attained.

The Chinese then we can reasonably dismiss without further ado. The Hindostanee, Malay, Mahratta and Bengali may deserve a little more consideration but if so, hardly very much. At most, young William may have come to understand that these are all derivatives of the original Sanskrit. But it is equally possible that we have heard of them only because the relatively uneducated Archibald was desirous to exhibit his own understanding of such learned matters to a friend.

This leaves Persian, Arabic, Chaldee, Syriac and Sanskrit — languages somewhat more esoteric than the Hebrew in which young William was clearly very proficient. Here we can allow him a proper basic understanding of the way in which these tongues were related and the probable, but unfulfilled, intention to specialise in each in later years.

Persian was certainly the language in which these early Oriental studies appear to have progressed most. There exists a Persian 'grammar' of about a dozen pages composed by Hamilton at the age of fourteen, one of which begins with a sentence remarkably typical of the later mathematician: "The reader will have perceived with pleasure the many similarities between the Persian and the English tongue."[23] Later in the same year, William was also to compose a hugely stilted and ornate letter in native script for the Persian Ambassador to Britain when that worthy man arrived in Dublin.

Hamilton however never progressed in Persian beyond this stage. His peak attainment was therefore comparable to what might be achieved by an ordinary pupil after about three years — if Persian were part of the average school curriculum. In other words, he was capable at a fairly elementary level, but certainly not at all highly proficient.

Comparing competence in Persian and Syriac, William's abilities were likely on a lesser level in the latter tongue. With Sanskrit, his knowledge seems even more elementary. Some evidence of his achievements here exist in a boyish manuscript wherein the alphabet is copied out. Later there are a few minor translations and beyond that no further evidence of esoteric languages at all.[24]

The facts available therefore force us to prune the legend of Hamilton's proficiency in thirteen languages rather drastically. He was certainly highly capable in Greek, Latin and Hebrew, a fact well proven by his later achievements in these subjects at university. And although this was not uncommon in an era when most studies were highly classical in emphasis, he was undoubtedly adept in these languages at a very early age. Of Persian, William knew enough to be able to compose a letter, though only with the aid of his textbooks.[25] In Syriac, he was probably slightly less skilled. And in Sanskrit, he knew at least enough to make out the characters and do minor translations — and probably relate the derivation of other tongues thereto.

Of modern languages, Hamilton knew enough French to read it without difficulty. He was never fluent enough to hold a conversation in that tongue however — a point which emerged at Dunsink many years later when he vainly tried to converse in French with a visiting Italian astronomer.[26]

Much later, Hamilton was also able to read German, though apparently not with the same facility as French. Again in Dunsink years after, we find him, with his sisters, taking lessons in German from a visiting tutor.[27] And his skills in Italian, which anyway resembles Latin, were probably at a similar or slightly lower level.

At the age of thirteen, Hamilton then undoubtedly knew three languages sufficiently well to read them easily. These were Latin, Greek and Hebrew. French, German and Italian, he was probably acquainted with at lesser levels. Of Persian and probably Syriac, he knew enough to compose letters, although laboriously. In Sanskrit and possibly Chaldee, he could make out characters, do minor translations and possibly trace the derivation of some descendant words.

The evidence then suggests that Hamilton's linguistic efforts (apart from English) peaked with proficiency in three classical languages. He had a much more elementary acquaintance with four Oriental ones. Of three other languages (French, German and Italian), he probably had a smattering. But beyond Archibald's single boastful letter, there is nothing to sustain the widespread legend that Hamilton ever knew anything like thirteen languages. That is, unless one chooses to interpret the term 'knew' in the weakest possible sense.

There is also of course one striking, and to some extent revealing, omission from the list of Hamilton's real or supposed linguistic feats. Apparently, it never occurred to anyone to add Gaelic or Irish to his repertoire, even though this was then the living language which over half the population still used. William could therefore dream of the ancient glories of Greece and Persia, while largely ignoring the strikingly eventful history and culture of the countryside immediately around. But this was a clear example of a highly blinkered perception of Irish society shared by the great majority of his co-religious; further examples were to become all too obvious in later years.

Super-gifted

To clarify the limitations of Hamilton's very real attainments in early language learning does not, of course, imply any derogation of his undoubtedly
great intellectual ability. Indeed it will become apparent later just how much
these early explorations of the roots of language seem likely to have
contributed to his own success in matters mathematical. Certainly it was all
quite different from Bell's uncomprehending fantasy of young William as
"one of the most shocking examples of a linguistic monstrosity in history".[21]

Mature and balanced consideration then indicates that Hamilton was
obviously more than just another very clever or gifted child. Instead he was
one of an even higher elite — those whom some psychologists now term
'super-gifted' individuals. These are the one-in-a-million children "who
start spouting Shakespeare at two, beat all the local chess masters at five,
write symphonies at ten".[28] Such children carry with them the capacity to
change all our lives and culture, but only if their potential is adequately
nurtured from an early age. In this respect, young William was doubly
fortunate in both his mentors and his surroundings, so that he duly went on
to achieve eminence in his chosen field of mathematics.

Super-gifted children may be expected to score above 180 in some,
though not all, IQ tests. They may for example excel in mathematics but not
in language. Curiously enough, the opposite is likely to have been true of
Hamilton at this stage. Since his classical attainments were clearly the equal
of many undergraduates twice his age, we can estimate that he would have
scored around 200 in any IQ tests involving such aptitudes.

Just how well the future mathematician might have scored in any similar
tests involving numeracy is, however, not at all so clear. If such tests had
been concerned with breadth of knowledge only, he certainly could never
have scored in the graduate range. Possibly because Uncle James did not
unduly stress the subject, young Hamilton's mathematical attainments up to
about fourteen or so can best be described as notably average!

This somewhat surprising conclusion is amply substantiated from various
letters around these years. At the age of ten and a half for example, he
informs his sister Grace as follows: "In arithmetic, I have got as far as
Practice and I have done near half the first book of Euclid with Uncle." By
thirteen, he has progressed as far as quadratic equations in algebra; a year
and a half later, his weekly study list mentions arithmetic and geometric
progressions. None of these could be considered in the slightest unusual for
any average boy of similar years.[29]

William's wide learning in so many other fields did however confer an
unusual breadth of vision and an almost superhuman capacity for
intellectual work. So that when eventually he began the study of
mathematics in earnest, he was supremely equipped for progress at a very
rapid pace!

3 THE BOYS' SCHOOL AT TRIM

"You perceive that in writing to you, I unite in some degree the poet with the astronomer. . ."

William to his sister Eliza, 1823

Hamilton's early academic excellence obviously owed much to the highly stimulating atmosphere in which he found himself at Trim. Here Uncle James was the dominant influence. He was a man who has often been unfairly pilloried for his methods, supposedly doing little but forcing an endless series of obscure languages into an all absorbent but undiscriminating youthful mind.[1]

In my opinion, these interpretations are based on inadequate understanding and as such, little better than a travesty of the truth. That James was probably over-enthusiastic about Eastern languages is true. But in a time of general learning in the classics, such an indulgence would not have seemed unduly strange. Otherwise, his own school records reveal young Hamilton to have been extremely widely educated rather than hopelessly over-specialised. (This is an important issue to be examined later in this chapter.) We also know that James taught his nephew swimming and at least some athletics, so that there is every indication that he planned to produce a well-rounded individual as well as a highly educated adult.

Although young William had been the subject of these aims from the age of three or earlier, Graves records that he did not begin schooling in the formal sense until about eleven or so. However, he had always lived in the schoolhouse so that likely his earlier education was more in the nature of private tuition from James and Sydney. This was common practice in those days before primary education became general. About the age of eleven, we do know that young Hamilton started lessons in a more formal manner, entering what we would now call the secondary or high-school stage. Here again of course, Uncle James was the dominant influence — this time in his capacity as Head of the Trim Diocesan School.

The exact size and nature of this institution has always seemed notably hazy in the account by Graves and later adaptations. But recent research by local Meath historians has now filled in this notable gap in the life of Hamilton. And from their work emerges a much clearer, even a startling, picture of what James was trying to do.[2]

27

The Boys' School at Trim, on the Boyne, with the Yellow Steeple to the right   *(Courtesy Irish Architectural Archive)*

We now understand that the Boys' School was first mooted in a Government Act of 1570, which foresaw a University for Trim in keeping with the town's large importance at that time. This school however did not really open its doors until 1658. Thereafter, it functioned at best sporadically, although it did count the future Duke of Wellington on its books for a time. There was however a determined attempt at revival in 1788 when Rev. Mark Wainwright was appointed and he was succeeded by James Hamilton after about a dozen years.

James got the commodious schoolhouse and its riverside garden to live in, together with a salary of £40 per year. He also had the living of the small parish of Almoritia some distance away which was worth £100 annually. In addition, he had another function as Curate of Trim. Here however he was under the Vicar Mr. Elliot and later Mr. Butler, men who enjoyed a living worth £600 per year. James was evidently hoping to succeed the former and great hopes were laid on a very eloquent sermon which he delivered when the Bishop visited the town in 1817.[3] The Bishop pronounced himself impressed and ordered that the sermon be printed for the record; nevertheless he still appointed the much younger Mr. Butler, just down from Oxford, as Vicar in 1819. There was a tendency to appoint English clerics to Irish livings around this period and patronage was dominant in the Established Church of Ireland at the time.

Diocesan records show that James had 14 day scholars in 1809, a roll which had expanded to 22 day pupils and 5 boarders by 1819. By then James had two assistants, presumably paid for entirely from the pupils' fees. Trim had at least six other educational establishments of similar standing around this period, a fact which would have meant that competition for pupils must have been keen.[4]

All of which gives further meaning to a remarkable advertising prospectus put out by James in 1820. This is a document which explains much that was previously mysterious about the nature and aims of young William's education and so its main points seem worth reproducing in abbreviated form:

PROSPECTUS of a course of instruction, to be pursued by the pupils under the care of the Rev. James Hamilton, Trim.

Reading and reciting with correctness, judgement and taste. Writing and arithmetic; the latter on principles more luminous and scientific than generally taught in schools, and followed up by an introduction to Algebra and Mathematical sciences.

Geography, ancient and modern, sacred and ecclesiastical, together with the use of the globe's history and chronology; including the Jewish, Grecian and Roman antiquities, and an enlightened view of heathen mythology.

A radical and grammatical knowledge of the Hebrew, Greek and Latin languages — an accurate, critical and familiar acquaintance with Latin and Greek classics —and the principles and practice of eloquence and composition. Including versification in Greek, Latin and English.

It is also hoped that to those tolerably well versed in the Hebrew, the elements of

Arabic grammar will promise affinity. It will be found no very difficult acquisition
— and one of no small importance on account of its connection with the Persian
—should the subsequent pursuit or destination of the pupil invite the study of that
and other Oriental languages.

That such a course as has been delineated — extending as it does beyond the
usual boundaries of school education — is nevertheless not beyond what the youth
of moderate ability may accomplish before entering University. Mr. Hamilton is
enabled to offer the most satisfactory proof, from the experience he can produce, of
the efficacy and success of the system of teaching he pursues.

In how superior a degree calculated, such a plan of education must prove, to open
the pupil to all the avenues of information and learning, to enrich the
understanding, cultivate taste and call forth talent — in short, to form the finished
scholar — it were superfluous to undertake to show.

N.B. Mr. Hamilton, being desirous as far as possible to initiate and form his
pupils throughout on his own system, is anxious to want to undertake the education
of such more particularly as not having been before at school, and that at as early an
age as parents may be disposed to commit them to his care.

In penning this advertisement, James was probably conscious of that other
Hamilton just then making his name with his radical new system of rapid
language learning already referred to (Chapter 1). In any case, several firm
conclusions concerning the early education of young Hamilton now emerge.

The first of these is that James was keen to start his pupils at the earliest
possible age, thereby affording yet another reason why our subject should
have been sent down to the country by his family before he was yet three.
Secondly, James planned to educate his pupils in the widest possible sense
of the word, fitting them for any future calling they might pursue. And the
fact that his nephew started out with languages, but later specialised in
mathematics, certainly indicates that this was a largely sensible approach.
Finally, James obviously believed that genius could be developed more or
less to order, although presumably even he would have recognised that this
required a certain minimum intelligence. Equally he was prepared to point
to his already locally famous nephew as proof that this idea was correct.

Whether or not genius can be produced to order is clearly still an open
question. Some very recent developments in our own time however suggest
that James was very likely more correct than otherwise.[5] At all events, this
recently unearthed Prospectus obviously does much to illuminate the early
education and indeed later achievements of young William Hamilton.

Given the latent promise in James' educational theories, it must remain a
matter of regret that he never really got the opportunity to test them
properly. Perhaps prospective parents were put off by his stilted manner; he
might have done better had he couched his Prospectus in less pretentious
tones. At any rate, the Trim Diocesan School did not attract sufficient
pupils to warrant continuation and it closed around 1823, the year when its
most promising student entered university.

Eight years later, James was offered the headship of a larger merged
Diocesan School at Mullingar, at a salary of £130 a year. This was

recognition of a sort but with several disadvantages which forced him to decline. By then, he was already over fifty and probably grown tired of the Establishment and its corrupt promotion paths.

Scholarship in Depth

The earliest extant letter of young William's refers to the time he started formal schooling. A stilted document of about 500 words in large and careful copperplate handwriting, it details, to his sister Grace, the course of his studies:

> *December 14, 1815:* I have for some time been reading Lucian and Terence, the Hebrew *Psalter* on Sundays and on Saturdays some Sanskrit, Arabic and Persian. I read at leisure hours Goldsmith's *Animated Nature* and any new history or poetry that falls my way. I like Walter Scott very much.
>
> In arithmetic, I have got as far as practice and I have done very near the half of the first book of Euclid with my uncle.
>
> I do the antient and modern geography of the different countries together. I do the second lesson every morning in the Greek Testament and, on Sunday after church, go over the Scripture Lessons of the past week with Dodderige's *Notes and Improvements*, and before church I read Secker on the Catechism, and in the evening Wells' *Scripture Geography*, a very entertaining book.[6]

Similar letters reappear at intervals over the next half-dozen years or so, their scholarly content expanding rapidly in concert with their writer's mental horizons. None of them gives any special prominence to the Oriental tongues of later legend and the bias if any is rather towards undue concentration on religious affairs. This however was probably only to be expected from a clerical household; but the general impression otherwise is one of wide and deep classical scholarship in accordance with the later Prospectus put out by James.

As yet however, there was still one striking gap in this rapidly developing picture of prodigious scholarship. At the age of ten, young William was obviously not unduly proficient in matters mathematical, indeed probably no more than average for his age. His great strides in mathematics did not begin until 1820 but then, they would have the advantage of a still youthful mind incomparably broadened by deep erudition in other spheres.

Graves gives a list of Hamilton's studies during the first quarter of 1820 and I have thought it worth including because it clarifies this issue.[7] Eight different areas of study are recorded in all:

(1) Religious studies from about a dozen sources, including the Psalms and Greek Testament in their original languages.

(2) Classical studies also from about a dozen texts, with blank verse translations of Homer and Virgil.

(3) Oriental languages — Hebrew, Arabic, Sanskrit, Syriac and Persian.

(4) Science — Euclid, theory of eclipses, algebra (arithmetic and geometrical progressions).

(5) Law — Blackstone's *Commentaries*.

(6) History from six standard works.

(7) English poetry from half a dozen authors, including Milton and Shakespeare.

(8) Miscellaneous reading including law, botany and biography.

This list is notable because it details the relatively minor part played by those two accomplishments for which Hamilton was later to become famous. His mathematical prowess was still relatively undeveloped, probably because James was not competent in that subject. And William's Oriental studies were similarly only one portion of a broad curriculum but, unlike the mathematics, they were never to progress much further.

Other manuscripts of this period enable us to assess Hamilton's Oriental attainments in more detail. There is for example an elementary Syriac 'grammar' of 30 pages compiled by him in early July 1817, which concludes with a concise summary of his knowledge:

> Thus far I have gone through what is necessary for reading and writing Syriac — the forms of their pronouns and of their regular nouns and verbs. Soon may be expected an account of their irregular and indeclinable words, etc. with a Syntax.

A similar treatise on Sanskrit followed in 1818 and there is a reference to another on Persian one year later. Records exist of some slight translations from both of these languages and we know that he was able to compose an address of welcome in Persian.[8] But in none of these studies did he ever show a mastery which remotely approached his competence in the classic languages.

William's interest in Oriental matters apparently peaked around this stage and there is little or no reference to esoteric languages thereafter. This change of interest was probably due to the growing pressure on him to prepare for university entrance. Another and more compelling reason was obviously his newly discovered passion for mathematics.

Before this happened however, a final and revealing little document of about 400 words on languages in general appears:

> *1820:* Comparison between the Persian and other languages: To trace the progress of the grammatical principles of any nation, from the first use of words to express bodily wants in infants or savages, to gradually acquired refinements capable of raising it (to higher levels), is and must be interesting, not only to the philologist, but also to the writer and lover of history.[9]

This extract is significant because it shows the way young William's thoughts were already running as early as fifteen. It is clearly the direct ancestor of similar speculations in geometry a few years later. These considerations would lead him in due course to ponder the origins of algebra and so eventually to his famed discovery of quaternions.

Early indications of great generality are also apparent in this and other writings of Hamilton about this time. And generality was later to be one of his most striking characteristics as a mathematician, a quality which led him straight to his most important discovery of all — the analogy between optics and mechanics, now indispensable in modern descriptions of the subatomic world.

Young William's studies in Oriental languages may therefore never have attained the heights attributed to him in posthumous legend. But neither were they the total waste of time which some commentators have uncomprehendingly assumed. To imagine such indicates slight understanding of the multifarious origins from which genius may eventually arise.

The Death of Archibald

About midway through his schooldays, young Hamilton also lost both parents in different years. Although various letters survive from him to his mother, she can hardly have been very important in his life by this stage. When she died (most likely in childbirth) on May 10, 1817, they had already been separated for about nine years.[10] At any rate, young William does not seem to have been very much affected by her death. A mere ten days afterwards, he was writing a cheeky letter to Cousin Arthur enquiring after his marriage prospects and declaring his interest in securing a good seat at the University Fellowship examination next day!

The death of his wife however had apparently left his father, Archibald, lonely and sad. So he invited his son to Dublin for the summer holidays, an event from which can be dated William's growing interest in the capital. These were also the holidays during which Archibald took his son on a tour of northern Ireland in connection with his business for the Fishmongers' Company, as mentioned earlier. From his diary of the period, it is evident that this first adventure into the wider world made a large impression on young William and indeed he was to remember it fondly until his last days.[11]

Archibald changed house from 29 to 18 Dominick Street the following year and his eldest daughter Grace became housekeeper at the age of sixteen. Thus began the role in which she was to serve her brother also in future years. William was now making progress reports to his father, much as he used previously to his mother Sarah; the tone of such letters as survive indicates regular communication between the two.

Archibald had been procuring books for some years to help William with his Oriental studies, but evidently even the young student could feel that all this learning might be a bit overdone betimes:

> *March 4, 1819:* I sometimes feel as if the bottle of my brain were like those mentioned, I think in Job, 'full and ready to burst'; but when I try to uncork and empty it, like a full bottle turned upside down, its contents do not run out as fluently as might be expected; nor is the liquor that comes off as clear as could be wished.
>
> Perhaps I am not long enough in bottle to be decanted. I fear the

vintage of my brain is yet too crude and unripe to make good wine of. When it shall have been more matured, I hope the produce of the vineyard you have planted and watered will afford some cups 'to cheer but not inebriate you', at least not shame you...

To putting Horace back into Latin I have now added the putting of Virgil into English blank verse. I hope it will help me a step up the hill of original composition, of which I confess myself at present at the bottom.[12]

By now however, Archibald seems to have had strong intimations of his own approaching demise; hints in the family records suggest that gout and alcoholism may have been the cause.[13] He made a conscious effort to gather his scattered family around him for what was to be a last summer reunion, the girls from their Moravian educators and William up from Trim. All stayed together at a large rented house in Booterstown, Archibald being then attracted to a widow named Barlow who lived nearby.

But before this, William had received two very long and hortatory epistles from his father. In the first he is urgently exhorted to remain humble, serious and pious always, taking good care to ensure that all his future studies and conduct are founded on good Christian principles. Perhaps Archibald felt alarmed by signs of wayward independence in his son's fast-growing scholarship. But either these worries were groundless or William took due heed of his father's fears. At any rate, he grew up as pious and orthodox a Christian as even James could have desired, remaining so until almost the very end.

Archibald's second letter of May 20, 1819 was more in the nature of an exercise in career guidance. An immensely long and obviously unedited epistle of more than 12,000 words, it inevitably begs comparison with similar effusions on different topics by his son in future years. If any model is required for these later, almost abnormal, vast outpourings by the younger Hamilton, it surely can be found in the earlier epistles of his father.[14]

In his career-guidance letter, Archibald ranges over all the possibilities open to his gifted son. Holy Orders is dismissed because of the need to court patronage in the Church. A legal career would be much more promising but if so, it should be directed towards the English rather than the Irish Bar. (The former was less corrupt and offered wider opportunities.) And the law might be used as a stepping stone to politics if so desired.

Alternatively, cultivation of the Oriental languages would serve for a career in India. Or they might equally be used for 'a totally new and enlarged study' through the medium of a Professor's chair. Concentration on Divinity would serve a similar purpose. The intellectual standing of Trinity College could thereby be elevated; the ultimate target should be the Provostship and a mitre. But generally a college Fellowship promised a good start for a young man of independent mind. In other words, young William was now being advised to aim for the highest possible academic rank. James had doubtless been saying the same thing to him repeatedly for many years before.

It is yet another instance of the striking adherence of Hamilton to early precepts that he went on to do just as his mentors had advised. Not even they, however, could possibly have foreseen that he would reach the top so rapidly.

During the 1819 holiday at Booterstown, we also see William's future familial pattern crystallise. Grace was there as housekeeper at seventeen, the eldest of the children. William was next in seniority, followed by the future poetess Eliza, then aged twelve. Sydney came after her as a lively nine-year-old and last came the 'baby', Archianna, at four. The rest of the family evidently found her still amusing and as yet there seemed no signs of future deficiency.[15]

It was about this time that Hamilton organised himself and his three oldest sisters into a body called the 'Honourable Society of Four'. This formal grouping can be considered in a context midway between his earlier organisation of role-playing and the later adult societies with which he became increasingly involved. The 'Society of Four' had a long formal constitution drawn up by William in obvious imitation of Archibald. This constitution and the formal accounts of the Society run to a document of over 5,000 words, so that the typical later pattern was already well established.[16]

Archibald describes his purpose at this time as "trying to brush (William) up, so as to unite a little of the gentleman and man of the world with the accomplished scholar". Obviously he was also trying to make as many useful connections as possible. To this end, William was sent out on the pretext of conveying a legal message to visit the Astronomer Royal, Dr. Brinkley, at Dunsink. This visit to Dunsink was Hamilton's first contact with his future post. Graves also records that "to his disappointment, the great man was absent and he had to be contented with being shown the instruments."[17] The importance of making the right connections was clearly being instilled in young Hamilton and this too was a practice which he would follow assiduously all his life.

His famous call on the Persian Ambassador a few months later was in the same vein. The potentate came to Dublin in November 1819 and Archibald, with an eye to an Oriental career, thought William's knowledge of Persian might gain him a useful introduction. The boy was therefore summoned up from Trim for the purpose, carrying with him a letter in Persian which he confesses had taken him much labour to compose:

> Accept, O illustrious visitant from Iran, a humble tribute to thy exalted merit from the weak and yet inexperienced pen of a schoolboy on whom, though far from thy ancient and renowned realm, a ray from the bright luminary of that paradise of regions, spreading light on this Isle of the West, has created in the soul of thy servant a heart-inflaming and daily increasing desire and love for the delightful literature of the East...[18]

And so on, for several increasingly tortuous but obviously quite serious paragraphs. Perhaps however we should be glad that the Persian

Ambassador pleaded other business and so was unable to receive William. His Persian script was apparently quite legible, a feat which must be considered as improbable as if some young Iranian suddenly appeared out of the blue writing a letter in Gaelic to an Irish traveller in Tehran! The potentate could easily have taken young Hamilton under his patronage at this point. And while the further history of Middle Eastern diplomacy would probably have been affected, the loss to mathematics would undoubtedly have been severe!

A few days later, William was summoned back to Dublin by his elder sister Grace to attend their father in his last illness. Archibald had contracted a somewhat mysterious and probably forced marriage to the Widow Barlow seven weeks earlier, but the whereabouts of his new wife at this point is not clear. At any rate, Grace and William were prominent at the bedside while the patient lingered for a few days in a coma. Then on December 10th, he died.

Whatever possessions Archibald owned may have gone to pay his debts or else to his new wife; at any rate, his son got nothing beyond "a few books and an old armorial seal".[19] Cousin Arthur along with Uncle James and the Huttons however immediately stepped in and the girls were soon dispersed among the various relatives. This still left William at fourteen nominally responsible for his four orphaned sisters, a charge which was to influence his thinking at several critical career points over the next fifteen years.

In dealing with this slice of early family history, biographers have usually not considered Archibald in a very kindly light. Hankins, for example, characterises him as grandiose, unctuous, egotistical and neglectful; Bell somehow conjures up a "jolly toper, the life of every party he graced with his reeling presence".[20]

In my opinion such interpretations are highly arguable at best. We know for example that Archibald was constantly aware, if somewhat over-boastful, of his son's prodigious scholarship. He tried to aid his progress by seeking out rare textbooks at considerable trouble and expense. There was evidently constant communication between James and himself, much of it probably concerning William, in the form of letters which have not survived. The education of his daughters was likewise conscientiously provided for. In short, the record suggests that Archibald was a very caring parent insofar as he was able; to imply otherwise seems unfair.

Poet and Dreamer

After the death of Archibald, William returned to Trim with a further motivation to his life. His favourite sister, Eliza, was now with Aunt Susan Willey, his maternal aunt at Ballinderry in County Antrim. And in Eliza, William now started to confide.

> *January 1820:* The hope of being, if we are spared, useful to my dear sisters will, I trust, stimulate, and the hope of God's blessing in doing so

animate, my exertions. Uncle encourages me to hope that with the
divine blessing they will be successful.[21]

From this point onwards, Hamilton's interest becomes increasingly fixed on
the university entrance examination. His previous attachment to Oriental
languages faded steadily under this ambition and the newly discovered
challenge of mathematics. Many of his other early habits also became more
firmly fixed with the onset of puberty, thereafter settling into patterns which
he was to follow all his life.

He used, for example, to walk up and down along the banks of the Boyne
while reading and scenes involving running water held a strong attraction
for him ever afterwards.[22] Other longer strolls through country lanes were
often given over to serious thinking and indeed it was on one such walk
many years later that his most famous discovery of quaternions was made.[23]

Psychologists like Jung have sometimes stressed the role of water as an aid
to creative thinking, an observation which perhaps only the truly creative are
properly qualified to evaluate. Others have stressed the beneficial role of
walking in terms of problem-solving, relating this to that important step
when the crawling infant first rises and knows that it can dominate the local
world. Whether or not such theories have any validity, we are probably still
not properly equipped to say. Here it must remain sufficient to record that
Hamilton formed such habits very early, thereafter adhering to them
faithfully throughout his years.

This was also the period when Hamilton began to develop an interest in
poetry, a subject which was at times to dominate his life almost as much as
mathematics. The poetry doubtless began with formal exercises in versifying
(as mentioned in the Trim School Prospectus), such exercises then being
common at all levels of the classical educational scheme.

Young William however soon began to soar far above such stilted
boundaries, a matter obvious from the last lines of his 1821 poem *To the
Evening Star:*

> Say lovely Planet! do congenial souls
> Quaff pure delight from thy etherial rills;
> And while unmixed their tide of pleasure rolls,
> Cast down a pitying glance on human ills?[24]

This poem also marks Hamilton's first consideration of the possibility that
other planets might be inhabited, a question which was to interest him
throughout his life due to his speculations on a possible physical location for
heaven. Eliza was the sister with whom he most liked to discuss and share
such ideas. Now aged fourteen and living with her relatives at Ballinderry,
she too would grow up to be a poetess in her own right. The fact that they
were separated orphans probably added an extra piquancy to the frequent
letters between the two.

For the same reason, occasional family reunions were treasured, as
recorded by William in his long poem in celebration of the feast of
Hallowe'en, 1822:

To me this day has highest charms,
It gives Eliza to mine arms;
Again our kindred spirits meet,
And every joy is doubly sweet;
And while my life flows smooth away;
This will have been my happiest day.[25]

Obviously such lines sound somewhat curious in our post-Freudian era. But doubtless they seemed wholly innocent in the context of their times. And a clearer picture of William's perception of their relationship emerges from a birthday poem he sent his sister on April 3rd, the following year:

Oh! tell me from what hidden ties
The charities of kindred rise,
Those softening feelings, mild, sublime,
That 'scape the withering blasts of time;
Like sister buds unsevered found,
Though rude the tempest raged around;
Those pure and holy loves that shed
Their mingling influence o'er our head,
While happy spirits from above,
With a benignant smile approve.[26]

Hamilton was also of course writing other poetry around this time, verses like a parody on Horace or lines on the inspiring associations of Trim. One final example from a poem called *The Dream*, written in June 1822, must suffice to show the general tenor of these verses:

Oft in the solemn midnight hour,
When things of other worlds have power,
The soul perhaps may take its flight
To regions of celestial light,
Once haply its own bright abode,
Ere earthly light was yet bestowed;
Mounting on incorporeal wings
May hear unutterable things;
See sights denied to human ken;
Meet friends, long wept for here, again.[27]

Throughout such writings of this period runs a strong sense of heightened awareness, a keen appreciation of matters like scenery, sibling ties, religion, astronomy. Writing to Eliza in early 1823, William noted that he now felt himself to unite in some degree the poet with the astronomer. This remark neatly summarises his two main intellectual recreations at this time.

The Emergent Scientist

For a boy as naturally inquisitive as young William, all the workings of Nature in their varied manifestations might have been expected to prove equally interesting. Curiously enough this was not so. The records reveal little or no interest in bird-watching, plants, rocks, magnets or home chemistry experiments. Perhaps Uncle James, in keeping with his classical Greek tradition, steered the boy away from such comparatively base or practical activities. At any rate, young William's early scientific activities were almost exclusively centered on mathematics and astronomy, the two fields with which he would be later most concerned.

In these circumstances it comes as no surprise to find that Hamilton's earliest extant scientific observation is prophetically enough concerned with light:

> *William to Grace, July 5, 1817:* As the lightning on St. John's Eve arose immediately over the bonfires, as it resembled a blaze rather than a flash, and as it was here unaccompanied by thunder, I even thought that it was not lightning![28]

A few years earlier, Cousin Arthur had bought William a telescope which he was accustomed to use for probing the heavens at night. Occasionally, he would wait up late or even rise at some unearthly hour to catch an expected eclipse, the Trim household evidently being accustomed to rising often at odd hours. In other contexts, Hamilton talks of rising in the middle of the night to help James with some particularly urgent sermon. His later habit of working through the night on occasions is then another of those characteristic individual traits in the adult scientist which can so readily be traced back to Trim.

William was much encouraged in his early efforts at astronomy by the Rev. John Willey of Ballinderry, the minister of the Moravian Church who was married to his mother's sister Susan. The Willeys took in some of the girls immediately after the death of both parents and they also took care of the slightly defective Archianna in later years. John Willey too was an amateur astronomer and was also apparently something of an astrologer — even though the latter would have been in direct contravention of his ultra-Calvinistic faith! At any rate, he helped young Hamilton with his early observations and continued to correspond with him throughout his lifetime. The archives contain many examples of his letters on astronomy, most of them complete with diagrams executed with great finesse and care.

Around this period, young William was led to use the gaunt Yellow Steeple (see page 28) just outside his front door as a marker for a giant sundial and a detailed interest in sundials would remain with him all his days. He also organised the older pupils in the school into a Senate of Four led by himself. This group can be considered midway between the earlier Society of Four set up with his sisters and the later learned associations with which he was actively engaged. The Senate of Four also helped with Hamilton's own design of telegraph or semaphore. This was still to the scientific forefront because of the Napoleonic invasion scare and also because electricity had not yet been applied. Indeed one famous version, by the local innovator R. L. Edgeworth, had recently been tested out on the nearby Hill of Collon. William was also reading a book on telegraphs at the time.

To design a semaphore system of his own was therefore hardly a

Hamilton's Semaphore and Code *(after Graves)*

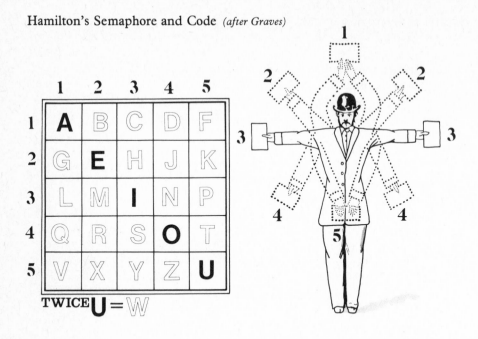

particularly original idea. Hamilton's semaphore scheme was however a simpler and far more practical system than that of Edgeworth; the latter was so complex that frequently messages could not be deciphered by the relatively uneducated operators then available.[29] In fact the real significance of young William's first innovation may lie in a more theoretical sphere. For basically, it involved a simple combination of optics and dynamics, and it was in this very area that Hamilton's later single most important discovery was made.

In any case, William was by now launching himself on a mathematical career. We have seen how prior to 1818 he was comparatively undeveloped in this field. But in that year, he was invited to meet Zerah Colburn, an American calculating prodigy, then visiting Dublin. Prodigies were at that time a subject of general curiosity and Zerah's father was trying to make money by exhibiting his fourteen-year-old son throughout Europe as a sort of mathematical Mozart. Dublin, however, was very proud of its own local prodigy and so a mathematical contest seems to have been arranged between the two.

Hamilton was well and truly beaten in this first contest, though "not without honour" according to Graves. Two years later, however, Colburn was back in Dublin. And now the tables were turned with a vengeance. On this second occasion, William was far more interested in how Zerah could perform such mysteriously involved calculations so rapidly — a process which, as William suspected, he did not really understand. But now, William's superior understanding enabled him to clarify the procedures totally. Colburn's calculations were basically a matter of an unusually developed memory and as such, unlikely to be of any great practical use!

Curiously enough, the academic pathways of these two youthful prodigies made a diametric intersection at this point. For soon afterwards, Colburn forsook his mental calculations and went on to become a professor of languages at Norwich University in America. Hamilton on the contrary gradually abandoned his earlier great interest in languages for the new fascination of mathematics — an interest which Colburn had fired. Later he would always date the real start of his mathematical studies from this point.[30]

Five months after his second meeting with Colburn, Hamilton was reading Newton's biography. Ten weeks after that he started on Newton's *Principia*, parts of which work were then on the university course. The following August, he went to Dublin to see the Irish visit of King George IV in 1821, a major public festival comparable with the arrival of the Pope nowadays. James regretted that time was being wasted and so sent along a new textbook on analytical geometry by Dionysius Lardner to be studied at spare intervals. William found the subject so fascinating that he was finally well and truly committed.[31]

The state visit of George IV was also to be important for young Hamilton in another outcome several years later. The city institutions and Trinity College put on such effusive displays of loyalty that the monarch was moved to pronounce himself well pleased. The Astronomer Royal, Brinkley, was apparently especially active in organising these displays of loyalty. Five years later, the King returned the compliment when the Bishopric of Cloyne fell vacant. Brinkley was thus promoted from science to religion and the way was clear for Hamilton to fill the coveted post.[32]

Meanwhile, young William's mathematical abilities were developing rapidly. His essays at this time reflect his preoccupations with such questions as the value of $0/0$ and similar issues, topics often notable for their bearing on basic but seldom examined questions. A good example is the following very profound early train of thought, one which is eventually stated more completely in his 1835 paper on *Algebra as the Science of Pure Time*:

> *March 13, 1822:* All the branches of Arithmetic are applied in a much more extensive manner than was contemplated by the inventors of them. By the introduction of negative and fractional quantities, operations that diminish are included under Addition and Multiplication, and others that increase under Subtraction and Division.[33]

Hamilton was now also contemplating Euclid — not just learning the formal theorems, but also speculating on the manner in which they might have been derived. His remarkably creative *Dialogue between Euclid and Pappus*, on the possible origins of geometry, dates from this period in summer 1823. The *Dialogue* is really a very revealing exercise in youthful imagination and, as such, better examined in conjunction with Hamilton's ideas on algebra in later chapters.

The sheer intensity and enthusiasm with which young William now threw himself into mathematics (and was obviously encouraged to do so) are also noteworthy:

> *William to Arthur, September 4, 1822:* I was amused this morning, looking back on the eagerness with which I began the different branches of Mathematics, and how I always thought my present pursuits the most interesting.
>
> I believe it was seeing Zerah Colburn that first gave me an interest in these things. For a long time afterwards, I liked to perform long operations in my mind; extracting the square and the cube root, and everything that related to the properties of numbers.
>
> It is now a good while since I began Euclid. Do you remember when I used to go to breakfast with you, and we would read two or three propositions every morning?[34]

The methods which William had learned from his meeting with Colburn were now also being applied to geometry:

> *October 12, 1822:* To return to Euclid, I have since read through the six books on this plan. When I am walking or otherwise prevented from graver pursuits, I glance at the title and work back from it, having resolved not to assist myself by text or figure until I conquer the difficulty by my own resources. In general I find this very easy, sometimes not.[35]

This offers another instance of the striking permanence of ingrained habit in Hamilton's character. For he never deserted these early practices. Indeed he always delighted in advanced and lengthy computation, both mentally or on paper, until his last days.

4 COLLEGE DAYS

"My life as a student has always to me been divided into two principal parts – preparation for Entrance; preparation for Fellowship."

Hamilton to Cousin Arthur, September 28, 1823

Long before even the start of his secondary schooling, young William's thoughts were being deliberately directed towards university. Archibald wrote his lengthy homily on the subject in 1819, but two years earlier his son had already begun to familiarise himself with the post-graduate stage of his intended career. At the age of twelve, he had started coming up to Dublin to attend the public examination where graduates could obtain a Fellowship; he did however have the grace to admit that most of the questions were still beyond him at this stage.[1]

The same thoroughness in preparation for Entrance becomes increasingly obvious as the date loomed near. Uncle James correctly stressed the formal examination course as his nephew's main priority at this stage. Other interests like poetry, astronomy or even mathematical speculation would meantime have to be relegated to second place. William's mentor was never one for letting slip an idle moment and his letters of this period continue to emphasise the necessity of adhering to the formal Entrance course.

By now however, these dictates were beginning to clash a trifle uneasily with Hamilton's growing passion for mathematical research. One of the candidates whose success in Fellowship William observed in 1821 was Charles Boyton. He was the son of a family friend and as such, was apparently chosen as the boy's future tutor at university. William began calling on him in this capacity whenever he happened to be in Dublin; Boyton reciprocated by advising him on the 'new' French mathematics as well as on suitable textbooks. Some of these books were obtained on loan from the Dublin Institution, a body then active in disseminating useful scientific knowledge.[2]

In this way, Hamilton came to read Harte's new English translation of *Mécanique Céleste* by Laplace. His competence at this level was soon demonstrated convincingly, when he discovered a previously undetected if somewhat minor error in the reasonings of the French author! This happened in September, but Hamilton had already demonstrated his mathematical ability in July by answering a problem which Boyton was unable to resolve.[3]

Another friend of the family who heard about William's correction of Laplace offered to bring it to the attention of a suitable authority. This friend, George Kiernan of Henry Street, was the son of a pharmacist who lived just around the corner from Hamilton's grandmother's original shop.[4] Kiernan was a member of the Royal Irish Academy and was thus acquainted with the Astronomer Royal, Dr. Brinkley; to him, he showed young William's correction of Laplace.

Whether or not Kiernan made this offer on his own initiative seems impossible to determine now. Remembering however Archibald's earlier unsuccessful attempt to introduce William to the astronomer in 1819, we can at least reasonably doubt whether Kiernan acted on his own. The Hamiltons were never slow in advertising the achievements of their prodigy and so we can perhaps suspect a quiet suggestion from Cousin Arthur, or one of the Huttons, behind Kiernan's generous offer.

At any rate, Brinkley pronounced himself impressed enough to wish to see the youthful student of Laplace. But William was unable to take up this opportunity immediately, possibly because he was then ill with a bronchial complaint at Trim. In fact he did not visit Brinkley until the Christmas holidays two months later, by which time he had written two original mathematical papers. Brinkley responded with an open invitation to visit him anytime and another useful contact for young Hamilton was thereby made.

It had originally been intended that William should enter College around the time of these developments in October 1822. He would then have been just over seventeen, about the average entrance age. Outstanding pupils however often entered earlier, as Uncle James himself had done at the age of fifteen. It is therefore a matter of some interest to determine why such an outstanding and already well-known prodigy should now hold back for yet another year.

Much later, Hamilton himself would cite "a trifling illness" as the reason for this delay. Graves agrees that the "determining motive (was) the state of his health, which during the spring and summer had caused much uneasiness." Hankins voices the more reasonable suspicion that William was held back deliberately in order that he might be assured of doing well.[5] Whether or not he really was ill, the youth was still obviously preparing himself with an almost heroic intensity:

William to Eliza, October 9, 1822: There is very little of the day that I am not reading, but I read a good deal standing and even walking. After dinner, I generally take out my book and walk up and down the top of our lower meadow.[6]

Evidently even the ordinary daylight hours were not considered enough:

William to Arthur, October 12, 1822: We have been getting up before five for several mornings, that is, my Uncle and I; he pulls a string which goes through the wall and is fastened to my shirt at night.[7]

But Uncle James was obviously still worried about those original

mathematical researches which the boy was even then preparing for
Brinkley, as is evidenced by a further passage in the same letter:

> In the conversation I had with my uncle on the subject of my
> deficiencies, he observed that since my time and thoughts had become
> most valuable, they had been taken up very much with mathematical
> studies — not without his approbation — yet which had diverted my
> attention, not only from the Classics, but the Science of the
> undergraduate course. This was a very just observation.

These admonitions evidently had their effect, at any rate to some degree.
Seven months later William could report as follows to Arthur:

> *May 31, 1823:* The time I have given to science has been very small
> indeed; for I fear again becoming infatuated with it and prefer giving
> my leisure even to less valuable reading, if it can be connected in any
> way to classical literature. I find however that I have not lost much
> ground.
>
>   In Optics, I have made a very curious discovery, at least so it seems to
> me...[8]

Although private scientific interests were then still intruding, William was
obviously making a determined effort to concentrate on the prescribed
courses — a policy which soon brought fruit. When he sat the entrance
examination five weeks later on July 7, 1823, he was placed first out of one
hundred candidates. And in addition, he received a premium or book prize
for excellence in Hebrew. These results were at once a vindication of Uncle
James' tuition and a harbinger of future unprecedented examination
triumphs.

Trinity College

The institution which young Hamilton was now about to enter differed
considerably from a modern university. When over two centuries previously,
Queen Elizabeth I had founded Trinity College as the nucleus of the
University of Dublin, she had two main objectives in mind. One was to
provide a suitable higher education for those in Ireland deemed worthy to
receive it. The other was to ensure an adequate supply of clerics for
administering the Established Church — which accounts for the large
clerical element among the staff even during Hamilton's time.

Trinity continued to fulfil its role with varying degrees of effectiveness for
two centuries after its foundation in 1591. Early in the eighteenth century,
formal courses in science were introduced. The first Professor of Natural
and Experimental Philosophy was Richard Helsham who was appointed in
1724. Fifteen years later, his lectures were published and remained in use as
a textbook for about a century. As such, he was one of the authors studied
by young William in pre-college days.[9]

Science at Trinity received another fillip when Francis Andrews was
appointed Provost in 1758. He was a barrister with a formidable reputation
among the ladies; since he was not an ordained cleric, a special dispensation

The Provost's House, Trinity College, Dublin, in 1817 *(after Cadell and Davies)*

was required to enable him to hold the post. Andrews built the present Provost's House before his untimely death at the age of 56 in 1774. And in his will, he bequeathed the sum of £3,000 to endow a new observatory and a related Professorship of Astronomy. This was the post in which young Hamilton would soon show an interest.[9a]

After some delay and a further subsidy, Andrews' observatory was duly constructed atop the long rise of Dunsink, about five miles northwest of the main College. Henry Ussher, a direct descendant of the famed Archbishop Ussher, was appointed in 1783 to supervise construction, but he died after a mere seven years in this work. Ussher's successor in 1790 was John Brinkley from Cambridge, then aged 29 years. His published textbook, *Elements in Astronomy* (1808), was used in early studies by young Hamilton. The reverend astronomer was however approaching the venerable age of sixty when William was first introduced to him in 1822.

Meantime Bartholomew Lloyd from Wexford had been appointed Erasmus Smith Professor of Mathematics in 1813. He was a man of boundless energy who set out to modernise his subject at Trinity. This he did by introducing the new 'French' mathematics into the curriculum, French mathematicians such as Lagrange and Laplace then being the most advanced anywhere. Similar moves were afoot in England where Euclid and Newton had long monopolised studies.

Lloyd wrote a *Treatise on Analytical Geometry* in 1819 and also persuaded other Fellows like Dionysius Lardner and Romney Robinson to write similar books. All these works were speedily assimilated by young Hamilton.

He was thereby preparing himself to add his own due quota to the extraordinary flowering of mathematical talent then just commencing at Trinity.[10]

A total of around 700 students were on the College books in these years, not all of them studious by any means. But the royal recognition, accruing from the visit of George IV in 1821, apparently boosted the College in public esteem and numbers increased rapidly afterwards.

Students from noble families could also graduate through a shorter course than the fee-paying pensioners or free-place sizars. The privileged status of the former was further emphasised by the more elaborate gowns they wore.[11] Pensioners and sizars however accounted for about three-quarters of the roll. So we can estimate that there were about 500 of these more serious students totalled over all years during Hamilton's time in college.

Providing for this student body, the Provost ruled over an academic staff of around twenty-five. Of these, one-third, the Senior Fellows, were primarily responsible for governing; the remainder were the Junior Fellows, more directly concerned with instruction. Fellows were never supposed to marry in keeping with Trinity's clerical celibate tradition; their close connection with the Established Church allowed many of them to become bishops in due course. The vow of celibacy was also often quietly ignored. But the realisation of its existence would soon inhibit Hamilton's assessment of his prospects in his earliest and most serious love affair.

A promising graduate could always compete for a Fellowship, these being awarded through an entirely oral examination held for four hours daily on four successive days. In 1824, the examination subjects were logic, mathematics, physics, ethics, history, chronology, Latin, Greek and Hebrew. The same spectrum of subjects features in Hamilton's own studies, as well as the Trim School prospectus, and as such was well representative of traditional education at the time. The Annual Fellowship Examinations were conducted entirely in public almost in the manner of a theatre. They were thus regarded as good intellectual entertainment by Dublin society and crowds as big as 500 might attend. Young William was often in this audience long before he had even entered university.

Given the relatively small student body and the even smaller academic staff, most people in Trinity in the 1820s probably knew each other by sight and name. There could have been none of the faceless anonymity often characteristic of any large and highly compartmentalised university of the present day. The entire senior staff likely knew every promising student personally from at least the senior freshman year. We can be sure that Hamilton must have been marked out with interest before long.

Examination Prowess

Some evidence of the widespread academic interest already created by young Hamilton at this point comes from much further afield. Writing just after Hamilton's death over forty years later, his future friend and confidant, de Morgan, had this to say:

> *September 5, 1865:* When I was an undergraduate not far advanced, and he must have been about nineteen years old, I heard of the extraordinary attainments of a very young student of Trinity College, which were noised about at Cambridge. This rumour was made more interesting by other rumours which also circulated about the same time concerning another young Irishman, then recently matriculated at Cambridge. This was poor Murphy, whose subsequent career, though great in mathematics, fell short in conduct and discretion. The appearance of the two at once in the field gave both an interest, and I was thus led to watch Hamilton's career before I knew anything of him personally.[12]

Of the unfortunate Murphy, we shall have more to say in due course, mainly because his subsequent career forms a striking contrast to that of Hamilton. For while it would appear that both young men were not dissimilar in mathematical ability, there was a vast difference in academic background, family upbringing and early general education between the two.

Meantime Hamilton was now well and truly launched into student life at Trinity. Characteristically however, he was already thinking far ahead to his post-graduate career. Evidence of this occurs in his letters of the period, as for example in the following confession to Cousin Arthur:

> *September 28, 1823:* My life as a student has always (seemed) to me to be divided into two parts — preparation for Entrance; preparation for Fellowship. The first part is over and I think the second has begun. For I consider Academic honours as not only valuable *per se*, but important as steps to the ultimate rank at which I aim. So you see I am trying to prove that in reading for premiums, I am really aiming higher.[13]

Premiums and certificates Hamilton duly obtained with almost total efficiency. The former were book prizes awarded each term for being first in a class of about 30 students, the latter being substituted if the candidate had already gained a premium that year. Separate examinations were held for Science and Classics in the first or freshman year, the two being combined afterwards. But in the final sophister examination, both subjects were again examined separately and a gold medal awarded to the outstanding student in each speciality.

During his first year, Hamilton came first in his division in each subject at every test. Twice, he gained the Chancellor's Prize for poetic composition. In Classics, he was awarded the further distinction of an *optime*, a judgement of excellence so rare that it was usually given only about once in every twenty years!

Hamilton did not reside in the College but with Cousin Arthur in South Cumberland Street, a mile away. His wide earlier learning meant that he was never unduly stretched in his studies and indeed he was able to pursue his own mathematical research more or less continuously together with the College course. He also had time to socialise quite considerably, attending fashionable dinner parties given by relatives or important figures to whom

Hamilton aged twenty-six: The Adare Bust by Kirk   *(Courtesy Trinity College, Dublin)*

he had been introduced. Sometimes these occasions extended into weekend visits to the country houses of the minor gentry and many of the friendships formed in this manner lasted throughout his life.

Maria Edgeworth was probably the most important of those whose acquaintance William made in this way during his college years. They met in August 1824 at her family seat in Edgeworthstown, Co.Longford, the youth being introduced by Mr. Butler who was Uncle James' superior at Trim. Hamilton seems at first to have been unimpressed by the diminutive appearance of the fifty-six year old woman who was Ireland's foremost authoress. Maria, on the other hand, had been forewarned by Brinkley that she might be talking to a second Newton.[14] In any case, the two soon warmed to each other and Hamilton was to consult Maria on various literary matters in later years.

Graves has given us an interesting pen-picture of what young Hamilton looked like during these student days. Broad-chested and medium-sized, he was strong and active in swimming and gymnastics. A combination of light blue eyes and dark brown hair, together with a certain harmony of features, "produced almost the effect of good looks".[15] But Hamilton's most striking physical feature was a countenance forever beaming with a simple happy cheerfulness and general acute alertness, a quality well captured in the bust by Kirk, reproduced here.

Hamilton in these early days, up to about the age of thirty, could then almost literally light up a crowded room by sheer personal radiance and magnetism. This was in notable contrast to his later years, when we can trace a striking change in personality as the portraits grow steadily more solemn, dour, sullen and almost grim.

Graves also records that Hamilton used to switch between two different voice tones according to circumstances. When delivering some solemn speech or lecture his tones were deep, rich, sonorous and rhythmical — a trait perhaps unconsciously copied from earlier memories of Uncle James. But when he was cheerful, ebullient or in the process of discovery, Hamilton's voice rose rapidly in pitch. A modern psychologist might chose to interpret these changes in terms of switching between the contrasting ego-states of solemn Parent and cheerful Child.

Hamilton's poetess sister Eliza was now at a boarding school just two streets away from Cousin Arthur's house and she too has left us a pen-picture which complements Graves:

> *October 22, 1824:* I had been drawing pictures of you in my mind in your study, with your most awfully sublime face of thought, now sitting down and now walking about, at times rubbing your hands with an air of satisfaction, and at times bursting forth into some very heroical strain of poetry, in your own internal solemn ventriloquist-like voice, when you address yourself to the silence and solitude of your own room, and indeed even at times when your mysterious poetical addresses are not quite unheard.[16]

Eliza obviously had still much to learn in punctuation, while William was apparently happy to talk to himself regardless of whether he had an audience or not!

Hamilton's second year in College was largely a repetition of his first. On December 13,1824 he submitted a highly original paper *On Caustics* dealing with light reflection to the Royal Irish Academy. But the consequences of this move were not immediately obvious. Meantime there were lectures to be attended and examination results to be achieved.

This time, however, matters did not proceed quite as smoothly as before. At the Easter examination in Classics, Hamilton failed to gain the expected premium or certificate, and in fact neither was awarded on this occasion. Graves obliquely suggests jealousy on the part of the examiner Mr. Kennedy, but William was probably downcast due to being disappointed in love. In any case, he resolved to do better next time and Uncle James seized the opportunity to warn against the dangers of relaxing in the scholastic race.[17]

Around the start of his third or junior sophister year, William was obviously ill. He did not sit the customary examinations in January 1826 and the circumlocution of the records suggest a serious bout of depression or even total nervous breakdown. If so, the rejection of his paper on light by the Academy — together with the loss of his first love — were probably more responsible than any examination trauma. Both these episodes will be examined in greater detail later. Whatever the proximate cause of this absence, Hamilton returned to sit his examinations on April 15.

In these examinations of April 1826, Hamilton secured his second *optime*. This time the subject was Science (really mathematics) instead of Classics and the examiner was his tutor, Charles Boyton. On the next occasion, the latter sought to get another Fellow to act as examiner, confessing that indeed his own mind had already been made up long before. But not even Kennedy was willing to take up this formidable challenge and Hamilton again gained his customary first place in October.

No student within living memory had ever gained two *optime* awards and Hamilton became the talk of Dublin as a result. He did not however allow his achievement to unsettle him, but instead set his sights on an even more exalted prize. If he could gain an *optime* in both Science and Classics, why not also the coveted Gold Medal or first place in the finals *in each*? Needless to remark, no one had ever seriously attempted such a feat previously.

To achieve first place in both finals would obviously require intensive study leading up to the examinations in Trinity Term 1827, a task which Hamilton undertook with his usual optimism and energy. But we will never know whether or not he would have succeeded for dramatic events originating elsewhere were soon to intervene.

Love Unfulfilled

Meantime, we can pause to consider how strongly his family background and early education influenced Hamilton in his constant pursuit of the Ideal.

221700

Summerhill Mansion, Co. Meath — the home of Catherine Disney
(Courtesy Irish Architectural Archive)

Those sermons preached by Uncle James specified the marks of an Ideal character to which ordinary mortals should aspire. The lives of numerous great men, perused by William in his schooldays, presented similarly idealised versions of reality. So too, in fact, was most of mathematics, a field to which the youth would soon add his own striking idealisations in due course.

The vision of the Ideal was at that time also prominent in romantic poetry, being there often associated with natural scenery and love. Young William's poems and letters began to reflect a heightened awareness of the former about the age of 16; the theme is well developed by early 1823 in compositions such as his *Verses on the Scenery and Associations of Trim*.[18] As yet however, love merits only transient and fleeting references, so that we can deduce that he had not so far met any worthy ideal female.

All this changed dramatically on August 17, 1824. That was the date when Hamilton first met Catherine Disney, an enchanted occasion which he would continue to recall with heightened nostalgia as he grew old. Ironically enough, Uncle James was the agent of their meeting, but we can be sure that he would have acted decisively to avoid the introduction could he have foreseen the eventual outcome.

Catherine Disney's father was a landlord's agent in the Langford estate at Summerhill, Co. Meath, seven miles southeast of Trim. The Disney family probably lived in the owner's residence whenever the latter was absent. Summerhill Mansion at that time was one of the wonders of Ireland, by far the most majestic and elegant of the great Palladian country houses built in the previous century.[19] It resembled a miniature Versailles set amidst the rolling woodlands of County Meath.

When one remembers William's admiration for the Ideal, it is easy to imagine his feelings as he approached this architectural masterpiece. His visit to Summerhill was really one of a series which he was making to various country houses at that time. But Summerhill was special because it was the greatest house in Ireland and also because within it, he first met the only woman he ever really loved.

From the moment of their introduction, William became totally and devastatingly infatuated with Catherine Disney and she apparently fell equally in love. And this first great infatuation was destined to shape the thoughts and memories of both throughout a lifetime afterwards. Long years later, it would lead them into conduct we would now regard as foolish, but which James would undoubtedly have then classified as 'sin'.

The classic theme of romantic tragedy however also demands that true love be constantly frustrated or even unfulfilled because of external circumstances. Such was to be the case with William and Catherine. And when eventually she mustered sufficient courage to break the rules and defy convention, it was only to find that he was by now determined to follow the dictates of the classic script to its bitter, empty end!

Graves has described Hamilton's feelings for Catherine as thoroughly as was possible within the circumspect proprieties of late Victorian times. He did however also leave sufficient clues for others to piece together the full story. Hankins has very properly followed up these clues with characteristic scholarship and so was the first to describe their story in unambiguous detail.[20]

Catherine Disney was one of a family of ten which included seven brothers, some of them older and some younger than herself. When they first met, she was most likely about eighteen or much the same age as Hamilton. Graves states that she was "by all accounts of singular beauty, amiable, sensitive and pious". We know that she was a blue-eyed blonde, as Hamilton mentions several times; we also learn from him that she could sing and play the harp. And finally, she must have had an unusually independent mind for her society and station as shown by later developments.

That William and Catherine were strongly attracted to each other was obvious to all. So engrossed were they in each other's company at their very first meeting that they all but ignored the other guests at the dinner table. Nor were Catherine's parents at first entirely disapproving, for they began calling on Cousin Arthur and Hamilton's sisters in Dublin.

William now started to cultivate those of Catherine's brothers who were fellow-students at Trinity, thereby commencing several friendships which endured through life. To strengthen the links with their sister, he also started to help the younger boys with their studies, a strategy he would again employ in future years. Much later, however, the objects of his pedagogic efforts and instruction would be Catherine's two sons instead of her brothers.[21]

Since Catherine was obviously so equally happy in William's company, the young couple met several times after their first meeting in August. But always, they must have been severely restricted by the conventions of their class and times. We know for certain that no kisses were exchanged at this stage and probably love was not directly mentioned either.

After a few months however, William certainly made clear his feelings in this *Valentine Ode* of 1825:

> Forgive me, that on bliss so high
> Lingers thrilling phantasie:
> That the one Image, dear and bright,
> Feeds thought by day, and dreams by night:
> That Hope presumes to mingle thee,
> With visions of my destiny![22]

Such forthright declarations however provoked a most unexpected conse-

LORETTE WILMOT LIBRARY
NAZARETH COLLEGE

quence. Either Catherine's parents became alarmed at the obvious direction matters were taking or a more desirable match for their daughter had by now been formalised. At any rate, and just immediately after this hopeful Valentine, Mrs. Disney informed William that their daughter was to be married by the end of May!

The marriage arranged for Catherine was to a man about fifteen years her senior. He was the Rev. William Barlow of a Dublin legal family and therefore presumably of suitably established status and means. Mrs. Disney had always been favourably disposed towards Hamilton, so it may have been her husband who regarded a settled clergyman as a better marriage prospect than an impoverished undergraduate. In later years, Hamilton claimed that Catherine was more or less dragged to the marriage altar, a possibility to some extent supported by her subsequent history.

At any rate, William's ego was now as shattered by Catherine's marriage as it had been elated by her discovery such a short time before. Finding his Ideal had roused him to new heights of ambition; losing her so unexpectedly now cast him down into corresponding troughs of despondency. And the memory of this first and greatest love would continue to haunt him ever after throughout a lifetime, one also sadly bereft of a suitable marriage partner. For Hamilton, Catherine would always remain an Ideal undiminished by any of the various imperfections of sad reality, one bright forever with all the promise of what might have been. Thirty-two years later, Hamilton would confess to his confidant P. G. Tait that at this point he had been driven close to suicide. He writes of an almost overpowering urge to throw himself into the local canal while on his way to one of his regular breakfasts with Brinkley at the observatory:

> I wish I could add that it was religion, or even generally my belief in the Bible, which protected me. My recollection has always been that it was simply a feeling of personal courage, which revolted against the imagined act, as one of cowardice. I would not leave my post; I felt that I had something to do.[23]

The loss of Catherine did however have other immediate and damaging effects. For even though Hamilton passed his June examinations just after her marriage, he did so without the usual high honours. And he seems to have been gravely incapacitated in his health towards the end of that same year. The accounts of the Stanley Society (a discussion group formed with his sisters and the other Disneys) refers to this illness. It was probably a severe form of depression, similar in its symptoms to that which recurred after he suffered another rejection in 1832.

Hamilton was too much of a gentleman and also too conventional ever to mention Catherine Disney by name again. He did however provide a very clear account of his feelings in a long poem called *The Enthusiast*. Written on January 21, 1826 and published in the Dublin Literary Gazette of September 1830, reprints were duly presented to any suitably understanding listener whom Hamilton would meet in later years.

The Enthusiast details Hamilton's early inspiration derived from poetry and nature, and describes the sense of heightened awareness of these catalysed by Catherine's discovery. It tells of the corresponding depression brought on by her marriage and ends with his eventual recovery from her loss:

> At length his bitter anguish passed away,
> But left him darkly changed. His mind awoke;
> Its powers were unimpaired, and the affection
> Of his fond friends could warm his bosom still;
> And he seemed happy; but his heart was chilled,
> And he was the enthusiast no more.[24]

The much more liberal relations between the sexes nowadays render it difficult for us to form a proper appreciation of the depth of Hamilton's feelings for Catherine. Perhaps we may regret that the Fates never saw fit to bring them together again in a situation where a more fulfilling romance might have flowered. Then we might know more about the inspiration derived from Catherine's real presence as distinct from her idealised memory — and also whether early infatuation could ever really have ripened into lasting love.

The Urge to Fame

From early days, young Hamilton had been imbued with a very strong ambition to achieve fame. The many great men whose lives were read during his schooldays doubtless served as models for emulation, while the various letters from his father Archibald further fuelled his ambition. Uncle James and Cousin Arthur also encouraged him. By seventeen, William's rapidly growing competence in mathematics therefore suggested the path by which such fame might most readily be achieved:

> *William to Aunt Mary, August 26, 1822:* Mighty minds in all ages have combined to rear upon a lofty edifice the vast and beautiful temple of Science, and inscribed their names upon it in imperishable characters; but the edifice is not completed: it is not yet too late to add another pillar or ornament. I have scarcely yet arrived at its foot, but I may aspire one day to reach the summit.[25]

In passing, we may note that this striking metaphor was very likely suggested by the monumental pillar just recently erected in honour of the Duke of Wellington by the townsfolk of his native Trim.[26] In any case young William's growing confidence in his own mathematical ability was soon reinforced by continuing encouragement from Brinkley. In his *Valentine Ode* to Catherine, written before he was twenty in 1825, Hamilton's urge to fame could therefore be more openly expressed:

> Perchance it may be mine to soar
> Higher than mortal ever before:
> Climb the meridian steeps of fame,
> And leave an everlasting name.

> If such my lot . . . O then how sweet,
> To lay my triumphs at thy feet.

One year later, Catherine was of course beyond reach, at least for the moment, but the same unabashed urge to fame could still be clearly expressed in *The Enthusiast*:

> . . . He longed to leave
> Some great memorial of himself, which might
> Win for him an imperishable name.

By this time also Hamilton's path along the rocky road to fame had been very clearly marked out. It lay through his application of the new 'French' mathematics to optics, that branch of science embracing the relations between vision and light. From the viewpoint of creativity, it is now a matter of considerable interest as to why young William should have centered so quickly on such a relatively fruitful area of research. Apart from his obvious intelligence, at least five factors can be discerned in this development.

In the first place, Hamilton was largely self-taught in mathematics, a fact which undoubtedly helped preserve him from that too early rigidity which conventional teaching often fosters. Secondly, his originality was probably enhanced by his well-recorded habit of continuously going over problems mentally while recasting them in different form. Newton attributed his own success to his habit of continuously 'thinking into' problems and Hamilton has left abundant descriptions of himself engaged in similar activity during long country walks.[27]

Thirdly, William had been trained from a very early age to seek out the philological roots of terms and meaning derived from ancient languages. Inevitably, when he came to mathematics, a similar process of searching and questioning was applied. This led him to consider problems normally taken for granted by most people. In the fourth place, Hamilton's continuous exposure to the concept of the Ideal in the classics generated that wider sense of intellectual vision which such studies can confer. His constant aim was therefore to seek results of the widest possible generality, a feature indeed characteristic of his later work. As early as 1822, he expressed to Eliza what he was seeking:

> . . . (some principle) in kind, though not in degree, as Newton's, when
> he found the one simple and pervading principle which governs the
> motions of the Universe, from the fall of an apple to the orbit of the
> stars.[28]

Finally and significantly, young William became highly proficient in mathematics while still youthful and therefore creative. In addition, he happened to come along at just the proper time; he assimilated the French mathematics when they were still relatively new and undeveloped. Nobody had yet attempted to apply the French mathematical approach to the principles of light — principles with which he was familiar from his early experience with telescopes and astronomy.

Undergraduate Research

The field in which young Hamilton was to make such a rapid name for himself derives from the work of the philosopher René Descartes about 1637. Descartes introduced a revolution in mathematics by forging a new link between geometry and algebra, demonstrating how the geometric properties of lines and spatial figures could be validly described by algebraic equations. At first however, these new Cartesian techniques were largely regarded as a useful adjunct to geometry, a situation in which the new branch of mathematics rested for over a century.[29]

It was the French scientist Gaspard Monge (1746-1818) who finally developed Descartes' technique as an independent branch of mathematics in its own right. Henceforth, it would be termed 'Analytical Geometry', a discipline distinct from Euclid in that no diagrams or constructions were required. The followers of Monge greatly extended this way of thinking at the end of the 18th century; their collective work was the new or 'French' mathematics, introduced by Bartholomew Lloyd at Trinity after 1813.

Hamilton was soon immersed in the new intellectual ferment in Dublin and he began reading the French mathematical textbooks as early as 1822. His discovery of the error by Laplace was one immediate consequence of this new interest. More important was his earlier experience with telescopes and the laws of light, which were universally still expressed in older or Euclidean terms. It was therefore quite natural that an inquisitive youth

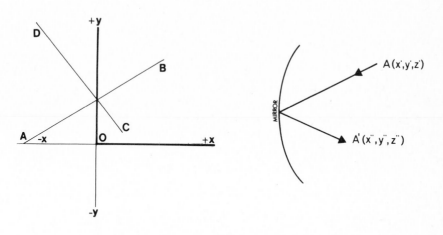

Hamilton's contribution to optical geometry

Descartes united algebra and geometry by expressing Euclidean diagrams in algebraic form, for example

AB can be expressed as $4y = 5x + 10$
or CD can be expressed as $5y = -4x + 10$

In his *Systems of Rays*, Hamilton began to apply algebra in similar fashion to the previously wholly geometric light reflection diagrams

should seek to apply the new mathematics to these older methods of describing the natural law.

During September 1821, William had drawn up a long original mathematical essay of twenty-one pages entitled *Systems of Right Lines*. This essay was the latest in a long series of summaries going back to his early Sanskrit and Persian 'grammars'. More recently, the content of such compositions had become almost exclusively mathematical, embodying themes such as an elementary summary of algebra or 'The Division of 0/0'. What is of most significance is that Hamilton's *Systems of Right Lines* was later acknowledged by him to be the direct conceptual ancestor of his theory of light rays.[30]

Right lines are of course perfectly straight ones and it is easy to see how any treatment of them could readily be extended to light rays. William apparently thought of describing these in terms of the new French mathematics almost as soon as he had begun reading the latter; at least, he mentions "some curious discoveries" to Eliza in a letter of September 23, 1822.[31] A letter to Cousin Arthur on May 31 following is much more definite when it asserts:

> In Optics, I have made a very curious discovery — at least it seems so to me...[32]

At first Hamilton believed that nobody before him had thought of describing light rays in Cartesian terms, until Boyton showed him a paper in which the French author Malus had attempted the same feat in 1809. Initial dismay however soon turned to relief as Hamilton realised that his own method was superior. The treatment of Malus was more limited in scope and his calculations more complex, requiring, for example, two equations where Hamilton required only one.

William continued his own researches along these lines during his first years in Trinity, aided by frequent encouragement from Boyton and Brinkley. His initial treatment was presented in a formal paper *On Caustics* submitted to the Royal Irish Academy (RIA) on December 13, 1824. Brinkley communicated the paper in his role as President of the Academy and William must have felt gratified in having his efforts thus recognised by Ireland's leading scientist.

The Academy referred the paper to a committee of three leading mathematicians, who duly reported the following June. They found the contents "novel and highly interesting" and also displaying "considerable analytical skill". But they considered that the paper was also too abstract and general, and that the derivation of some formulae was far from clear. In short, it was prophetically like many of Hamilton's later publications, requiring to be considerably simplified if it were to be published in a useful form!

Hamilton probably felt cast down by this rejection, especially as it came just one month after Catherine's marriage in May. Eventually however, he roused himself from his depression and simplified his methods as the referees desired. The result was his *Theory of Systems of Rays* presented to the RIA on April 23, 1827. This contribution was recommended to be printed without further ado and Hamilton's first peak on the ascent to fame was thereby well and truly scaled.

The Geometry of Light

In a letter to Coleridge written five years later, Hamilton described himself as striving "to remold the geometry of light".[33] This he had intended to do in a series of three papers of which his earliest, the 1827 contribution, would be the first. It dealt with the simplest case of light reflection, but considered by means of the Cartesian or algebraic method, instead of in the older Euclidean or geometric framework. Part Two of the series would have dealt with the more complex case of light refraction as in lenses; Part Three would have been a generalised summary which also included more specialised examples. But the contents of these two later papers were already listed in Part One and Hankins has proved convincingly that they must have been already written when it was submitted.[34]

In any event, Parts Two and Three of the intended series were never published until a century afterwards, mainly because Hamilton soon improved on his original plan. The improvements appeared in two Supplements to the first paper, which were published during 1830, and in a third more general Supplement, issued in 1833. The Third Supplement also contained Hamilton's dramatic prediction of the previously quite unsuspected phenomenon known as 'conical refraction', a discovery considered further in Chapter 7. This was the discovery which above all others brought him immediate widespread fame.

Hamilton also provided a general account of his theory for those not skilled in mathematics; this account is given in full by Graves and can be considered by us in abbreviated form:

A Ray, in Optics, is to be considered here as a straight or bent or curved line, along which light is propagated; and a *System of Rays* is a collection or aggregate of such lines.

To investigate the geometrical relations of the rays of a system, of which we know the optical origin and history, is to study that System of Rays.

And to generalise this study of one system, so as to become able to pass to the study of other systems, is to form a *Theory of Systems of Rays*.

Towards constructing such an application it is natural, or rather necessary, to employ the method introduced by Descartes for the application of Algebra to Geometry.

The first important application of this algebraical method to the study of optical systems was made by Malus in 1807, many of which conclusions, along with many others, were also obtained afterwards by myself, without knowing what Malus had done.

But my researches soon led me to substitute, for this method of Malus, a very different and (as I conceive that I have proved) a more *appropriate* one, for the study of optical systems.

Instead of employing the *three* functions (of Malus), or at the least their *two* ratios, it becomes sufficient to employ *one function*, which I call *characteristic* or principal.

And thus whereas he made his deductions by setting out with the *two equations of a ray*, I on the other hand establish and employ the *one equation of a system*.[35]

Through an idea conceived at 17 and published before he was 22, Hamilton had therefore succeeded in applying algebra to optics in the widest possible way. This achievement is directly comparable to that of Descartes in his elaboration of a wholly new complement to Euclid two centuries before. Almost immediately, British astronomers would start to compliment Hamilton for having made an entirely new science out of the older geometric diagrams for optics which were all that had existed previously.

While still an undergraduate, Hamilton had therefore contributed the single most important paper that the Royal Irish Academy had received since its foundation or very likely ever since!

PART II

MATURITY

5 APPOINTMENT TO DUNSINK

"Now will you go and settle quietly there with your sisters?"

Charles Boyton to Hamilton, June 1827

Astronomy in Ireland had traditionally displayed a strong interest in chronology ever since Archbishop Ussher's famous calculation that the world was created in October 4004 BC.[1] Ussher, an early graduate of Trinity, was appointed Archbishop of Armagh in 1625, thereafter establishing himself as one of the greatest scholars of his age. He calculated the date of Creation by adding up the ages of the Bible patriarchs. And even though we may now smile at such credulity, his attempt must also be seen as the first numerate attempt at an overall chronology for the universe.

A century after Ussher, literal belief in the Bible was still only slightly challenged by the growing rise of science. Even Newton could not bring himself to contemplate that the world might be more than sixty thousand years old at maximum. By 1780, however, new perceptions from geology were beginning to challenge such beliefs. And in the resultant controversies, Irish chronologists were again prominent in a traditional or Creationist role.[2]

This was the background against which astronomy emerged as an important academic discipline in Ireland. As Trinity College evolved from its largely classical origins, astronomy was introduced naturally as one of the earliest science subjects. Helsham's Professorship of Natural Philosophy of 1724 was followed by a Chair of Mathematics in 1762.[3] Twelve years later, Provost Andrews made his bequest of £3,000 to fund the professorship of astronomy and build the necessary observatory, the latter being duly established at Dunsink during the 1780s.

The Rev. Henry Ussher was, until his death in 1791, in charge of the early stages of introducing astronomy in Trinity. And when the Royal Irish Academy was established in 1785, at Lower Grafton Street just opposite the Provost's House, he contributed its first published article on Dunsink's layout and plans.[4]

Some further idea of how astronomy was then regarded emerges from the notebooks of a student who attended some nineteen lectures on the subject in 1777. As with most lectures of that period, these were cast in a question and answer form:

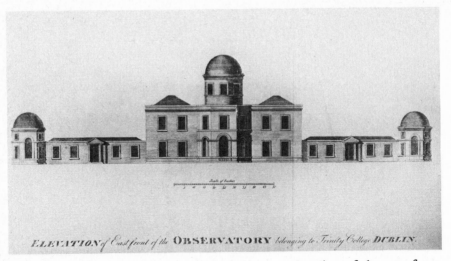

ELEVATION of East front of the **OBSERVATORY** *belonging to Trinity College* **DUBLIN**

The original plan for Dunsink Observatory — elevation of the east front
(Courtesy Royal Irish Academy)

What is the use of studying astronomy? Without it, we would have no geography or chronology of consequence, no certain declaration of history. Besides, it wonderfully pleases and recreates the mind.

What is the moral use of studying astronomy? Because it leads us to entertain just notions of the wisdom and goodness of our Creator.

Can we from this, our earthly habitation, take an accurate view of the motions and phenomena of the celestial bodies? No, for our bodies are, as it were, chained down to our earthly mansion. Yet our minds and imagination may ascend through the heavenly regions and thence contemplate the surprising system of the Universe.[5]

Fifty years later, the viewpoint expressed in such lectures was probably very little changed. It is therefore not surprising to find young Hamilton imbued with the same way of thinking — a fervent belief that scientific advance must inevitably give proof of the infinite wisdom behind God's plan for the Universe.

Meantime, and even while Dunsink was being built, there were similar developments seventy miles to the north at Armagh. There a new Ulster University was envisaged by Archbishop Robinson after his appointment in 1765. To this end, a school and library (and also a prison) had already been planned by 1773. Around this period Robinson met the great astronomer William Herschel. From him the Bishop probably got the idea of an observatory as yet another nucleus for his intended University. Armagh Observatory was therefore begun in 1789, its first director, Rev. J. A. Hamilton, being appointed the following year.[6]

It was originally hoped that Armagh and Dunsink, in co-operation, might come to rival Greenwich, a hope which, due to later developments allied to uncertain funding, was destined to be largely unfulfilled. The end of the eighteenth century did however witness a sudden upsurge of interest in astronomy among private individuals throughout the British Isles. Country vicars like Hamilton's uncle, the Rev. John Willey, often liked to study the stars. And large country houses, like Edgeworthstown, might have an attic room fitted out as a private observatory. Occasionally these private hobbies even developed into a full-time calling, as when Sir James South in 1816 gave up his lucrative medical practice to establish a well-endowed private observatory of his own at Southwark in the London smoke.

Ireland also had its own amateur astronomers who were equally dedicated. Of these, William Parsons, third Earl of Rosse (1800-1867), is certainly the most famous; he began building telescopes in 1827 and had progressed to the world's largest reflector by 1843. His example probably stimulated another rich landowner, Edward Cooper (1798-1863); his private observatory at Markree near Collooney, Co. Sligo, had the largest object-glass then in existence (13.5 inches in diameter). Rosse discovered the spiral nature of the nebulae with his reflector, while Cooper with his refractor went on to catalogue over 50,000 new stars. These were very impressive achievements for which both men received due honour from various learned societies during their lifetimes.[7]

Brinkley's Post

Meantime, the Rev. John Brinkley had been appointed to succeed Ussher at Dunsink in 1792. He was 29 at the time and had earlier served under the Astronomer Royal, Maskelyne, on whose recommendation he received the Dunsink appointment. It may also have been due to Maskelyne's influence that the title 'Astronomer Royal for Ireland' was added to the post from this date.

Brinkley found Dunsink fitted only with a transit instrument, a telescope equipped solely for observing the passage of heavenly bodies across the meridian. In 1808, or twenty years after it had been ordered, a vertical circle was set up, permitting the determination of stellar distance in angular degrees. Brinkley was now at last able to commence practical astronomy in earnest and within two years, he was able to announce an annual parallax of 2″.52 for the star Alpha Lyrae. Similar results of even greater magnitude were announced for other stars over the next few years.

Parallax is, of course, a measure of stellar distance, so that Brinkley's results were of acute interest in an age when the distance to the stars was still unknown. Unfortunately, the Dunsink results did not prove reproducible, testing at Greenwich proving consistently negative. But Brinkley at Dunsink continued to report parallax and a restrained academic debate on the subject continued until 1824. It now seems that Brinkley's error lay in defects of his instruments and the end result was a general tightening up of procedures in observatories.

The proud title of Astronomer Royal also effectively conferred recognition as Ireland's chief scientist. While this doubtless conferred a certain political and social cachet, it was of little immediate benefit. Indeed the total salary for the Dunsink post was only £240 annually, although there was also a free house and eighteen acres of ground. This salary was less than half the income of a Senior Fellow at Trinity, so that the post of Astronomer Royal was really little more than the equivalent of a junior lectureship in financial terms.

Brinkley however was able to augment his income from clerical sinecures. In 1806, he had been given two minor benefices and two years later became Archdeacon of Clogher. He was probably active in Church politics when the usual keen competition for preferment became more blatant than usual during the effusive welcome given by Trinity to George IV in 1821. On September 28, 1826, he was therefore elevated to the bishopric of Cloyne, the see where the great philosopher Berkeley had been installed a century before.[8] These two appointments, a hundred years apart, are yet another illustration of the fruitful connection between intellectual life and the Established Church in Ireland.

Obviously it must have helped young Hamilton to have known such an important figure from 1822 onwards and William often availed of his standing invitation to call out to the observatory at any time. Brinkley encouraged his research and tried to direct his reading, submitting Hamilton's first paper *On Caustics* in his capacity as President of the Royal Irish Academy. In fact, he seems to have done his best to assist the youth in every possible way.

There was nevertheless one eventuality to which neither Brinkley nor his protégé seem to have given any special thought. Apparently it never occurred to either of them that Hamilton might succeed his sixty-three year old patron to the Dunsink post! For one thing, the youth was still an undergraduate and indeed unlikely to have completed his studies by the time the vacancy would have to be filled.

Others, however, soon grasped the possibility. Hamilton's tutor, Charles Boyton, planted the idea among the Trinity hierarchy that William was ideally suited to become Brinkley's successor. Thereafter he worked vigorously behind the scenes to ensure that this should come about.[9] And from Armagh Observatory came a cordial invitation to Hamilton to visit during the 1826 Christmas holidays. The Observatory was under the Rev. Romney Robinson's direction for the previous three years. At thirty-four, he probably felt closer to young Hamilton than the relatively aged Brinkley. Robinson too was a former child prodigy and sometime poet, features which would have strengthened the links with Hamilton.

Uncle James was immediately eager that William should make the most of yet another potentially useful contact:

> *December 1826:* I hope you will by all means lay yourself out to be able to accept Dr. Robinson's invitation at Christmas, and that none of the sympathies, which that season is apt to awake in your social bosom, will

sway you to forego the benefits of establishing a connexion as close as possible with the Armagh as well as Dunsink Observatory.[10]

Hamilton however did not go to Armagh immediately and early in 1827, Robinson renewed his invitation in far clearer terms: "I hope when you come here that you may . . . get a first lesson to prepare you for being successor to the Bishop of Cloyne."

Despite all this, Hamilton was nevertheless still an undergraduate and there were many people with proper formal qualifications interested in the post. Among them were Henry Harte and Dionysius Lardner, who had refereed his first paper for the Academy. Another candidate was George Biddell Airy from Cambridge, already at twenty-six Lucasian Professor of Mathematics there.

The Lucasian chair however, affording only £190 annually, was another of those posts which were more prestigious than financially renumerative. Airy at this point badly wanted a salary sufficient to impress his prospective father-in-law and he travelled to Dublin to sound out Dunsink's possibilities. However, he largely lost interest when informed of its low renumeration and wrote that he could not consider it for less than £500 a year.[11]

It would appear that Hamilton first met Airy on this occasion at Bartholomew Lloyd's dinner table where there occurred the first of a series of lifelong arguments between the pair. In general Airy was a strikingly negative person who later would denounce both Babbage's calculating machine and Thomson's improved compass; his negative attitudes helped lose Britain the glory of discovering the planet Neptune in 1846. On this Dublin visit, he contested some of Hamilton's conclusions in his new or algebraic approach to optics, but the latter was more than able to defend himself effectively. The same pattern however was to recur repeatedly in future encounters and it is easy to understand what a fundamental clash of temperaments there must have been between the two.

At any rate, this first meeting with Airy probably afforded Hamilton further confidence in his own abilities. Boyton, while furthering his cause behind the scenes, continued to urge him to apply for the post. On June 8, he was able to state that the Board of Trinity were favourably disposed, while at the same time warning against consulting Brinkley. Maria Edgeworth also heard the rumours about William's chances and wrote to encourage him, but her letter arrived too late for the election on June 16. In any case, Hamilton had finally made up his mind to apply the week before.

William did not inform Brinkley of his decision until the application had gone in, probably calculating that Cloyne's remote situation would preclude dissuasion until it was too late. In any case the Bishop immediately replied, expressing his doubts to his former protégé, doubts that were eventually destined to prove all too soundly based:

> However creditable it may be to you to be appointed so early, I fear it would eventually be injurious to you. If you be precluded from looking for a Fellowship, I think no one can doubt it will not be for your interest

to accept the Professorship. You cannot be certain until you have made yourself acquainted with the business of an observatory, whether you would be likely to continue to pursue with satisfaction Practical Astronomy. Having a Fellowship, you can have time to look about you and select the paths of Science which may appear to you most inviting.[12]

In other words, Brinkley was now advising his former protégé to delay awhile before fixing his future too firmly into one restricted mould! Astronomy at that time was mainly a very laborious business of collecting data followed by routine calculation, and Brinkley doubtless appreciated its high content of sheer drudgery more than William did. The Bishop recognised much better than his would-be-successor that work of this lowly nature could hardly appeal for very long to Hamilton's wide-ranging mind. William would never be suited for the patient accumulation of minor data, his largely divergent imagination being intent rather on seeking general theories on the widest possible scale.

Hamilton however had other and not strictly scientific concerns to throw in the balance, factors doubtless emphasised by his counselling relatives. He was after all still nominal head of an orphan family, responsible for four sisters whom he had long ago promised to support. And even though these same sisters were well looked after by their various aunts and cousins, Dunsink offered a very desirable country residence for the entire family. It would obviously be years before he could hope to obtain anything as suitable through the slower progress of a Fellowship. The opportunity to reunite the scattered Hamilton family in such ideal surroundings must then have weighed heavily on William in making his final decision to apply.

The Board apparently had no misgivings whatsoever about the proper course, for Hamilton's academic history together with his recent publication on optics doubtless offered sufficient testimonials. On June 16, 1827, he was elected unanimously to the Dunsink post, just one week after his application had been received!

William was of course still an undergraduate, although his final B.A. examinations were now very near. These he passed a few days later, duly emerging with his degree. Although he was therefore appointed as Astronomer Royal while still an undergraduate, the anomaly was largely a temporal technicality. Had the Board's election meeting been held a week or two later, William would have been a graduate candidate. Of greater relevance for comparison is the fact that Hamilton was appointed full professor while still not quite twenty-two. While sheer luck in the date of Brinkley's departure undoubtedly played a part in this, other appointments of the period suggest that this was not atypical at the time. Airy for example was appointed to the Lucasian chair at 25 and Kelvin in Glasgow was also a full professor at the age of 22. Outstanding scientists in nineteenth-century Europe often advanced faster than is usual today.

Partly because the house was being refurbished, Hamilton and his sisters did not move to Dunsink immediately. Instead he went to Cloyne for practical discussions with Brinkley, some of them concerning the Greenwich parallax dispute. William wanted to test the uniformity of the great meridian circle, then generally supposed to be the most accurate anywhere. Like many an old man, Brinkley was full of practical objections, but yet he did not succeed in discouraging William totally.

The Bishop was also as negative as ever about the wisdom of Hamilton's career choice. He still thought that Hamilton had been hasty and imprudent, and cannily warned him against depending on the generosity of the Board. He almost implied that they had been looking for cheap labour in appointing William and still felt that waiting for a Fellowship would have been the wiser course.

It must have been a decided relief for the new appointee to encounter the more robust optimism of Robinson in Armagh. He travelled there after leaving Cloyne in response to yet another invitation and soon was busy immersing himself in technical details. Robinson's general enthusiasm for most things scientific struck an answering chord in William; Robinson and Herschel were the astronomers whom he was to find most congenial in later years.

Robinson and Hamilton also intended to visit other parts of Ulster where the first great Ordnance Survey of Ireland was now just getting underway. This travel plan however was cut short by the unexpected arrival of Alexander Nimmo, a renowned public engineer who still enjoys semi-legendary fame along the western coast.[13] Nimmo had not met Hamilton previously and was some twenty-two years his senior; he nevertheless invited his new acquaintance on an immediate inspection tour of his various works throughout the British Isles!

This two-month tour, initiated by Nimmo, was a splendid education for the previously untravelled Hamilton. The engineer sent him down in a diving bell into the Shannon at Limerick to inspect underwater bridge foundations and William found himself impressed "by the great condensation of the air which was felt in a very painful manner". They visited the Lakes of Killarney and various towns along the south coast, concluding with an inspection of Nimmo's new pier and lighthouse at Dunmore East, Co. Waterford. From there, they rowed out to one of the new steam paddle ships just recently introduced between Waterford and Bristol, landing on the English coast next day.

Hamilton and his friend progressed north by coach from Bristol, pausing to inspect several manifestations of the Industrial Revolution at various points along the way. The many iron manufactories with their vast fires struck William's classic mind as modern versions of Vulcan and the Cyclopes. At Dudley, they were almost lost underground while exploring stone caverns, suggesting the ancient vision of Hades. These adventures obviously impressed William greatly for he wrote a long account to Eliza with a suggestion that it be read out to Mrs. Disney and other members of the Stanley Society.[14]

At Liverpool, Hamilton sought out the Misses Lawrence, middle-aged ladies who kept a girls' school there and whom he had known earlier in Dublin. One of the sisters, Arabella Lawrence, was a very realistic critic of William's poetic tendencies. Poetry indeed was still very much an integral part of William's interests and so he was delighted to travel further north into the beautiful Lake District, so closely associated with famous poets and writers.

Here Hamilton and his party met the ageing William Wordsworth, at the house of a local clergyman near Ambleside. The poet was then aged 57 and widely famous, while Hamilton was just turned 22 and still relatively unknown. The two however obviously took to each other immediately, so that this meeting would thereafter come to be regarded as one of the major formative influences in Hamilton's life.

The exciting news of meeting with Wordsworth was duly relayed to Eliza, herself an aspiring poetess who would, presumably, appreciate such things. In his letter, Hamilton details how they walked back and forth between each other's houses repeatedly, thereby conveying vividly that sense of high intellectual stimulation evoked by contact between kindred minds:

> *September 16, 1827:* He (Wordsworth) walked back with our party as far as their lodge; and then, on our bidding Mrs. Harrison goodnight, I offered to walk back with him, while my party proceeded to the hotel. This offer he accepted and our conversation had become so interesting that when we arrived at his house, a distance of about a mile, he proposed to walk back with me on my way, a proposal which you may be sure that I did not reject; so far from it that when he came to turn once more towards his home, I also turned once more along with him. It was very late when I reached the hotel after all this walking . . .[15]

Wordsworth also gave Hamilton a letter of introduction to his neighbour Southey, but there was apparently no similar sense of kindred feeling for Hamilton in this encounter. Southey was clearly struck by Hamilton's renowned exuberance and he has left an account of a young man "so full of life and spirits . . . I believe that for the sake of making a tour among the stars, he would willingly be fastened to a comet's tail."[16]

These stimulating events again inspired Hamilton to poetry; once more he was moved to express his seldom forgotten feelings for his lost Catherine:

> It haunts me yet, that dream of early love!
> Though Passion's waters toss me now no more;
> And though my feelings, like the ark-banish'd dove,
> In wandering that sinking ocean o'er,
> Hail with sad joy signs of a coming shore.[17]

This long and somewhat negative poem of ninety lines Hamilton immediately sent to Wordsworth, along with some of Eliza's verses. The poet replied promptly with incisive criticism, highlighting the many points where "the workmanship (what else could be expected from so young a writer?) is not what it ought to be." A similar theme runs through much of their later and fairly regular correspondence.

William Wordsworth in old age   *(Courtesy National Portrait Gallery, London)*

Generally Wordsworth seems to have felt it his duty to steer Hamilton gently away from poetry — a field in which his efforts might best be described as competent, if undistinguished. This would allow more time for science where he was obviously outstandingly capable. The older man also tried to advise his young friend on romantic matters, a field wherein he was not without suitably relevant experience himself.

From the Lake District, Nimmo and Hamilton went on to Edinburgh and there they are said to have conducted a revealing experiment in phrenology. The story goes that the engineer introduced his young friend to a leading phrenological consultant, pretending that he was contemplating hiring him as a man-servant. But the expert, after due examination, pronounced the supposed servant as quite unsuitable because of his obvious low intelligence.[18] Nimmo, in his own way, was apparently as divergent as Hamilton ever was and we can imagine that the two of them had a good laugh at this episode. Phrenology however remained on the fringe of William's interests afterwards and was to enter his life again in various ways.

Life at the Observatory

The new Astronomer Royal and his sisters finally came to live at Dunsink on October 13, 1827. The spacious building on the long low ridge five miles northwest of Dublin was part-observatory and part-country house; besides its telescopes, it did not differ significantly from other country houses such as Dunsinea and Scripplestown nearby. They kept a cow, a pig and a greyhound named Smoke which Sydney called the 'Dear Dark Dog of Dunsink'. There was also a goodly stock of wine and provisions, together with several servants for the household.

Grace was twenty-five by this time and soon settled into her usual role in charge of domestic arrangements. This was a task she had been accustomed to undertake, both at home and in Cousin Arthur's, since the death of their mother ten years before. Eliza, not quite twenty, was the best educated; as perhaps befitted an aspiring poetess, she was of a somewhat excitable temperament. Sydney, at seventeen, was an untrained assistant at Rhodens Girls' School near Belfast, where she also cared for the twelve-year-old Archianna. But Sydney too would join Dunsink the following summer, although Archianna was mostly cared for by the various relatives.

These same relatives continued to support the reconstituted Hamilton family in various ways. From Trim, Uncle James kept weighing in with advice, even though now we can suspect that he must have felt somewhat redundant with all his early ambitions for William so suddenly achieved. In Ballinderry and later at Cootehill, Uncle John Willey continued to pursue astronomy more enthusiastically than ever; he would assume prime responsibility for Archianna eventually. And wise old Cousin Arthur, with his legal counsels, had his own room at the observatory, frequently calling out to keep an eye on things when William was away.

The maternal relatives, the Huttons, were also comparatively well off and they made various bequests to the sisters in later years. Indeed even Hamilton himself apparently would later have occasion to borrow money from them.[19] The sisters however had no worthwhile dowries around the age of 20, so that their prospects of marriage must have been very slim. In any event, none of the four ever married; genteel poverty as governesses or lady companions among the less affluent middle-class Irish Protestant families would summarise their future lives.

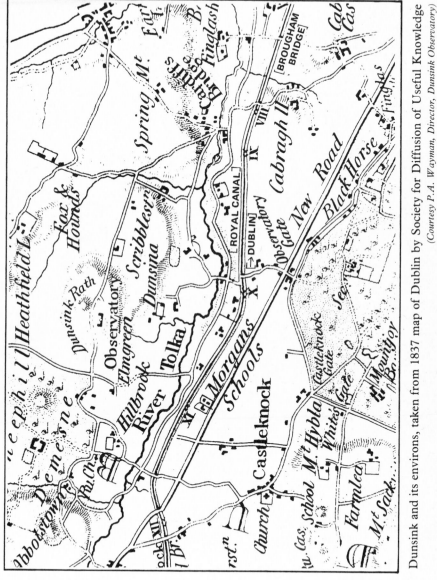

Dunsink and its environs, taken from 1837 map of Dublin by Society for Diffusion of Useful Knowledge

(Courtesy P.A. Wayman, Director, Dunsink Observatory)

Hamilton's typical enthusiasm initially envisaged the sisters as co-operative partners in discovery, companions along the uphill road of science which he intended to travel. Earlier meetings of the Stanley Society, during his undergraduate days, probably helped form this idea. The girls had then formed a willing audience while he expounded on abstruse matters like Berkelian metaphysics or the particle concept of light.[20] And since Eliza was the most educated and also the sister closest to him, she doubtless seemed the most suitable scientific partner of all.

Soon after his appointment to Dunsink, Hamilton put this idea in a letter to his obviously reluctant sister:

> You know how desirous I have been that you should learn Astronomy, both for your own sake and mine ... Feeling thus deeply, the almost insuperable difficulties of that enterprise in which I have nevertheless determined to engage, I would not willingly augment those difficulties by neglecting to arm myself with the aid of friendly and female sympathy.[21]

Nowadays, we would simply conclude that William needed a girl-friend for inspiration and understanding; relationships were more restricted and therefore more complex to a man of his upbringing in nineteenth-century society. At any rate, Eliza proved cold towards William's repeated declarations on the attractions of shared astronomical discovery, thereby at least demonstrating that she had a mind of her own. Grace proved somewhat less negative and Sydney, positively enthusiastic. So it was to the latter that Hamilton finally turned in his efforts to encourage his sisters towards an active interest in his work.

However, William himself soon tired of practical astronomy just as Brinkley had feared. He worked very hard at the telescopes for the first year or so, and progressively less after that. Nearly all the routine observations after 1831 were carried out by Brinkley's former assistant, Charles Thompson. Hankins has demonstrated that Sydney and Grace did much of the observing up to the time they left the observatory, as their initials in the official record book show.[22] Hamilton may even have succeeded in having his sisters paid by the Board of Trinity College as computists without revealing their identity.[23]

Such was the household and institution to which many learned letters poured in and where various distinguished persons visiting Dublin called out. Not all of these visitors were primarily interested in science by any means. Dunsink's situation, on top of the rise at the end of its long lane, inevitably attracted favourable comment because of its natural beauty and sense of restful solitude. If genius requires empathy with nature in order to maximise its powers, then Dunsink was certainly an ideal place for a creative person to reside.

Hamilton therefore had facility for solitude as required, but still had no need to feel isolated from the world. Like any country gentleman, he soon began calling on the neighbouring big houses and in one of these, he would eventually find himself a wife. Two miles further on, across the tiny river

Dunsink Observatory during the early Hamilton years
(Courtesy P.A. Wayman, Director, Dunsink Observatory)

Tolka and the new canal, lay the Phoenix Park. There the Ordnance Survey was just setting up its headquarters — effectively the most organised and extensive scientific effort Ireland had yet seen.

The Park also housed the Viceregal Lodge. It was the official residence of The Crown's Deputy in Ireland, the Lord Lieutenant. The Lodge was the scene of regular levees, balls and state dinners — functions to which Hamilton in view of his official position was often invited as a matter of course. Two miles further afield lay Trinity College and the headquarters of the Royal Irish Academy, the intellectual milieu in which most of his endeavours were conceived.

Hamilton obviously enjoyed his new position and residence, allowing him as they did full scope for his creative aspirations as well as his natural exuberance. He often walked out along the parapet of the observatory because he found the view of distant Dublin much better from that vantage point. He took lessons in horsemanship from Lalouette, a fashionable riding-school instructor of the time. He loved to gallop his horse, Planet, in great sweeping orbits through the surrounding fields. And he also liked to walk in the woods along the Tolka or along the many lanes in the vicinity, perusing his books or contemplating mathematical issues with that strong sense of visual imagery which he had learned to cultivate at Trim.

Books had always been a very large part of Hamilton's life since his infant days. They lay around at Dunsink in great profusion, often open and ready to be picked up again where William or one of the sisters had left off. Readings of poetry or the latest novels vied with mathematics and philosophy in this highly intellectual household. Normally, William took several books to bed and sometimes rose in the middle of the night to continue reading; a carpetbag of his current favourites usually accompanied him on his travels. Hamilton continued to read as fancy pleased him on canal boats, coaches and paddle steamers, while the various houses he visited were likewise treated as convenient study rooms.

One gets the impression from some of this more public reading that Hamilton rather overdid things, as if he were consciously acting out the 'learned professor' role. Similarly, he was forever rushing to make connections during travel, as for example in this account of a trip to England:

> *Carlisle, August 20, 1838:* After leaving you at Dunsinea, I was very hard set to be in time for the five o'clock train, and in fact should not have been so had it not been for poor old Brownie. As it was, the Post Office clock struck five before I reached Carlisle Bridge, but I determined to try whether any favourable chance might befriend me, and found that lately the trains, for some reason or other, set out after their nominal times, by about ten minutes, which exactly met my case. The steamer started in less than two minutes after I got on board...[24]

Hamilton also liked to compose poetry on the relatively tedious voyages across the Irish Sea, sometimes expressing grandiloquent emotions as his native coast again came into view.[25] Doubtless these activities were yet another genuine expression of his almost continuous mental effervescence. But again, one cannot help wondering as to what his more mundane fellow-passengers must have made of it all.

The Arrival of Adare

Apart from the usual stream of visiting scientists and Dublin social callers, there were several more significant visitors to Dunsink in the early days. The first of these came after the Lord Lieutenant, Anglesey, had summoned Hamilton to the Viceregal Lodge in April 1828; he wanted his two sons, then aged ten and twelve, to be tutored at the observatory.

The one-legged veteran of Waterloo presumably thought that his sons would gain from acquaintance with such an accomplished intellect. Doubtless he was unaware of Hamilton's genuine difficulties in simplifying his thoughts. His proposal also meant a desirable addition to Hamilton's small income and in any case the Board would have welcomed the recognition involved from such a prestigious source. The two boys were therefore immediately installed as residents at the observatory under the care of William's sisters. A few days later, their father called to check on the arrangements, taking the opportunity to discuss the connection between science and religion with Hamilton:

'And you', said he, 'do you find confirmation of your creed while studying the book of nature?' To which I answered that I found continually new evidence of design and goodness in studying the structures of the Universe.[26]

Hamilton's friends, including the reconciled Brinkley, stressed the great advantage which could be expected to accrue in due course from the Lord Lieutenant's patronage. Maria Edgeworth also understood, even though Anglesey had just forestalled her own similar request that Hamilton tutor her stepbrother, Francis. The latter was then a student at Cambridge and not succeeding at mathematics. But even if Hamilton felt unable to serve him as a tutor, the two now became firm friends involved in many important discussions on poetry and philosophy.

In any case, the Anglesey boys did not stay long at the observatory, their father being recalled to England nine months after they had commenced. The following August, Wordsworth arrived in response to a suggestion from Hamilton, this being the poet's first visit to Ireland. The sage had long wished to view the Irish scenery but felt himself endangered by the unsettled state of the country, but evidently Hamilton was able to reassure him sufficiently.

At Dunsink, the three sisters were awaiting the arrival of the Great Man just as eagerly as William; Eliza has left a commendably frank account of her impressions.[27] She found the poet to be somewhat rustic and even awkward in company, not so much loquacious as reserved. He was tall, grey, elderly and serious, but "with an indescribable superiority, both intellectual and moral, stamped upon him in his very silence". Wordsworth was evidently eloquent in what psychologists would now term 'body language'! And yet Eliza's impressions were completely contrary to her preconceptions of the man. Indeed they were so different that she felt herself involuntarily parodying the first lines of his own poem *Yarrow Revisited*:

And this is *Wordsworth*! this the man,
Of whom my fancy cherished
So faithfully a waking dream,
An image that has perished!

The visitor stayed several days at Dunsink, discussing his own compositions and Hamilton's attempts at poetry. He laid much stress on the great effort of craftsmanship that must be undertaken to produce a proper poem after the initial inspiration; his young friend's similar experience with mathematics doubtless helped him understand this point. In short, the craft of poetry demanded a full commitment if one were really serious and so a divided allegiance, shared with some other calling like science, could not be entertained. The younger man apparently drew the obvious conclusion from these observations by an expert and poetic compositions became for him thereafter more of a diversionary pastime than a possible career.

Wordsworth and Hamilton also discussed Science on this Dunsink visit, finding themselves very largely in agreement. The poet deplored the mere collection of facts for their own sake as worse than useless, because it tended to extinguish Imagination. But that higher form of Science which raised the mind to the greater contemplation of God in its newly discovered aspects was certainly worthy of high praise. William found these sentiments admirable, while still stressing the value of Intellect as well as Imagination. He believed mathematics to be a connecting link between man and higher beings. And he also thought that the triangle and circle had a real existence in the minds of these higher beings as well as in the nature of things, being more than mere creations or arbitrary symbols invented by the human mind.

From Dunsink, Wordsworth went south to visit the Lakes of Killarney, proceeding thence to Edgeworthstown. There he again met Hamilton for a few days, finally departing by a northern route. He certainly made a large impression during his Irish visit, although it must also be recorded that Ireland does not seem to have made any similarly major impact on the poet's works.

Even while Wordsworth's visit was being arranged, Hamilton was also engaged in other negotiations following the departure of the Anglesey pupils. Again the proposal was that he should act as tutor; again the request came from a nobleman of major influence and importance. Lord Dunraven was very wealthy due to his Welsh wife's family connections and lived at Adare in County Limerick; now he wished to have his son prepared for entry to Trinity College.

The young Lord Adare was then just turned seventeen and, following an Eton education, was displaying wide general intelligence with a special interest in astronomy. His future career was confidently expected to be promising, as well as highly favoured through family connections and wealth. Dr. Kyle, the Provost, was naturally anxious to secure such a desirable advertisement for the University; it may even have been he who suggested that Hamilton be sought as tutor.[28]

Initially, Hamilton professed himself as reluctant to compromise his regained freedom from tutorial duties, while his sisters did not welcome the upset which Adare and his manservant would entail. But, as with Anglesey, suggestions or approaches from such high sources were not to be lightly set aside. In any case, there was the extra income which tuition would bring in. Also William's various advisers again approved of the arrangement, notably Robinson at Armagh who envisaged the venture as generating future support for astronomy. At any rate, the seventeen-year-old Adare arrived to stay at Dunsink early in February 1830, thereby commencing another important influence on the life of Hamilton.

6 THE EARLY ASTRONOMER

"As a Mathematician, you will probably have no equal in Britain; as an Astronomer, some superiors."
Romney Robinson to Hamilton, May 1831

Another young man who visited the observatory around this time was Robert P. Graves, the person destined to become Hamilton's future biographer. He was the younger brother of John and Charles Graves; the former would become Professor of Jurisprudence at London University and the latter, Bishop of Limerick. Both of these elder brothers were primarily highly accomplished mathematicians and, as such, important in Hamilton's scientific career. John in particular had begun correspondence almost as soon as William was appointed at Dunsink.

Robert Graves, who showed no skill as a mathematician, made his future career entirely within the Church. As a biographer, he was acute and thorough in his observations as well as adept in expressing them. Nor did he shrink from detailing the negative aspects of his subject as seemed necessary. This blend of personal reminiscences seasoned with occasional acerbity renders his biography all the more valuable; without it, many aspects of Hamilton would inevitably have remained less clear.

Robert was also an early student at Hamilton's lectures on astronomy, one of the relatively few College duties associated with the Dunsink post. This annual course of just twelve lectures began in November with an Introductory Lecture of the widest possible generality. Here Hamilton allowed full rein to his soaring imagination combined with his undoubted erudition. History vied with metaphysics and classical references in his utterances, the whole delivered in an enraptured manner befitting the oratorical tradition of Edmund Burke. The annual Introductory Lecture was obviously regarded as good intellectual theatre, so that professors and Fellows sat on the benches along with undergraduates. Literary figures and even society ladies also joined in the audience. Hamilton, during these early years, was an orator whom people flocked to hear.

Graves relates how William appeared quite carried away on such occasions, absorbed as if in reverence of the solemn truths which it was his privilege to declare.[1] Such talks were delivered in those deep sonorous tones mentioned earlier — a public voice derived perhaps from unconscious

79

Page of a letter written by William to his Uncle James on December 24, 1834. The immediate context concerns the Board's plan to exclude women from attending Hamilton's astronomy lectures by stationing 'a porter at the foot of the stairs' . . .

(Courtesy Royal Irish Academy)

imitation of Uncle James as he spoke from the Trim pulpit years before.

Subsequent lectures in the astronomy course were naturally quite different and more mathematical in content. These were delivered with less solemnity in a more ordinary tone, one which nevertheless tended to break into a higher key whenever its owner became carried away by his own enthusiasm. It does not require much psychology to postulate the childlike traits of eagerness, enthusiasm and discovery frequently taking over at such times.

Nevertheless Graves also voices our reasonable doubts as to whether Hamilton's students ever derived much really worthwhile instruction from his lectures. For one thing, he had the annoying habit of diverting into whatever flight of fancy was suggested by a passing reference or stray idea. Neither was he conscious of the need to explain to lesser minds the various stages through which his thought sequences rapidly developed. He did take the trouble to rehearse his lectures beforehand with his assistant Thompson or any other suitable listeners whom he could rally at the observatory. Even so, the end result does not seem to have been very instructive. Hamilton then undoubtedly stimulated his listeners through oratory, spectacle and sheer personal example. But still the evidence suggests that as a lecturer he was hardly a great success!

The contents of his Introductory Lectures in the early 1830s do however tell us much about Hamilton's thinking at the time. They show that he recognised no logical conflict between truth and beauty, but thought that the true scientist should always give the latter precedence. He allowed that there may occasionally appear a transient conflict, but this is probably because our limited intellects compel us to separate and pursue unevenly these differing aspects of the one reality.

Indeed Hamilton thought that the full development of science may eventually call for faculties higher than the merely human; some idea of its beauty can nevertheless still be grasped through suitable study by the average mind. Scientific activities of this nature strive to record and explain appearances, to classify and then generalise as far as possible.[2] But always the end aim of such activities is:

> ... to discover the secret unity and constancy of nature, amid its seeming diversity and mutability; to construct, at least in part, a history of the outward world, adapted to the understanding of man; to account for past and to foresee future phenomena; to learn the language and interpret the oracles of the Universe.

Hamilton stressed Astronomy as the prime example of this way of thinking, offering this as the reason why the College had ordained its study first. It was a suitable introduction to those other sciences not yet properly developed. Patient collection of facts by astronomers had taken place over the centuries; these now enabled the mind to reduce the great diversity of the heavenly movements to the identity of a few simple laws. And from these general principles, reliable statements about future phenomena could in turn be made.

Imagination was of course a vital element in progress of this kind. Newtonian natural philosophy was widely accepted because it continued to predict phenomena reliably and did so in an ideal, logically strict and internally consistent manner. And yet to Hamilton:

> ... it seems to belong to imagination also and to bear analogy to a production of the arts. It is, like them, an imitation, not a copy, of

Nature. It is a creation of the mind, so framed as to resemble, in an immense number of particulars, what we know of the external universe, yet perhaps differing from its archetype in a still greater number of things as yet unknown.[2]

On various other occasions, Hamilton repeated this concept of Newton's Laws as perhaps only an approximation to the truth. Almost a century later, Einstein did in fact replace Newton's Laws by laws of greater accuracy, so here Hamilton must be regarded as curiously and prophetically indicative.

This however was only one of several instances in which his vivid imagination leaped notably far ahead of the scientific thinking of his time. For example during the 1850s when the future Baron Kelvin was planning the first transAtlantic cable between Ireland and America, Hamilton suggested that it might be possible to communicate across the ocean without any need for wires at all.[2a]

But meanwhile, Hamilton also noted that Newton's interpretation of the solar system still served as a good example of the scientific method at work. The sun and planets "lay under the oppression of facts material, unintellectual, disjointed". The old Ptolemaic simplicity had been destroyed without the creation of anything comparable to take its place. Then when Newton came:

> ... he meditated on many laws and caused many ideal worlds to pass before him; and when he chose the law that bears his name, he seems to have been half determined by the mathematical simplicity and consequent intellectual beauty, and only half by the phenomena already observed. While therefore I do not pretend that the Newtonian philosophy is likely to make men better painters or sculptors or poets, I yet consider the structure of that philosophy as bearing much analogy to the productions of painting, sculpture and poetry, and as being not less than they an intellectual and imaginative creation.

These general views on scientific method were delivered during 1831 and 1832, and Hamilton himself was just then engaged in producing a striking example of the same process at work. This was his famous prediction of conical refraction — an episode to be examined further in subsequent chapters.

Meantime, one cannot but express regret that William's views on the scientific method never reached a wider and perhaps more advanced audience. Maybe Hamilton should have subsumed his Introductory Lectures into a book on the philosophy of science!

An Adventuresome Decade

The decade which started with these viewpoints was also by far the most adventurous and creative in Hamilton's career. It began with the arrival of Adare as a pre-College private pupil and ended with Hamilton serving in his country's most eminent academic position — as President of the Royal Irish Academy. In the interval, he had again become seriously infatuated with another young lady, only to lose her through timidity as before. Soon afterwards, he married and very unsuitably, selecting a wife who was to remain a semi-invalid all her days.

Even while these events were unfolding, Hamilton was knighted for his scientific work — the first Irish scientist to be so honoured. Such developments brought Hamilton more and more into the limelight as a public figure, but did not diminish in any way his personal commitment to scientific research. Science in its widest possible context remained his greatest interest, but mostly in so far as its laws could be expressed in terms of his own highly original mathematical research. Primarily, Hamilton was therefore a pure mathematician, a scientist who never felt the necessity to carry out even one practical experiment in his entire life!

Throughout his early years at Dunsink, he continued to refine and develop with great energy his novel application of algebra to the geometry of light. This encapsulated the principle enunciated in his original paper on *Systems of Rays*. While engaged on such developments, he happened on the totally unexpected phenomenon of conical refraction, a discovery which immediately served to advertise his name. Around the same period he further advanced the generalisation of his new treatment of optics, by applying it to dynamics. This was a major innovation which is now considered to be his most important work.

Somehow in the midst of these major achievements, Hamilton also managed to advance his highly novel thesis of *Algebra as the Science of Pure Time*. From this would eventually come his famed discovery of quaternions. The latter is the most widely known of Hamilton's innovations and was also regarded by himself as the most important; it is therefore more than a trifle ironic that later generations have not agreed with this assessment.

Besides these primary researches (which we shall be examining in more detail in the next chapter), Hamilton had several other well-defined areas of interest. Poetry probably came second to mathematics, but increasingly after the early years only in a recreational or therapeutic way. In close competition with poetry came metaphysics, an interest to be expected in a scientist of his wide erudition who was also a graduate of Berkeley's university. When Hamilton perused Berkeley, Kant or Boscovich during these early years, he was pleased to recognise opinions which he had himself already formed.

Hankins, however, has pointed out that Hamilton was one of the first English-speaking scientists of stature who had read these writers and taken them seriously. As such, he was one of the earliest to reject the purely mechanistic picture of the Universe, inclining towards the more metaphysical modern interpretations inherent in present concepts such as wave particle duality.[3]

Meantime, there were other more routine matters concerned with astronomy and the Dunsink post, such as co-operative projects proposed by other observatories. Hamilton was never very partial to the routine labours involved in such activity. He was more disposed towards the establishment of new, privately funded observatories, projects like that of Edward Joshua

Cooper at Markree or that of the Earl of Rosse at Parsonstown. Both these were wealthy young men of similar age to Hamilton and it is quite possible that his example may have helped to encourage them.

Other academic business flowed into Dunsink at a steady pace, much of it originating in England. Dionysius Lardner, his first referee and then rival for the Dunsink post, vainly requested an article on light for his new *Cabinet Encyclopaedia*. Captain Everest called to visit on one of his periodic trips back from the Orient: he wanted William and Airy together to review his work on the New Indian Meridian. Hamilton refused this task also; he might have reacted differently had he known that his visitor would later be immortalised through discovery of the world's highest mountain.

Everest had been introduced to Hamilton by Captain Francis Beaufort, the cartographer of Asia Minor who was then modernising the Hydrographic Service of the British Navy. Beaufort was much older than Hamilton though from a very similar background, having been born into an intellectual clerical family at Navan, County Meath, in 1774. Indeed he learned the rudiments of science at Dunsink as a student under the first incumbent, Ussher, and was also related through marriage to the Edgeworth clan.[4] His notes to Hamilton were always commendably brief and succinct, and he certainly served as a useful contact, being well placed in the higher echelons of English science.

Two other routine matters of importance took place during these early years in Dunsink. The first was a proposal from the College in 1829, soon after his appointment, that Hamilton be allowed to compete in the normal manner for a Fellowship. The Board may have already been entertaining doubts about his suitability as an astronomer or perhaps it was ashamed of his relatively small salary of £240. In any case, Hamilton was still very much a youthful idealist in many ways. So since he had forsworn the chance of a Fellowship in electing for Dunsink, he could not bring himself now to change the rules of the game.[5]

In May 1831 however, a different and more attractive proposal materialised. Bartholomew Lloyd was now in the process of being elected Provost of the College, in succession to Dr. Kyle who had been appointed Bishop of Cork. As a result, the Professorship of Mathematics became vacant and a proposal emerged that Hamilton should be transferred. He himself was attracted because his salary would be more than doubled, to £600: his only regret lay in "giving up a residence so pleasant for my sisters".

By this time also, Robinson's earlier enthusiasm for Hamilton's appointment to Dunsink had evidently waned. So his letter from Armagh was now decisively in favour of the change:

> *May 14, 1831:* Your course appears to me so clear that there can be no hesitation. As a mathematician, you will probably have no equal in Britain; as an astronomer, some superiors; for you certainly have not the practical enthusiasm which is essential to make one sustain the uniform progress of observing.

I had hoped that Lord Anglesey would have given you some of the Government benefices when you were in orders (many of which as you know are sinecures), but such you can hold as well when Professor of Mathematics.[6]

The new Provost was also active in seeking to promote the transfer, but formal difficulties due to Hamilton's lack of a Fellowship arose. Eventually in November, the Board raised his Dunsink salary to full professorial level of £700, out of which was deducted £100 for the assistant, Thompson, and £20 for the gardener. Hamilton would be debarred from taking private pupils henceforth, a stipulation which probably caused him some relief. He also gained permission to devote himself mainly to mathematics — a point which was to cause some difficulty in future years.

Travels with Adare

Hamilton's sole private pupil at this juncture was of course young Lord Adare, the seventeen-year-old youth who had come to the observatory with the Provost's blessing, on February 10, 1830. Perhaps unexpectedly, the new arrival soon proved himself a very eager student. Indeed he even exhibited a passionate interest in astronomy and immediately started observing with all the enthusiastic intensity of youth. Hamilton soon realised that he now had an eager listener and suitably intelligent sounding-board; the many manuscripts which he would later write for his pupil's instruction also helped to clarify his own ideas.

Adare was well connected among the nobility and was also probably more socially skilled than his tutor. Hamilton, on the other hand, had ready access to the higher echelons of science and so was able to introduce his pupil to the most famous figures of the day. The youth reciprocated by introducing his tutor to some of the nobility, so that they complemented each other in such respects.

It was in this manner that master and pupil travelled together to visit Armagh one month after they had met. Adare was anxious to see Ireland's other main observatory and Romney Robinson was equally desirous of meeting him. His hope was that the rich young man would found yet another private observatory in Ireland and Adare's obvious passion for all things astronomical sustained this idea. To further this interest, Robinson took his visitors out to dine with Dr. Beresford, Archbishop of Armagh, and also the observatory's main patron.

Hamilton however had other and more private reasons for wanting to visit in this vicinity. His first love, Catherine Disney, was now living not far away as wife of the Rev. Barlow, near Carlingford. Adare took William to call on Lord Gosford at Markethill and the latter lent them horses so that they could visit the Barlows. William met the husband and their several children, but found Catherine herself apparently none too happy; she reciprocated by coming to visit him at Armagh a few days afterwards.

Hamilton offered to show his first love the telescope, as was his usual

T. Romney Robinson, Director of Armagh Observatory

(Courtesy Royal Irish Academy)

stratagem with lady visitors. On this occasion, however, he became so agitated that he broke part of the mechanism and we can assume that Catherine remained the more self-possessed of the two.[7]

The predictable result of all this was that William again fell into one of his customary bouts of depression, once more attempting to exorcise his agony with the usual poem:

> We two have met, and in her innocent eyes
> A meek and tender sorrow I have seen;
> Ah! then, the change which my glad light put out
> And threw a gloom over my once bright way,
> Has not to her brought perfect happiness . . .[8]

Here one cannot help feeling that William seemed almost a little glad to find his lost love apparently not wholly satisfied with her lot; developments many years later would clearly confirm the accuracy of this early judgement.

Meantime the lovelorn poet felt himself in need of a sympathetic listener and this also he soon gained through an introduction by Adare. Lady Campbell was a daughter of the famed Irish patriot Lord Edward Fitzgerald and now the wife of the military commander at Armagh. Her mother had often visited A. H. Rowan's town house in Dominick Street when Hamilton's father, Archibald, was prominent there during the 1790s; this common background helped to create an immediate bond between her and William. Lady Campbell was also a highly intellectual woman, knowledge-able in literature and interested in the latest scientific developments. So it was little wonder that she soon gained William's total confidence. Indeed he began to form the idea of her as a sort of intermediary between himself and Catherine. This hope however never materialised because her husband was soon afterwards posted to Dublin. Lady Campbell thereby became one of William's closest friends in the city, but he never had any real further contact with Catherine for another fifteen years.

Meantime, Wordsworth was now in regular correspondence and Hamilton, together with Eliza, returned his visit of the previous year. They travelled to the Lake District in July 1830. Wordsworth spent many hours shut up in a summerhouse with Eliza, presumably discussing poetry; his advice may have given her sufficient confidence to produce her own volume of poetry which appeared in 1839.[9]

Another poetess to emerge on this occasion was Mrs. Hemans, a lady in her late thirties well known for her edifying religious verse. She was an enigmatic figure whose husband had fled in mysterious circumstances and left her with a young family. Most women detected affectation in her manner, but men were invariably impressed. Hamilton was no exception in this respect, so when Mrs. Hemans moved to reside with her brother in Dublin soon afterwards, she too became a regular visitor to Dunsink.

Not long after this second visit to Wordsworth, Hamilton travelled to Adare Manor in County Limerick. There, entertainments typical of a country-house weekend were organised. These included boating on the river complete with musical accompaniments, poetic readings and visits to historic ruins. Hamilton as usual borrowed books from the library; Adare's mother, Lady Dunraven, provided entertainment on the harp. Soon she began to exhibit that strong maternal instinct which William often evoked in older women.

Hamilton now began pulling strings for his protégé Adare in earnest and quickly introduced him to the Royal Irish Academy. There, the seventeen-year-old was unanimously elected a full member as a matter of course. The Academy at this period was evidently just as deferential as Trinity towards nobility and was equally conscious of the advantages which acquaintance with the ruling class might bring.

Things were no different in England with the newly formed Astronomical Society. There, Hamilton arranged for his pupil to be introduced by the great astronomer John Herschel, with Beaufort and Robinson to back up the proposal if required. He did not tell his pupil of these moves until all had been duly arranged, so that the excited Adare received his membership as an unexpected Christmas present for 1830.

The winter of early 1831 was an unusually severe one and the residents of Dunsink found themselves temporarily cut off by the snow. Hamilton and his sisters took due stock of their provisions and found them adequate, their only lack being bread because the baker could not call. William cheerfully proposed that they make their own bread from sawdust according to the latest scientific recipe, being further confident that snow makes excellent pancakes![10] Sometimes even the most learned scholar can unwittingly display a total ignorance of other scientific spheres.

The following summer, Airy visited Dunsink and Hamilton found the experience an unusually depressing one. Evidently the English astronomer's great personal dullness and strict adherence to factual detail drove him close to despair:

> *Hamilton to Adare, August 23, 1831:* On the whole, his mind appeared to me an instance, painful to contemplate, of the usurpation of the understanding over the reason, too general in modern English science.
>
> The Liverpool and Manchester Railway, he said, playfully perhaps but I think sincerely, he considered as the highest achievement of man.
>
> When shall we see an incarnation of metaphysical in physical science? I am chilled by this recent visit of Airy, and could find it in my heart to renounce science, in deep despair of sympathy.[11]

Ellen de Vere

The chill of Airy's dulling presence was soon dispersed in the warm welcome accorded to Hamilton during a second visit to the Adare home. This time William travelled by passenger boat along the Grand Canal and down the Shannon, a novelty duly described in graphic letters to his sisters. Again, there was boating on the River Maigue which flows by Adare Manor and this time the future revolutionary William Smith O'Brien toppled overboard at a shallow spot. Hamilton joined in the fun by jumping in fully clothed at a deeper point, thereby proving to himself that he could still swim as strongly as he had been taught by James at Trim. Lady Dunraven fussed over her wild young charges with true maternal instinct and later there was a grand dance in the old oaken hall.

But the real highlight of this second visit to Adare Manor was William's sudden infatuation with local beauty Ellen de Vere. She was a daughter of the neighbouring Hunt family who lived at Curragh Chase. They were then in the process of changing their rather homely surname for the somewhat grander title of de Vere.[12] Her father was a country gentleman, given to writing drama and historical poems and his family had similar interests.

Although Hamilton had met Ellen two years earlier at the Abbotstown residence near Dunsink, she had apparently much matured meantime. Now she was probably aged about eighteen to his twenty-six years and William felt himself immediately "smitten by her mind"! Her feelings on poetry were so intense that he even found them superior to his own. Conversation with her seemed like being in another world. Obviously another poem was the only proper method for feelings of this intensity to be expressed:

> Oh lovely one! who o'er thy Sire's domains
> Glid'st light and free, the Spirit of the place!
> In thy sweet presence an enchantment reigns.
> And all injurious bonds of Time and Space
> Do I forget, when on thy mind-lit face
> A momentary gaze I dare to rest.[13]

Hamilton returned from Adare in deep infatuation with Ellen, the first really entrancing marriageable prospect he had met since Catherine seven years before. He was obviously all too ready to read too much into some of her casual remarks. Nor did he shrink from resurrecting his old dream of a female partner in astronomy, in a somewhat Freudian letter to Adare:

> *September 23, 1831:* ... finding that in astronomy too, I can sympathise with a mind like hers, and thus throw around the austere nakedness of the science the robe of human interest; to her who is not a mathematician, the reasonings of astronomy may be a useful mental discipline, such as even the exercise of taste and discrimination in poetry might not be able to supply.[14]

Clearly, William was lonely in his intellectual abstractions and deeply conscious of his need for a sympathetic female partner. Wordsworth was speedily informed of this exciting new infatuation and was showered with verses relating to her over the next few weeks. Once more, the poet grew alarmed lest poetry should again seduce his young friend from the path of Science, "which you seem destined to tread with so much honour to yourself and profit to others". He also cautioned wryly against wearing rose-coloured spectacles in matters of the heart. Nevertheless, Wordsworth deduced that William was at least three-quarters in love with Ellen despite his platonic protestations. So he advised him to pursue the full course without unnecessary delay.

Adare had now recently entered College and Hamilton's salary had just been doubled; he was therefore for the first time able to contemplate marriage realistically. So in December, emboldened by Wordsworth's advice and his new financial status, he sallied down to County Limerick once again. His aim was to propose to the exciting Ellen whom he had met briefly just three months before!

Lady Dunraven guessed William's intentions and probably supported them. The de Vere parents and family also seem to have been favourably disposed, excepting the strong opposition of their third son Aubrey. Ellen herself was likely not unawares and she even travelled over from her own residence at Curragh Chase to call on Hamilton.

Then she let fall the casual remark during conversation that she "could not live happily anywhere but at Curragh." William immediately took these words quite literally, another example of his usual tendency to read too much into things where women were concerned. Now he construed that Ellen was adopting this means to gently dash his hopes! All thoughts of marriage were immediately abandoned and again the timid suitor took refuge in composing more despairing poems!

In writing of this episode fifty years later, Graves concluded that William should have been more forceful in his approach. Delicate soundings from the now long-married Ellen supported this idea. Of the three women really prominent in his life she would probably have made the best wife for Hamilton. As it was, William retired into yet another depression, engaging in highly exaggerated reconstructions of his pitifully transient acquaintance with Ellen de Vere. Where love was concerned, we are forced to conclude that he had an undeveloped vision of reality and also a marked inferiority complex.

And even though William construed himself as totally rejected by Ellen, they did not say goodbye immediately. Instead he came to stay for a few days on her invitation to the de Vere home. Here he did not seize the opportunity to pursue his original intentions as many another might have done. Rather he struck up what was to become a lifelong friendship with her brother Aubrey. He was a youth widely renowned for his handsome features and also ironically, that member of the family most opposed to William's intentions towards Ellen.

The friendship of Aubrey de Vere and Hamilton most certainly had its peculiar moments and nowhere is this more obvious than at the start. Just what the accomplished mathematician of twenty-six should have in common with a privately tutored youth not yet turned eighteen is far from clear. Perhaps it was their mutual interest in poetry, an area in which Aubrey would later achieve fame. It may be that Hamilton still felt more at home with younger and more enthusiastic minds rather than with the more settled companions of his own age. Or possibly he sensed yet another young disciple to whom he could expound on metaphysics, since Aubrey's later interest in this sphere can hardly have been highly developed at this point.

It is also possible that William really wanted to keep in touch, even at second hand, with his newly lost love. He had of course adopted the same stratagem with Catherine Disney's brothers and indeed in their case this policy would eventually bear fruit of a kind in future years.

More might also be made of the further point that Hamilton was in regular contact with three very similar young men from the minor nobility around this period. De Vere, Adare and Francis Edgeworth were all at least five years younger than Hamilton and each of them had a general or dilettante interest in the wider aspects of science. None of them at this stage however tried to master even one science topic to professional depth. But all of them were also members of the gentry and as such held in superior social regard.

It may then very well have been that the often childlike Hamilton felt most at home with younger minds like these. Or maybe he just really wanted to fraternise with the nobility — a supposition strengthened by the notable lack of more plebeian acquaintances so constantly favoured with his innermost ideas!

Hamilton returned to Dunsink at the start of 1832, a sadder if not wiser man. He fought the gloom occasioned by his dashed hopes with new research and calculation, and it was at this point that his *Third Supplement* was begun. He wrote to Wordsworth about his disappointment and to Adare about research. And from the eighteen-year-old Aubrey, he received solemn exhortations to continue searching for a suitable marriage partner:

> You may remember, in some of our conversations on this subject, I was very anxious that you should give your affections to another, even though a less worthy object, but one with a mind so entirely unworldly and disinterested as to please you at once by the power of contrast and harmony... Surely amongst the young, amongst the undefiled, the visionary, there are many such. I hope you will very soon write to me on this subject.[15]

William replied by return post in a similar vein. The general impression is of two inhibited personalities, attempting to conceal their own inadequacies concerning the opposite sex by outpourings of a suitably exalted kind:

> We agreed that habits of comparative seclusion were almost (if not altogether) necessary for preserving the youthful simplicity and innocence of female character, and keeping it unburdened and unspotted from the world. I cannot think myself allowed to expect that I shall ever again meet in a character of so much delicacy as your sister's so much innocence and frankness of manner; overcoming at once my own secret caution and reserve, getting as it were within my guard...[15]

Here the two were referring to Aubrey's theory of love, one which required prospective partners to seek out opposites so that a fuller combined character might ensue. This theory does not seem to have been based on very much practical experience; it says something about de Vere's theories that he remained unmarried, but very devoted to worship of the Virgin Mary in his later years.

Dora Wordsworth met Ellen and Aubrey soon afterwards and, in the

light of recent findings, her observations shed much light on the relationship
between the pair:

> What an interesting creature she is, but "I think of her with many
> fears" ... how she is wrapped up in her brother Aubrey! and tho' it is
> beautiful to witness, one cannot think without trembling of the sorrow
> and distress even this may bring upon her — but it is wicked to
> anticipate evil ...[16]

An early poem by Aubrey also illustrates the curious ambiguity with which
he saw himself and his sister:

> A golden bow the brother carries,
> A silver flute the sister bears;
> And ever at the fatal moment,
> The notes and arrows fly in pairs...
> With hands into each other woven,
> And whispering lips that seemed to teach,
> Each other in their very motion,
> What still their favourites learn from each.[17]

Here Aubrey was obviously inspired by those images of cherubic Cupids
common at the period; but one does not have to be a committed Freudian to
conclude that he was also, at least subconsciously, in love with his sister. If
so, his latent opposition (but also the continuing correspondence) to
Hamilton becomes more clear.

A Meeting with Coleridge

William's upsurge of creativity to compensate for his disappointment over
Ellen did not last more than a month or two. After that he began to neglect
himself and lie in bed for half the day. Even so he made up for this wasted
time by reviewing his algebraic and geometric problems mentally. He found
the geometry more relaxing because it required less discursions calling for
paper and pen. Hamilton was therefore still following his earlier practice of
visualising mathematics, a process begun with Zerah Colburn a dozen years
before. Like Newton, he continued to 'think into' his scientific problems;
indeed his dramatic discovery of conical refraction before the end of the year
may really have been set in train around this point.

Meanwhile however, Lady Dunraven and her son were much concerned
about William's current depression over Ellen. So she suggested that
Hamilton should travel to London in company with Adare and another
youth. They travelled in early March 1832 via Liverpool, where he saw his
first railway. The Liverpool to Manchester line excited and amused him,
but he still could not quite regard it as the 'greatest achievement of human
intellect', like Airy did!

At Liverpool, Hamilton also called on his old friends, the Misses
Lawrence. One of them had known Coleridge in his younger days, thirty
years before; now she gave William a letter of introduction to the famed
poet-philosopher. On the day following his arrival in London, Hamilton

Samuel Taylor Coleridge in later years *(Courtesy National Portrait Gallery, London)*

sought out the master in his Highgate lodgings and a suitable appointment hour was arranged.

Coleridge in his prime had been a famous critic as well as poet; in philosophy, he was a follower of Goethe and Schelling and so opposed to materialism. All of these were matters of great interest to Hamilton, even though now at the age of 60 the sage was greatly enfeebled both in mind and body by his opium habit. William nevertheless still professed himself impressed by the encounter, an event which seems to have consisted of a monologue by the master on the idea of the Holy Trinity.

But the idea of trinity or triads was always of large importance to Hamilton and now the triadic mathematical classification of plus-zero-minus was impinging on his thoughts. This he would soon equate with that other triadic classification of past-present-future, in his interpretation of Algebra as the Science of Pure Time. And ten years after this first meeting with Coleridge, he developed his own triadic philosophy, one based on his three fundamental classifications of Will, Mind and Life. Ternary rather than binary logic was generally more important in Hamilton's scheme of things.

William met Coleridge again in London, a few days after their first encounter, and also the following year in Cambridge. The master offered to loan him books and Hamilton explained his new approach to the theory of light. Various letters passed between the two until Coleridge's death two years later, but William's relationship with the Sage of Highgate was never as close as with Wordsworth.

A far more vivid and informative picture of Coleridge at this period emerges from a letter of Adare. He called on the master with a letter from William, two years after the latter's first visit:

> *June 30, 1834:* In one corner was a small bed, looking more like a couch, upon which lay certainly the most remarkable looking man I ever saw; I found it so difficult to follow him that I cannot recollect what he said, but even less can I remember what I should say were the subjects of conversation: this I think arises from a great want of method; but I say this, feeling I do him an injustice; still it strikes me he rambled on.
>
> All I can tell you is that his book is on logic of some particular kind, and is a sort of introduction to his great work, as he calls the one which Aubrey says exists only in his brain.[18]

Coleridge and Hamilton shared more traits than a common philosophy and their similarity would become more obvious as the years went on.

A Marriage of Sorts

During this London visit of March 1832, Hamilton first met many of the leading figures in British science — men whom he would meet at many later meetings and some of whom would become firm personal friends. At Slough, he peered through John Herschel's famous twenty-foot reflecting telescope; in the City, he inspected Sir James South's magnificent private observatory. Mr. Babbage invited him to see his new calculating machine and Captain Beaufort gave a dinner; there was also a party sponsored by the Duke of Sussex in his capacity as President of the Royal Society.

The same round of visits and parties was repeated at Cambridge, where they stayed with Airy at the Observatory. Here Hamilton met the geologist Adam Sedgwick and the mineralogist William Whewell; with the latter he was to strike up particular rapport because of their similar philosophical views. At Cambridge he also met that other Irish mathematician and former prodigy Robert Murphy, who was now alas heading towards decline; this is the only recorded instance of contact between the two.

Throughout this socialising, William, with his newfound financial independence, was keeping a weather eye open for any eligible young ladies he might meet. When none were encountered he relapsed into feelings of self-pity, a state which can be deduced from some of his poetry at this time.[19] But science and travel soon revived his spirits; later he journeyed back to Oxford to attend the second meeting of the new British Association for the Advancement of Science (BAAS). Thereafter Hamilton attended most of the BAAS meetings and took a leading part in its proceedings, a move which helped compensate for the relative isolation of the Dunsink observatory.

But now, Dunsink held additional attractions because a possible marriage prospect had lately drifted by. At twenty-nine, Helen Bayly was two years older than William. She sometimes stayed with her two married sisters at Scripplestown and Dunsinea where they had met previously. But his sudden infatuation with Ellen de Vere had displaced Helen from his affections. In any case, Helen was as different from either Ellen or Catherine as could possibly be.

William immediately reported to Aubrey de Vere, his customary consultant on matters matrimonial:

> *November 7, 1832:* A dim perspective of possible marriage has floated past me within the last few days. If the thought had been formed when you were here, I would have spoken of it then. The person is not at all brilliant, but one whom I have long known and respected and liked, although the thought of marriage is so recent.[20]

At least there is no immediate idolisation this time; it would appear that Hamilton's thoughts had turned towards Helen because she had been dangerously ill at Scripplestown during most of the summer. Whether this illness was anything more than psychosomatic may reasonably be doubted; Helen was to suffer from vague and ill-defined nervous complaints throughout her life. Indeed the circumstances which brought her to William's attention were an unhappy portent of their unfortunate future. Within a week however, William was indulging his customary fantasies:

> Never before the dark luxuriancy
> Of cloud-like tresses rich, o'er snowy brow
> Gently descending, stirred my heart as now
> The meek and spiritual majesty
> Of those dark looks: my fascinated eye
> Almost forgets the loveliness below.[21]

But not even these new visions could entirely efface the memory of his earlier longings and attachment. In another poem, he therefore thoughtfully, or perhaps thoughtlessly, informs his new love that old memories still remain:

> The ancient images shall not depart
> From my soul's temple; the refined gold,
> Well proved, shall there remain, though newer mould
> Of worth and beauty fill another part.

Hamilton followed these poems by a regular barrage of similar outpourings at daily intervals; by November 22nd, Helen had responded to all this ardent wooing with the unprecedented intimacy of a kiss. (He wrote an especially long poem about that too!) The kiss must have done wonders for William's somewhat battered ego and indeed it was probably the first such that he had ever received in all his twenty-seven years.

All this excitement made Helen ill again and she withdrew from the scene awhile to consider the formal proposal which had now been made. William too found the occasion suitable to submit a more objective appraisal to his confidant Aubrey:

> *November 26, 1832:* As to her beauty, I may consciously exaggerate that in my present state of feeling, and I must own that it did not strike me at first or always, although lately it has much impressed me. But her mind I was pleased with from the first, and after a long impartial study I do not think it very possible that I should be mistaken there.
>
> Spirituality, including but not confined to religion, appears to me to be its characteristic; and though she is not a person of brilliant or highly cultivated intellect, yet I have always found that I converse with her with pleasure . . .[22]

Helen seems to have been the more realistic of the two and wondered whether her recurring illnesses might not present a problem. William reassured her that he had taken that also into account, concluding that: "Our Heavenly Father may have provided this new pain as a successor to the now finished pain of unreturned affection. That pain has preyed upon me for almost nine years; it is over now."

Evidently, he still felt the loss of Catherine Disney almost as keenly as his rather desperate hunger for consolation from any suitable female. And even though Helen was neither cultivated nor very intelligent, he still planned to introduce her to literature and even astronomy. Hamilton had unlimited faith in his own enthusiasms and abilities, but sadly little awareness of the more limited potential of many others in such affairs.

Helen went to her widowed mother's home at Bayly Farm near Nenagh for Christmas and there, at her family's urging, she accepted Hamilton's proposal. The marriage date was duly arranged for April 9th and letters passed with great regularity between the two. Characteristically, William's letters are full of enthusiasm for classical and scientific matters, mixed up with increasing daring and suitably refined intimacy. His plans for introducing his fiancée to the greater glories of science are numerous and one can sense that here at last he had found a woman to whom he did not feel subconsciously inferior.

Helen's replies on the other hand are notably more formal. They are also invariably subdued and unenthusiastic, as well as being strikingly unsophisticated and limited in tone. Had Hamilton been more experienced in such matters, he would have instinctively recognised the warning signs!

However, if William was blind to Helen's obvious unsuitability, his relatives and family advisers were not. From the outset, his sisters would not countenance sharing the same house with her. Cousin Arthur was still giving sage advice on many matters, but we have no record of his thoughts on the proposed marriage. Uncle James however was evidently receiving bad reports and tried to advise his nephew accordingly:

> *January 13, 1832:* Love at first sight is one thing, marrying in the same haste, another. Self-confident revelation of Divine guidance and abandonment of that to passionate and wayward impulse characterises schools of Unchristian philosophy![23]

This letter evidently refers to William's earlier dejection over Ellen, but it also recognises the danger of him committing himself too readily on the rebound to the first available female.

None of his relatives attended Hamilton's marriage to Helen Bayly at Nenagh on April 9, 1833. His honeymoon must have seemed somewhat circumscribed because it was spent at his new mother-in-law's cottage. Lady Dunraven invited the pair to spend a few days in the lovely surroundings of Adare Manor, but Helen would not go. William had brought along his usual mass of papers and continued working on them during his fortnight's honeymoon at Bayly Farm.

The newlyweds returned to Dunsink to find workmen building two massive pillars through the house for the observatory dome. Grace, Sydney, Eliza and most of the servants had all decamped during William's absence; however they were apparently thoughtful enough to leave the simple-minded Archianna behind.[24]

Hamilton was due to attend the third British Association meeting at Cambridge two months later, but Helen tried to persuade him not to go. During his absence, she duly fell ill and Cousin Arthur became so apprehensive that he wrote advising William to cut his Cambridge visit short. Grace's former efficient organisation of the Dunsink household had degenerated into chaos by October; Hamilton was pleased, but Helen fearful, when Mrs. Bayly came up to sort things out again.[25]

And such was to be the general pattern of daily life at the beautiful observatory henceforth. It was to become an extraordinary blend of domestic incompetence at the lowest possible level, coupled with mathematical achievement on the highest possible plane!

7 MATHEMATICIAN EXTRAORDINARY

"Perhaps the most remarkable prediction that has ever been made is that lately made by Professor Hamilton."
G. B. Airy, June 1833

The mathematical researches which Hamilton continued right up to his last days were numerous, intensive and diverse. Indeed they were so diverse that it is still difficult to comprehend them in their entirety. The difficulty is compounded by his untidy work habits and by his tendency to use the nearest paper to hand. In his manuscripts, vast masses of secondary calculations are juxtaposed with important new principles; papers and letters were frequently redrafted many times and then copied with all the earlier versions likewise preserved.

All too clearly, Hamilton lacked the desirable discipline of ordinary office routine. Characteristically, the mind which sought to bring new order to the universe was blind to the same requirement at the more mundane level of everyday paperwork. Most of his major publications exhibit similar defects.[1] He might have done better to emulate at least some of the despised routines of Airy, a man so addicted to office routines that he carried on filing in his dotage, long after his other intellectual faculties were gone.[2]

Because of these difficulties and his own lack of facility in mathematics, Graves was never able to convey an adequate idea of Hamilton's scientific achievements. He does however list the one hundred and thirty-five papers and two books produced by him. To these must be added the four volumes of collected papers published during the present century.[3] Hankins however has achieved admirably what was beyond Graves' competence. He has unravelled the sometimes tangled threads of Hamilton's scholarship, relating his contributions to the academic climate of the times. This achievement will therefore stand as a landmark of permanent significance in the history of science and mathematicians especially will remain in Hankins' debt. Non-mathematicians however will hardly feel qualified to understand completely his more technical passages on what exactly Hamilton achieved.[4]

The present work therefore aims at something less ambitious, though possibly more difficult. Our goal is a valid restatement of Hamilton's accomplishments in terms which will be reasonably comprehensible to the non-mathematical public. And if such an aim necessarily implies some slight diminution of scientific rigour or mathematical accuracy, the expected gain in wider communication still promises to make the effort well worthwhile.

Seven Main Contributions

In summary, Hamilton made at least seven distinct creative innovations, or new contributions to scientific thought, as a result of his lifetime's work. However, all of these innovations were not of equal importance and at least two were of minor significance. But their relative order of importance did not become obvious until long after his death. To avoid confusion about such aspects, the easiest procedure is therefore to treat Hamilton's innovations chronologically. Each separate contribution can then be examined later in more appropriate detail.

Hamilton's first contribution was therefore the application of algebra or Cartesian methods to the properties of light. Before him, these had inevitably been described with diagrams using Euclidean geometry. This use of Cartesian methods was the innovation described in his first paper *On Caustics* in 1824 and elaborated in the *Theory of Systems of Rays* submitted in 1827. The algebraic approach to light was greatly developed in two further *Supplements*, submitted to the RIA in 1830, and then by a *Third Supplement* presented in 1833. This last was really a summary of all that had gone before and it is important also because it embraced William's second major creative discovery — conical refraction.

Hamilton's second innovation was, of course, recognition of the phenomenon of conical refraction, a natural happening so unexpected that nobody had even contemplated it before. Essentially, conical refraction involves passing a single ray of light into a crystal under certain strictly qualified conditions; when this is done, it is found that a *hollow* circular beam emerges. Hamilton predicted this phenomenon entirely on the basis of his new algebraic approach to light. And when the effect was quickly verified by his colleagues at Trinity in 1832, the general viability of his new method was strikingly confirmed.

Meantime, Hamilton was also engaged on his third innovation, the one which eventually proved to be the most important of all. Through further mathematics, he was able to apply his new approach to light to the dynamics of moving bodies. The connection arises because light in Hamilton's treatment could be regarded either as a form of wave motion or a stream of moving particles. The latter is of course mainly a matter of dynamics, so that Hamilton was able to extend his light treatment into this region by his two papers on *General Methods in Dynamics* submitted in 1834.

Nobody, not even Hamilton, saw any really major advantage in his analogy between optics and dynamics when it was first published. In 1926, however, the General Method proved to be tailormade for the new quantum mechanics, then being introduced by Schrödinger, to describe the inner structure of atoms. As a result, it has since become indispensable for the modern physicist.

Hamilton's fourth innovation was a much more controversial question and one which is still debatable. This was his idea of Algebra as the Science of Pure Time, expressed in a paper of that title in 1835. He formed this notion as a follower of Kant, who believed that space and time were the prime determinants of reality; since geometry was obviously the science of space, Hamilton proposed that algebra would serve a similar role for time.

Hamilton may have been overly optimistic in his thinking here. He does however seem to have been the first scientist anywhere to propose that a separate science of time was required. The need for such became generally obvious only with the advent of relativity in 1905 and still more specifically over the last twenty years.[5] In any case, his thinking did lead him to the first valid algebraic expression of 'imaginary' quantities such as the square root of –1. Before him, the $\sqrt{-1}$ symbol had seemed impossible to comprehend in any logical real sense, hence its description as 'imaginary'.

Continued concern over certain unresolved aspects of imaginaries eventually led Hamilton to his fifth, and in some respects, most famous discovery — the Theory of Quaternions. This discovery happened in an historic flash of inspiration while he was out walking on October 16, 1843. Quaternions are a related group of four factors which enable any line in any direction in space to be transformed into any other; in many ways they are an almost uncanny forerunner to Einstein's later concept of four-dimensional space-time.[6]

Quaternions however were also an entirely new mathematical language or method of notation, one capable of replacing many existing methods beyond the fairly elementary level. Hamilton therefore saw them as the direct route to fame of a kind which would endure as long as Euclid. And so indeed it might have been but for the fact that other mathematicians found quaternions far too difficult to use!

Hamilton's fifth discovery of quaternions was then certainly a major innovation, but one which was unfortunately not obviously superior to existing methodology. The real significance of quaternions lay in the fact that they were the first new or unconventional algebra radically different from the conventional kind then used. Ironically, Hamilton did not see that once he had invented one such novel algebra, there would soon be many others. And some of these inevitably proved superior to the one discovered first by him. So Hamilton spent the last third of his life more or less totally devoted to developing his new mathematical language which seemed so easy only to himself. But even while so doing, he remained creative otherwise, producing two more, though lesser, discoveries.

The hodograph was the sixth of Hamilton's main innovations and also the one most exclusively relevant to astronomy. It involved a valuable new method of describing planetary orbits which he announced in 1846. Astronomers previously had always drawn the changing velocity vectors of a planet at suitable points around the orbit, but now William transferred all these vectors to a common origin. The extremities of these vectors then define another curve, the path of which is called their hodograph.

Hamilton's final innovation came in 1856, at the age of fifty-one, when he invented the Icosian Calculus and its related 'game'. In modern terms, this was really a mathematical treatment of nets or graph theory. It solved the familiar puzzle of passing through all the various points and lines on a network diagram without repeating any path. The Icosian Calculus was eventually marketed as a commercial 'game' for which Hamilton obtained £25, but it never really took off commercially.

Such then were the seven main innovations which Hamilton produced in a lifetime of dedicated if occasionally spasmodic work. Doubtless only advanced mathematicians are capable of appreciating the sheer ingenuity and poetic qualities of these discoveries in entirety. Here it seems more fitting to consider each innovation in somewhat larger detail through the rather inadequate medium of ordinary words.

Algebra and Light

This first major section of Hamilton's researches began while he was still an undergraduate and lasted for about ten years. Almost as soon as he had grasped the new techniques of algebraic or analytical geometry about 1822, he formed the idea of applying them to optics or the properties of light. His first paper *On Caustics* was really more about lines in general than light beams specifically, but light enters more definitely into his *Systems of Rays*, submitted in 1827.

At first, William was disappointed to find that the French army officer, Malus, had partly anticipated him in the novel attempt to use algebra for describing light beams. Then he realised that his own method was far superior to Malus because it was less cumbersome. Where the Frenchman for example needed two equations to describe even a single ray, Hamilton eventually required just one master equation which could encompass any optical system.

Hamilton could do this because he was able to extend a basic principle of optics far beyond the point where Malus thought it held. The latter believed that light rays emitted from a point source and reflected from a mirror will still all be perpendicular to a second mirror sited suitably. But he did not think that the perpendicular law applied to other mirrors in subsequent reflections.

Hamilton however soon demonstrated that the perpendicular law applies to *any number* of mirror reflections; it also works for any number of refractions and even when the rays are curved! Through such methods, he eventually arrived at a very important new mathematical concept which he termed the *characteristic function*, denoted by the symbol V. When V is manipulated by other appropriate symbols, one arrives at equations such as:

$$\left(\frac{\delta V}{\delta x}\right)^2 + \left(\frac{\delta V}{\delta y}\right)^2 + \left(\frac{\delta V}{\delta z}\right)^2 = 1$$

Obviously equations of this nature must remain unintelligible to the non-mathematical reader. So here it is sufficient to grasp that suitable manipulation of V describes the total path of a light ray passing through *any* optical system. The system can comprise anything from a simple mirror to a compound telescope. The characteristic function, V, is therefore at the core of just one key mathematical equation through which all optical systems can be described.

At the age of twenty-two, Hamilton had thus gone far in his early ambition to emulate those imagined superhuman beings whose superior intellect could comprehend the entire universe at a single glance. In the more limited universe of light at least, he had successfully achieved this aim.

All this was obviously very exciting for those few advanced mathematicians capable of following his analysis. The problem was that the characteristic function, V, proved difficult for most people to derive, much less manipulate. In fact, it proved so difficult in practice that the older methods still seemed superior if less elegant!

Accordingly, apart from a small band of *cognoscenti*, Hamilton's highly original application of algebra to optics at first caused little stir. The general reaction was "Beautiful, but useless!"[7] If however such reactions seemed unduly negative, William had only himself to blame. Whether or not he wrote his *Systems of Rays* to attract a new scientific following, we cannot now really know. But if indeed such was his aim, he paid remarkably little attention to the problems these potential followers might face. His papers provide no diagrams, examples or explanations for less agile minds attempting to follow his reasoning. In his constant urge towards the absolute minimum in mathematical description, he seems to have adopted a similar, though quite unnecessary, economy in words.

On the other hand, Hamilton just possibly may have been striving to impress his audience by a degree of erudition above the level of more ordinary mortals. Whatever his motive, he certainly succeeded totally in mystifying most people. And in so doing, he must have very soon lost many potential disciples.

Hankins also notes that Hamilton's papers on light lack the vital element of proportion. Less interesting aspects are examined in great depth at the expense of more important elements. This resembles a treatise on human anatomy devoting whole chapters to minor appendages like a toe or little finger, while at the same time confining discussion of important features, like the skull or spine, to a single paragraph! The fact is that truth implies a more or less direct proportion between perceived importance and depth of description, but Hamilton was very often deficient here. In the end, however, he may have been most interested in the expression of reality as it appeared to him. Whether or not this reality is palatable, digestible or even perceptible to others is often a secondary matter for the true artist or discoverer. And so too may be such relatively minor matters as presentation in a popular way.

There was also the final irony that the Royal Irish Academy was not well known in the 1820s and therefore its papers were not widely read abroad. In fact, Hamilton's first publications were not even sent to the French Academy of Sciences, the intellectual milieu where his ideas originated and where they might naturally have caused most stir!

Conical Refraction

Given these unfavourable circumstances, Hamilton was then clearly lucky as well as brilliant when he came up with a highly dramatic new physical phenomenon. This was the discovery of conical refraction which he predicted from his new optical method in 1832. Its almost immediate concrete verification dramatised his rather esoteric theorising most convincingly, so that Hamilton and his algebraic method quickly became more widely known.

Hamilton's normal practice was to draft and redraft his more important writings perhaps a dozen times: it was during one such redraft for his *Third Supplement* (to the *Systems of Rays*) during 1832 that he chanced on the phenomenon of conical refraction. It developed as a special case in biaxial crystals (those which contain two axes of optical symmetry).

Ordinary refraction — the phenomenon by which a stick appears bent when placed underwater — was first clarified by Snell early in the 17th century. Much later, Huygens and Malus investigated double refraction, whereby an object affords a double image when viewed in certain directions through crystals such as Iceland spar. Now Hamilton's theory predicted that a ray of light entering certain other crystals under some circumstances would emerge as an expanding cone or hollow circular light beam. This was a phenomenon so unexpected that nobody had even contemplated it previously.

In fact, Hamilton concluded that there would be not one but two distinct types of conical refraction depending on the nature of the incident ray.[8] Once he was sure of his figures, he informed the RIA on October 22, 1832; on the following day, he requested Humphrey Lloyd to verify the prediction he had made. Lloyd had some difficulty in getting a suitable crystal, but after about six weeks a suitable specimen of arragonite was found. So on December 14, he was able to write to Hamilton that he had found the cone and also that its angles were in good agreement with those foretold.[9]

Hamilton immediately started preparing for publication and also wrote to Herschel and Airy about this dramatic new discovery. The latter at first replied that it had nothing at all to do with Hamilton's optical theory! Here Airy was probably displaying that characteristic negative attitude towards novelty which would later lose Britain its chance of discovering the planet Neptune.[10] At any rate, this time he was instantly corrected by Hamilton and so was fulsome in his apology:

January 28, 1833: Allow me to thank you for your last note, which is all very comprehensible and true; and if I had not been very dull, I might

Conical Refraction simplified

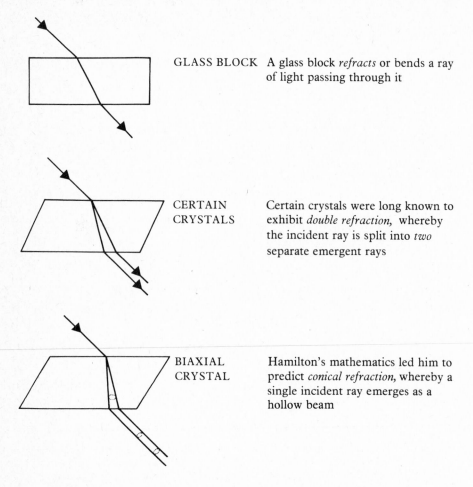

GLASS BLOCK   A glass block *refracts* or bends a ray
of light passing through it

CERTAIN   Certain crystals were long known to
CRYSTALS   exhibit *double refraction,* whereby
the incident ray is split into *two*
separate emergent rays

BIAXIAL   Hamilton's mathematics led him to
CRYSTAL   predict *conical refraction,* whereby a
single incident ray emerges as a
hollow beam

perhaps have guessed at some of it before. There were parts of the
previous letter that were altogether mysterious to me, and were likely to
remain so, except I could divine or you explain.[11]

Meantime, trouble was also brewing from another quarter, one from which
Hamilton was to suffer frequently henceforth. Later we will meet
MacCullagh who engaged in minor political machination before Hamilton's
election as President of the RIA. But his general jealousy had started long
before. A brief look at his record readily suggests how this may have
occurred.

James MacCullagh was born in 1809, four years after Hamilton, and also
developed as a child prodigy. Unlike the latter, however, he never had a
favoured background, his father being a small farmer at Upper Bodoney in
County Tyrone. MacCullagh nevertheless persevered and entered Trinity in
1824 as a sizar or free-place student; at the age of fifteen he came in just one

year after Hamilton. Thereafter he progressed rapidly and became a Fellow in 1832.

MacCullagh however never fitted in well with the Trinity establishment; he was always very much a loner and was probably unduly conscious of his humble origins. He seems to have deeply envied Hamilton's academic achievements and wide social contacts. And were it not for the presence of Hamilton, he would also undoubtedly have been regarded as Trinity's greatest mathematician of the early nineteenth century. MacCullagh had indeed come very close to discovering conical refraction two years earlier in a paper which had been refereed by Hamilton. As a result, he duly published in July 1833 what he regarded as the basis of his claim to priority:

> When Professor Hamilton announced his discovery of Conical Refraction, he does not seem to have been aware that it is an obvious and immediate consequence of the theorems published by me three years ago . . . That the indeterminate cases of my own theorems, which optically interpreted, mean conical refraction, of course occurred to me at the time . . . Business of a different nature, however, prevented me from following up the inquiry.[12]

Whatever the real value of MacCullagh's ideas on this score, he was of course to be faulted for not having followed up such an important consequence had it been truly recognised by him. Lloyd moved tactfully to point out these aspects and so the dispute was peacefully resolved. MacCullagh, however, remained sensitive on this issue, so that his sense of grievance was to surface on various occasions over the following fifteen years.

Meanwhile, Hamilton's prediction of conical refraction and its confirmation by Lloyd elicited high praise generally. At Cambridge, the philosopher William Whewell opined that "few things have been more remarkable" in the general development of science. Airy was moved to go even further in his praise when he declared that "perhaps the most remarkable prediction that has ever been made is that lately made by Professor Hamilton."[13] This was unusual praise indeed to be heaped on what is after all a fairly minor curiosity among the many such in optics. It is therefore of interest to consider what rendered Hamilton's discovery unique.

Conical refraction was of such importance simply because it was a previously unimagined natural phenomenon, predicted solely on pure mathematical grounds. And, in addition, it was not only qualitatively but also quantitatively verified.

Three similar unexpected predictions, derived entirely from mathematics, were to follow over the next century. One was the discovery in 1845 of the planet Neptune, inspired by calculations conducted by Adams and LeVerrier on perturbations in the orbit of Uranus. Another was the prediction of radio waves from James Clerk Maxwell's electromagnetic theory of 1864. Thirdly, there was Einstein's prediction, derived from his 1915 theory of general relativity, that light would bend under gravity.[13a]

Hamilton's prediction was at once the least important but also the first of these purely mathematical predictions and so its influence for all future science was profound.

The Search for the Ether

One of the great advantages of Hamilton's optical treatment was that it did not matter whether light ultimately consisted of waves or particles. If light progressed in waves, the moving wave front was always perpendicular to all the rays, as both the law of Malus and Hamilton's treatment required. But if, on the other hand, light progressed as a series of moving particles, they too would always arrive simultaneously at a surface perpendicular to their direction of motion.

This was a matter of great importance in view of the great controversy over the nature of light which then raged. Newton had thought that light rays were streams of corpuscles emitted from their source, like little bullets; his corpuscular or emission theory of light was largely accepted throughout the eighteenth century. From about 1800 onwards, however, scientists like Thomas Young and Augustin Fresnel began to investigate phenomena like interference fringes; these strongly suggested that light rays were not propagated as corpuscles but in a wave or undulatory form.

The dispute raged through Hamilton's youth and early years at Dunsink and, after some hesitation, he sided with Airy and Herschel in supporting the wave theory. By 1840, most scientists agreed with them. And in 1850, Newton's particle theory received what seemed to be its death blow when Foucault showed that light moves more slowly in water than in air.

This still left the problem of how the light waves could be propagated; to explain this, the idea of a lumeniferous ether was conceived. The properties of this ether had to be very curious and almost metaphysical if they were to explain its function in the wave transmission of light. It had to be tenuous, elastic and all-pervasive, being also apparently immune to verification by experiment. And even though it was quite imperceptible to the senses, it also needed a solidity resembling that of steel!

During the 1830s, Hamilton and other scientists sought to create models of this strange material apparently required by theory to support their waves of light. MacCullagh was one of the most successful because he started from the experimental facts instead of preconceived assumptions. However, the outcome was a theoretical picture which proved almost impossible to accept. Hamilton, in contrast, set out from his metaphysical idea of an ether composed of point masses with interacting forces. But in spite of all his undoubted mathematical powers, this viewpoint never led to any real advance.

Through such considerations however, Hamilton pondered for a while a radical new idea: "Much has been done, perhaps in the dynamics of light; little I thought, in the dynamics of darkness . . ."[14]

Here Hamilton proposed to consider a problem to which none of the other ether theorists had given much thought. Their calculations concerned an ether already filled with light waves; he wanted to know about the ether when no light was there. This wholly new area Hamilton proposed to term the 'dynamics of darkness'. Herschel approved and suggested 'skotodynamics' as a more attractive term.

Although the history is still controversial, MacCullagh most likely came closest of anyone to solving the theoretical problem of the supposed ether. In any case, interest in the ether as a mechanical basis for light propagation declined rapidly following the publication in 1864 of James Clerk Maxwell's electromagnetic theory. Seventeen years later, Michelson and Morley showed that light has the same speed in all directions, thereby calling the very existence of the ether into question; in 1905 Einstein disposed of the concept entirely.

Ironically, we now know that light is both corpuscular and also wavelike in its propagation properties. Both sides in the 'great light debate' of the 1830s were therefore in a sense correct. But the search for the ether was entirely unnecessary, a great scientific wild-goose chase, dictated by the wholly mechanistic thinking of the times.

Optics to Dynamics

Although Hamilton's consideration of the ether then proved to be unsuccessful, a much more fruitful development had occurred just before. His original approach to optics readily allowed light rays to be considered as streams of moving particles and thus not really different from other speeding objects in the natural world. The similarity with dynamics (the science of force and moving bodies) was therefore clear.

Hamilton apparently began to develop this analogy in 1826, the year when he extended his early simple treatment of straight lines into the more complex description of curved rays. By 1832, his optical treatment was largely completed with the conclusion of the *Third Supplement*. Now he was free to extend the principle further and this he did in his two famous papers on *General Methods in Dynamics* which appeared in 1834. However, he did not present these papers to the Royal Irish Academy as he had done with earlier works. Urged on by Uncle James, he sought a wider audience this time. So he submitted his papers on dynamics, with Beaufort's aid, to the Royal Society of London where the first part was duly read on April 10, 1834. No scientist of any standing could validly plead ignorance of a publication from such a body, so that this time Hamilton's work immediately became widely known.

While writing these papers, he explained his purpose very clearly to Uncle James:

> *March 12, 1834:* It is my hope and purpose to remodel the whole of Dynamics, in the most extensive sense of the word, by the idea of my Characteristic Function or central law of relation; not indeed that I

pretend to do more now than to distinctly sketch a plan by which this great task may be accomplished.

I am not now offering so great a work as that would need to be, in which Dynamics and Optics should be treated expressly as corollaries of one common principle.

It may be mentioned that this Dynamical principle is only another form of that idea which has been already applied to Optics in my *Theory of Systems of Rays*.[15]

Here again, the precise mathematical nature of Hamilton's new contribution is adequately conveyed by Hankins in specialist terms.[16] Equally again, its highly abstruse mathematical content renders elucidation in non-mathematical terms difficult. We can however derive some comfort from the fact that even Herschel found himself unable to understand it at times: "Alas! I grieve to say that it is only the general scope of the method which stands dimly shadowed out to my mind amid the gleaming and dazzling lustre of the symbolic expressions in which it is conveyed..."[17]

It may then be sufficient for the reader to grasp that Hamilton had now extended his earlier optical characteristic function into dynamics. Here it becomes transformed into a new and more general function denoted by the symbol S. This again can be manipulated by suitable methods, affording equations such as the variational formulation:

$$\delta S = \delta \int_0^t L dt = 0$$

The characteristic function, S, is now the core of a new and mathematically important method of stating results, one which became widely known as Hamilton's Principle. Soon after Hamilton's papers were published, C. Jacobi in Germany adopted and extended the method still further. The resultant theory then became known as the Hamilton-Jacobi Principle or Theory. It has been suggested that Jacobi did not understand Hamilton's intentions properly, but at any rate he was the main developer initially associated with the method.[18]

As happened earlier, the outcome of Hamilton's research into this area was greater generality and simplicity on a theoretical plane at least. A good example of this process concerns the determination of the ten planetary orbits around the sun. Previously, their description had required the solution of either thirty or sixty differential equations according to complexity. Hamilton's new method reduced these many calculations to just two equations involving his characteristic functions.

This major theoretical simplification is perhaps best expressed in his own words:

The difficulty is therefore at least transferred from the integration of many equations of one class to the integration of two of another; and even if it should be thought that no practical facility is gained, yet an intellectual pleasure may result from the reduction of the most complex of all researches respecting the forces and motions of body, to the study of one characteristic function, the unfolding of one central relation...[19]

For almost a century however, Hamilton's great method was generally more praised than used. It seemed more elegant than practical, nor was there any great reason for employing it where time-honoured methods would serve just as well. Such was the position until Schrödinger introduced his revolutionary wave-function model of quantum mechanics to describe the atom in 1926. Then Hamilton's method proved to be the one form of previous classical theory that could be applied directly to the new wave mechanics and associated ideas!

Quantum mechanics have been remarkably successful in elucidating the electronic structure of the atom, as well as the internal forces within its nucleus. Prior to this, Hamilton's discovery — that the laws of light and moving particles could be expressed in the same form — had seemed to be little more than a curious analogy. Now it emerged as a very important property of matter at its most basic level.

In other words, Hamilton's urge to unify and generalise had in fact uncovered a very important natural law. But tragically, he would never know this, simply because those developments in physics requiring his method were still ninety years ahead in time.

Schrödinger has expressed Hamilton's significance in these matters quite unequivocally:

> I daresay not a day passes — and seldom an hour — without somebody, somewhere on this globe, pronouncing or reading or writing Hamilton's name. That is due to his fundamental discoveries in general dynamics. The Hamiltonian Principle has become the cornerstone of modern physics, the thing with which a physicist expects every physical phenomenon to be in conformity ...
>
> The modern development of physics is constantly enhancing Hamilton's name. His famous analogy between optics and mechanics virtually anticipated wave mechanics, which did not have much to add to his ideas and only had to take them more seriously ... If you wish to apply modern theory to any particular problem, you must start with putting the problem *in Hamiltonian form*.[20]

Both sides in the great wave/particle debate on light in the early nineteenth century were therefore ultimately correct. It is easy enough for us nowadays to understand how light exhibits dual characteristics, both wave and particle properties. But in the 1830s, not even Hamilton with his vivid imagination could have dared to dream that such might be. Apparently he never suspected that his curious optical-mechanical analogy was much more than mere analogy after all. As far as we know, he did not realise that it was in fact an extremely important and very practical basic manifestation of the natural world.

8 ADMINISTRATOR

"Any man who is fit for original research has no business to be a president or secretary or treasurer."
De Morgan to Hamilton, February 1846

When Hamilton first met the leading men of British science during his London visit of 1832, a new sense of excitement was in the air. This arose from the first meeting of the British Association for the Advancement of Science (BAAS), held at York the year before. The BAAS had its origins in the discontent felt by many at the power held by titled non-scientists, such as the Duke of Sussex, within the Royal Society. The new body also raised hopes of enlisting proper state support for science as was already common on the Continent.

It was also considered that a yearly gathering of scientists, visiting each of the main cities in turn, would help to educate the public towards these ends. Famous figures like Charles Babbage, David Brewster and John Herschel were soon prominent in their support of this Association, to which Hamilton also was quickly attracted. In late 1831, he was invited by the organiser, Vernon Harcourt, to join the BA's new local committee in Dublin. Hamilton agreed enthusiastically while passing over the job of secretary to Humphrey Lloyd; at this stage, he tried to avoid most extra administrative duties of a minor kind.

On June 16, 1832, he attended the second Association meeting at Oxford as the sole Irish representative. On behalf of the Royal Irish Academy, he read a paper for MacCullagh on spheroids and another by himself on functions of zero; he also sketched an outline of his *Systems of Rays*. All this provided good exposure for the new scientific upsurge at Trinity and Hamilton seized the opportunity to invite the Association to Dublin for 1834. The Dublin visit was eventually deferred to 1835, but while at Oxford Hamilton was also called upon for a farewell speech.

In this address, he compared the idea of Association meetings to the early Olympic Games, a regular event in which diverse factions might still assert their common identity. He declared himself as an Irishman first within the greater statehood of the British Isles and this would remain his political and cultural stance throughout his days.

At the third meeting of the Association, in June 1833 at Cambridge, there was a much stronger Irish presence. With Romney Robinson and Hamilton came Provost Bartholomew Lloyd and his son Humphrey. The main topic of discussion was Hamilton's recent discovery of conical refraction at Dublin and again he was called on for a speech. This time his bride of two months was much on his mind; she was seriously ill with one of her mysterious neurotic maladies back home in Dunsink. But still he was able to rise to the occasion as demanded, expressing in his usual rhetoric the delegates' general satisfaction with the new upsurge in science now underway.[1]

Hamilton also met Coleridge at this meeting and spent an entire evening in his company. Nothing much of interest must have transpired however, for he left no records of the event. But he made a more important contact in the person of Monsieur Quetelet from the Brussels Observatory. He was editor of a widely read periodical and now asked Hamilton for a summary of his method — a notice which was to make his work far more widely known on the Continent.

Hamilton's first child, William Edwin, was born on May 10th of the following year. Four months later came the fourth Association meeting at Edinburgh. This time, the Irish contingent was strengthened even further by the presence of Dionysius Lardner and John Graves. Hamilton attempted to explain his new and important extension of the optical method to dynamics as best he could; his eloquence must have been much appreciated because again he was called upon for the customary speech.

The Irish delegation returned from Edinburgh in triumph, the Association having chosen Dublin as its venue for the following year. Effectively this decision confirmed a recognition that Ireland was now a growing focus of scientific development; it was undoubtedly due to Hamilton that such transpired.

The Dublin Meeting

William returned from Edinburgh to find that his wife and newborn son were still on holiday with her mother in the south, where they had gone before he went away. Ireland at this period was in some civil disorder as the Catholic majority struggled for equal rights with the Protestant minority and Helen was timorous of the relative isolation of Dunsink. In addition, however, she was likely seeking some excuse to return to mother because otherwise, she could just as readily have stayed with either of her married sisters who were living only a few fields away! At any rate, Hamilton now journeyed south a hundred miles to see his wife and child. He stayed for a fortnight, while his assistant Thompson carried on with the usual observatory routines. But William put his holiday to good use by completing large sections of his *Second Essay on Dynamics*. Curiously enough, he always found his mother-in-law's residence a very creative place in which to work!

When William returned to Dublin for his course of Introductory

Lectures, Helen still persisted in staying on at Bayly Farm. For half a year or more, Hamilton was constantly making the arduous public coach journey back and forth to Nenagh to visit her. Helen finally returned to Dunsink in the following May; three months later their second son, Archibald, was born.

As might be expected, Hamilton found all this needless travel highly wearying as well as expensive; for a period, he was again depressed to be so much on his own at the observatory. Now he realised that he could not function properly under such hermit-like conditions. His ideas flowed best in constant company from which he could retire and return at will. Meantime however, there was always the organisation of the forthcoming British Association meeting at Dublin to keep him occupied.

Hamilton also utilised his frequent journeys up and down to Nenagh to visit the new giant telescopes then being assembled by William Parsons in his ancestral seat at Birr. Parsons then held the title of Lord Oxmantown and did not become the Earl of Rosse until 1841. Just how the elder Herschel had manufactured his giant speculum telescope mirrors was still a secret; starting in 1827, the 26-year-old Parsons decided to make better ones on his own. Now Hamilton was able to see the latest three-foot mirror inserted in its casing and, in a letter to Helen, reported himself suitably impressed:

> *February 22, 1835:* When the tube was nearly, but not exactly, adjusted to Jupiter, so strong a light was thrown upon the side by the reflexion from the mirror, that it reminded me of the light thrown upon the ground by a coach-lantern; and it happened that I was the first to point it at a celestial object, which will be something to remember (if I live) in after-years.[2]

Meantime, the date of the Association meeting was fast approaching and Hamilton and Humphrey Lloyd shouldered most of the responsibility as local secretaries. They met once a week at the Royal Irish Academy to discuss progress; as might be expected, Lloyd did most of the actual organising work. Hamilton's function was more to invite and persuade the various eminent figures with whom he was in contact so as to ensure a worthwhile attendance. There were fears that Dublin's relative isolation across the Irish Sea might keep some of them away.

In the event, these fears proved groundless for the fifth meeting of the British Association, at Dublin in 1835, was generally agreed to be the most worthwhile yet. It opened on Monday August 10, with the Provost, Dr. Lloyd, as President; it fell to Hamilton as Secretary to read the customary Annual Report. Newspapers record that the Provost spoke in so low a voice that it was impossible to hear him; Hamilton however rose to the occasion in characteristic fashion and was received with enthusiastic demonstrations of applause. From a visiting American science reporter we learn that "he gave us a beautiful and eloquent address of an hour long, exactly hitting the tone of the occasion, and the wants and feelings of a large popular audience. I was delighted with it, and it produced a fine effect."[3] Hamilton was obviously in his element on this occasion and the cheering effect which his early great

The Great Birr Telescope, constructed by William Parsons, 3rd Earl of Rosse   *(Courtesy National Library of Ireland, Lawrence C5676)*

enthusiasm usually exerted on company of any sort was evidently still at work.

The proceedings of the meeting were divided into the usual six sections, these being accommodated in suitable buildings around Trinity. Almost all the eminent British scientific figures of the day were present except Brewster and Herschel; the former likely stayed away through pique, while the latter had already begun his five years of observation in the southern hemisphere at the Cape. The Arctic explorers Ross and Franklin were both present and Babbage was head of Section F on statistics. The venerable John Dalton of atomic theory fame also came over, exciting much popular interest as he appeared in traditional Quaker garb.

A selection of the papers read to the various sections affords us a taste of the general scientific flavour of the times. Professor Davy read a paper on metals in seawater; Griffiths exhibited his famed new geological map of Ireland, which was then the most detailed of its kind available. Local engineer Robert Mallett explained his use of the new electromagnet for separating scrap iron from copper; he had not yet advanced to his major work as the future father of seismology. Sir John Ross advanced his theory, based on Arctic observations, that the Aurora was caused by the reflection of sunlight from high clouds. This interpretation however was not generally well received.

There were also the usual fringe activities often associated with such gatherings, one of which led to a highly indecorous incident. It so happened that just before the meeting the local River Poddle, which runs under St. Patrick's Cathedral, had overflowed; during the subsequent repairs, the coffins of Dean Swift and his beloved Stella were unearthed. A group of phrenologists who were attending the meeting seized on this unexpected opportunity and they were duly given permission to examine the disinterred skulls.

Everybody in Dublin soon knew that Stella's skull still had one tooth remaining and that her organ of amativeness was considered to be very prominent. According to Oscar Wilde's father, writing fourteen years later, both skulls were "carried to most of the learned, as well as all the fashionable, societies of Dublin" during the following ten days.[4] Evidently they were among the highlights of the Association week.

Down in the country, Aubrey de Vere was greatly shocked to hear of such incidents and he wrote to Hamilton to record his disgust. The latter took care in his reply to acquit himself and the Association of any responsibility, which seems at variance with other accounts of the incident. It would appear that Hamilton was simply trying to evade the issue.

In any case, the episode of Swift and Stella was probably just an unwise inclusion in a general civic programme designed to honour science. There were for example free trips for Association members on the new Dublin to Kingstown Railway; scientists could thereby disprove by personal experience Lardner's famous contention, that people would suffocate if they travelled at over thirty miles per hour! There was also a constant round of fêtes, receptions and garden parties, so that the delegates were probably as much impressed by Irish hospitality as with the new enthusiasm for science.[5]

The Association meeting culminated in a grand dinner given by the College for three hundred Association delegates and various local dignitaries. This function was held on August 15 in the magnificent Long Room of Trinity Library. Before dinner the Lord Lieutenant, Musgrave, summoned Hamilton and in an unexpected simple little ceremony dubbed him Sir William Rowan Hamilton!

This was the first knighthood which had been awarded in Ireland for scientific merit. As such, it was therefore yet another sign of recognition by the establishment that science was now being taken seriously. Hamilton himself seems to have been genuinely taken by surprise, indeed so much so that his usual eloquence quite deserted him. On this rare occasion he had nothing at all to say.

Knighthood at the age of thirty on that August night in Dublin was also in a real sense the crowning apex of Hamilton's career. Four of his five main contributions to science had been already made, and now only quaternions remained.

The Long Room of Trinity College, Dublin, where Hamilton was knighted in 1835   *(Courtesy PDI, Dublin/Trinity College, Dublin)*

Interestingly also, Hamilton's most public honour was achieved within three days of the exact chronological centre of his life. This was a curiously fitting instance in career symmetry — one which William, with his perpetual interest in dates and coincidence, would undoubtedly have appreciated could he but have known.[6]

Learned Societies

Hamilton's knighthood however was not an unmixed blessing. For one thing, it probably intensified the petty jealousies so common in most restricted academic communities and in his case most obviously exhibited by MacCullagh. In addition, it cost him £74 in registration fees (a sum equivalent to six weeks' salary), which he duly paid on September 16. Since Hamilton was never rich and was permanently overdrawn at his bankers, Bruce and Syme, this fee must have represented a considerable sacrifice.[7]

Hamilton was also a member of various other learned societies in many countries and eventually there would be at least two dozen in all. Proof that he valued such honours highly is evident in the fact that he saw fit to list all of them on the frontispiece of his *Lectures on Quaternions* published in 1853.[8] Many of these foreign societies also required an entrance fee; some were quite substantial, as for example the five guineas' subscription to the Northern Society of Antiquaries of Copenhagen.[9]

All of which renders more than a trifle mysterious the fact that Hamilton was never a member of the most prestigious learned society of all. In the Royal Society, he had many prominent friends, such as Beaufort and Herschel, who had on several occasions in the early days offered to recommend him for membership. To Sabine in 1847, Hamilton privately pleaded poverty, stating that he could not afford the required £5 subscription.[10]

The poverty plea however hardly makes sense in view of his similar contributions to lesser societies. Perhaps William felt that his enthusiastic identification with the BAAS, combined with neglect of the Royal Society, might help to advance the standing of the newer group. Or perhaps he felt something similar about his association with the Royal Irish Academy, possibly even making the silent point that to belong to the latter body sufficed! In the end we are forced to conclude that Hamilton's lifelong neglect of the Royal Society remains a minor mystery, one of the many such in his career which future scholars may resolve.

In any case, the Royal Irish Academy was of course the single learned society with which Hamilton was most concerned. Founded about 1785 from two College societies known as the Palaeosophers and the Neosophers, its headquarters were at Lower Grafton Street, just opposite the Provost's House, until 1852. Then it moved to the present location in Dawson Street but Hamilton during his career was most concerned with the earlier building.

Some idea of conditions at the old Academy headquarters during this period is conveyed in a letter by librarian Edward Clibborn. In it, he seeks reimbursement for the sum of £26.18.0d spent on his own initiative:

> *July 4, 1840:* On entering into office, I found the house in such a filthy state that I took immediate steps to have it cleaned. I had the carpets taken off and taken out to my place in the country where they were cleaned; but that in the parlour was so decayed, I found it not worth putting down again.
>
> The floor I had repaired, with decaying floorboards removed. But the old carpet had such an intolerable smell from dried saliva and other filth that I could not put part of it in the gallery library as intended.
>
> Before this, the parlour was intolerable and no lady or gentleman could remain in it for ten minutes without a feeling of sickness, unless the window and door were open . . .[11]

At this period the RIA had about 150 members, many of them inevitably associated with Trinity College. There was a ruling Council which served under a President elected for life, an office held by Brinkley from 1822 until 1835. Young William duly joined in 1824 and it was the President who introduced his first premature paper *On Caustics*. Doubtless patronage from such an august source was a considerable help to the ambitious undergraduate.

Hamilton in turn proposed MacCullagh for membership just after the latter had gained a Fellowship in 1832. Some idea of the newcomer's often abrasive personality comes across in his acknowledgement note: "I was never anxious to become a member of the Royal Irish Academy, but the honour of being proposed by you is too flattering to be rejected. . ."[12]

Brinkley died just one month after the great British Association meeting in Dublin and Hamilton duly read his eulogy to the Academy on November 9. Provost Bartholomew Lloyd was now elected President in an election where Hamilton secured just three votes.[13] Apparently however the newly knighted William was proposed against his will in this first contest.

Meantime, the newly titled Lady Hamilton had again decamped to be with her mother soon after their second son, Archibald, was born on August 5. A few weeks earlier, William's favourite poetess sister Eliza had gone abroad on a Moravian mission to heathen Turkey. So altogether, 1835 was certainly a momentous year for Hamilton.

President of the Royal Irish Academy

Provost Bartholomew Lloyd did not last very long in his new role as President of the Academy, for he died suddenly of apoplexy after spending two years in the Chair. The main contenders for the succession were Hamilton and the late incumbent's son Humphrey; another serious candidate was Richard Whately, a distinguished Oxford economist who had been appointed Church of Ireland Archbishop of Dublin.

Intensive lobbying was now begun on behalf of all three candidates. The main fear of the science faction was a split vote which would let the relatively unpopular Archbishop win. Lloyd had the support of most of the Fellows because of his influences within the College; Hamilton was better known and far more popular among the non-College members. Lloyd thought that Hamilton had a more deserving claim, but the latter offered to stand down in his rival's favour.[14]

MacCullagh was busy in these matters behind the scenes, allying himself with the Senior Fellow, Dr. Wall, in active opposition to Hamilton. He now gave Lloyd to understand that Hamilton had withdrawn his name to give the science faction a united front, thereby persuading the former to let himself be formally proposed. In fact, MacCullagh had visited Hamilton earlier and told him that Lloyd was determined to go forward in any case and it was this deliberate lie by MacCullagh which had persuaded Hamilton to withdraw!

Once this piece of byzantine intrigue became apparent, Hamilton's friends insisted that he press his claims again. A straw poll was therefore proposed among the electors to see who would be the likely winner; now MacCullagh reported that it would probably be the Archbishop unless Hamilton withdrew!

In the event, all three major candidates finally went forward and the results must have afforded little confidence in MacCullagh's mathematical abilities, as a pollster at least. Hamilton secured forty-five votes and Lloyd thirty-six, while the Archbishop scored fourteen and others two. MacCullagh evidently still saw himself as a politician of the academic variety despite this reverse. Indeed it was probably disappointment over another more public election ten years later, in which he stood unsuccessfully as the nationalist candidate, which may have led to his eventual suicide!

Immediately upon his election, Hamilton took care to smooth over any ruffled feelings by nominating both Lloyd and Whately as Vice-Presidents. His friendship with the former therefore remained unabated, while relations with the Archbishop improved from this point on. He also embarked on a conscious policy designed to liven up the Academy generally, a policy which proved successful in many ways.

Before embarking on these measures Hamilton wrote to various persons for advice. As originally conceived in 1785, the Academy was meant to concern itself with three distinct departments — Science, Polite Literature and Antiquities. In practice, a proper balance between these three divisions had been difficult to maintain, a situation which Hamilton now set out to rectify. He felt himself competent to administer an enlightened policy for science, while being equally conscious of his deficiencies in the other two.

Concerning literature, Hamilton wrote therefore to four suitable authorities of his acquaintance for advice. Wordsworth was not much help because he opined that official patronage only helped to subsidise laziness among creative men. Hamilton however still thought that learned societies had a valid function in publishing works too academic or recondite for commercial consideration. In fact he enquired whether the poet himself had any such

Hamilton in 1842 as President of the Royal Irish Academy
(after The Dublin University Magazine, June 1842)

which the RIA might be honoured to sponsor, but here again the answer
was negative.

Maria Edgeworth, as Ireland's most distinguished authoress, also
considered that academies were not much use in furthering artistic
endeavour. Even awards were too difficult to decide equitably because they
tended to foster divisions and jealousies. The RIA could nevertheless help
stimulate the literary spirit of Dublin by introducing topics which would
then be discussed at greater length outside. As President, Hamilton would
be well advised to hold himself aloof from the more routine discussions in
the Academy.

Aubrey de Vere's father, who was also a prominent literary figure,
thought that the Academy should try to promote indigenous cultural
subjects: "They should effect for their own country, as respects its ancient
history, institutions, popular traditions, literature, manners and language,
what cannot be looked for elsewhere."[15]

From Trim, the Rev. Richard Butler (the man who did more than any other to seek out the true history of the many ruins in the vicinity) replied in similar vein. Specifically, he suggested that the Academy should print such ancient Gaelic Annals as were still in manuscript, thereby helping scholars to shed new light on Ireland's glories during the period before English rule became supreme.[16]

Hamilton duly took heed of all these suggestions, proving himself a conscientious President as well as an able administrator during his term. This latter administrative skill may seem surprising in view of his relative neglect of observatory routines. The records nevertheless show that he was very familiar with the Academy's constitution and also illustrate his careful attention to minute detail. In science, he broadened the range of publications by shifting away from the previous emphasis on mathematics and physics — those two fields where he himself excelled. In literature, he arranged honorary memberships for Wordsworth, Maria Edgeworth and also the Scottish science writer Mary Sommerville.[17]

It was however in the general sphere of antiquities that the RIA probably made most striking progress during Hamilton's reign. He encouraged the preservation of ancient manuscripts as Dean Butler had suggested, repeatedly petitioning the Chancellor of the Exchequer for £1,000 so that the important monastic Annals of the Four Masters could be printed.

Private collections of antiquarian value were acquired and purchased during this period and here MacCullagh was especially enthusiastic. In 1839 for example, he presented the Academy with the wonderful and ancient Cross of Cong, which he had purchased on his own initiative. Petrie's account of this episode some years later throws a new and surprising light on MacCullagh's character:

> I communicated to my friend my opinion as to its great historical interest and value; and without having ever seen it himself, or having received any further information relative to it than that which I had communicated to him, he, who could not be called a rich man, determined, if possible, to become the purchaser, and this without any regard to its cost.[18]

This incident, supported by other evidence at various points, reveals that MacCullagh was certainly more than the single-minded theoretical mathematician generally assumed.

Adare's earlier enthusiasm for astronomy was now veering towards antiquities, so that Robinson's earlier hopes — for yet another private observatory in Ireland — were never fulfilled. However Adare embarked on a very fruitful partnership with George Petrie (1790-1866) in the study of Ireland's many ancient ruins. The latter was superintendent of the antiquarian section of the Ordnance Survey from 1833 to 1846, and in this capacity made the first scientific survey of ancient buildings and ruins. Adare and Petrie also shared a common interest in the mystery of Ireland's many surviving round towers and together they formed the Irish Archaeological Society in 1840.

Hamilton also instituted a system of yearly medals for the best publications in each of the Academy's three sections. In 1838, the first medal for Science could easily have gone to himself, but he made sure that it was awarded to MacCullagh. This move evoked so much admiration from the Trinity faction which had earlier opposed his election that Hamilton was invited to an all-night party the same night in Lloyd's rooms.[19] It was about this time that William began to exhibit carelessness in his drinking habits, a trend which was to lead to trouble with his public image even before his term as President was over.

In the proceedings of the Academy, he encountered other problems as well. In 1838 for example, Sir William Betham had submitted a paper claiming to connect ancient Gaelic with the Etruscan language via the Phoenicians. When the referees refused this paper, Hamilton felt bound to uphold their decision. The following year, Petrie was awarded the annual medal in antiquities for his paper on *The Hill of Tara;* during this presentation, Hamilton characteristically delivered himself of a lengthy oration stating his own views on the subject.

Betham was evidently still rankling over the rejection of his pet thesis and now, he objected that the President was talking too much on a topic about which he knew little or nothing. He may in fact have delivered a very telling point here. For Hamilton was indeed too often accustomed to lend what he saw as his superior intellect to the more struggling efforts of workers in other fields. In 1839 for example, he offered his own suggestions gratuitously on a paper by Dr. Apjohn about the specific heats of gases; in 1841, he did the same with a chemical paper on the properties of litmus by Robert Kane.[20]

Kane was gracious enough (or more likely sufficiently wise) not to enter into any chemical discussions with the President. But a perusal of Hamilton's views as preserved in the archives suggests that they were of little value to say the least. Possibly the constant tributes to his intellect and appeals for all sorts of knowledge from every side may have begun to develop impressions of omniscience. At any rate, one is left with the clear conclusion that William would have been well advised to confine himself more strictly to his own specialities.

Hamilton's name was also occasionally invoked without permission for the sake of greater authority in dispute. On one occasion, he was represented as having advised publication of a correspondence with Apjohn in an academic controversy. He felt the danger of a possible slur on his honour so keenly that he issued a printed broadsheet for circulation to all concerned, clarifying his role.[21]

Dissatisfaction with Hamilton's Presidency of the Academy is stated more clearly in another pamphlet circulated anonymously to members in February 1840. This very likely emanated from Betham; its contents nevertheless still shed an interesting light on certain aspects of Hamilton's tenure:

> That the meetings of the Academy have of late been conducted with little dignity or decorum is a matter of fact well known ... Indeed to

such an extent has disorder at times prevailed as to take from the meetings much of that interest they would otherwise have afforded; while the dictatorial consequence afforded by a few individuals has so disgusted many really learned men as to induce them to absent themselves altogether.

The business of a President is to hear patiently the opinions and arguments of others, to regulate debates and keep order. But it is no part of his business to speak on the merits of the questions in discussion or to occupy the time of the assembly by long dissertations on the subject before them.

While therefore every allowance should be made for amiability of disposition and kind benevolent feeling, it is suggested that some individual possessing (other) prerequisite qualifications should be elected to fill the Chair for the following year.[22]

Hamilton had never contemplated filling the Presidency for life in any case, even though this had been general practice before he came. But now, in addition, his personality was beginning to change very noticeably. Obviously the cares of an unsatisfactory marriage were beginning to dull his once-famed exuberance, a trend which becomes more obvious if one studies his various portraits through the advancing years.

The early realisation that he was of unusual intellect had also made William very introspective from early boyhood; Graves notes that this tendency began to assume unhealthy proportions from about 1839 on. No longer was he the uninhibited character who a decade earlier could jump fully clothed into a river with wild abandon. From now on, his conversation became almost apologetic, often needlessly defensive, and increasingly directed towards the past. Ten years earlier, Hamilton had declared that he felt himself already an old man in some respects and now, from the age of 35 onwards, we observe him beginning to age rapidly in some, though not all, respects.

This change for the worse very likely had its origins in a domestic life which was becoming increasingly more miserable. His mother-in-law, Mrs. Bayly, died at the observatory on September 30, 1837; this death removed the last constraint on her daughter's increasingly neurotic and probably slovenly tendencies. William gave Helen long lectures on religion and still wrote her letters while on his travels. But inevitably, she left the children with the servants at the observatory and stayed with her sisters whenever he was away.

In January 1839, the country was shaken by the political murder of Lord Norbury; Helen seems to have left the observatory in terror of its loneliness soon afterwards. She may have gone awhile into lodgings with Grace, now tending sick Cousin Arthur at 6 Drumcondra Hill, four miles away. William stayed at the observatory and arranged a semaphore system to keep in touch. Apparently, he would look through one of the telescopes at a predetermined hour to see if his presence was required:

William to Grace, September 12, 1839: Today, at about 20 minutes after midday, I noticed your white handkerchief, and I think, a red shawl on the end of a stick, out of your bedroom window. If Cousin Arthur wishes me to visit him on any day, then a white handkerchief may be waved from his bedroom window...[23]

The following summer Helen was again pregnant, but suitable city lodgings could not be found as the event approached. So their third child, Helen Eliza, was born at Dunsink on August 11, 1840. The mother stayed in her room for three weeks afterwards and then departed to one of her sisters at Scripplestown House across the fields. Four months later, she travelled further to another married sister at Shrewsbury in England and there she stayed for over a year. William was left with three infant children to care for, as well as his normal duties and the Presidency of the RIA!

Graves tells how domestic arrangements fell into great disorder around this period. Hamilton apparently carried on with his studies as usual while the children more or less ran wild. Helen's departure for England brought at least a temporary improvement in these affairs. Now Hamilton's capable governess sister, Sydney, was summoned and she rapidly instituted regular mealtimes as well as manners for the children. But William still craved Helen's company and travelled to England to bring her back in January 1842. Sydney then left the observatory on their return and the Dunsink household seems to have begun a permanent slide into increasing disarray from that point on.

Hamilton's three children grew up with personalities distinctly flawed in various ways and it has been customary to cite their famous father's eccentricities for these defects. Simple common-sense however suggests that a neurotic mother, who abandoned them repeatedly during the crucial early stages, was probably far more to blame.

Henceforward, Hamilton would often have no regular mealtimes and indeed sometimes no meals at all. Alcohol, mostly in the form of porter, gradually became a convenient substitute. The various official dinners he attended were also noted for their many toasts and general good cheer. Hamilton prided himself on matching drinks with the best of them, but finally one night he went too far. At the annual dinner of the Geological Society on February 11, 1846, he became so violently incapable that he had to be restrained.[24]

This event caused quite a stir among the Dublin gossips and for a President of the Royal Irish Academy, such conduct was obviously unthinkable. In fact Hamilton already wished to retire in order to devote more attention to his new discovery of quaternions; he had even offered to do so three months before. Following the February incident, he duly handed in his resignation on March 16, 1846; his former rival, Humphrey Lloyd, was swiftly elected in his stead. And henceforth, the term of the Academy Presidency would be limited to a maximum five years.

Lloyd ensured that Hamilton remained on the Academy's ruling Council and also nominated him as one of the four Vice-Presidents. William's connection with the RIA however grew steadily more tenuous thereafter; in 1858, he was struck off the Council for non-attendance at meetings although reinstated the following year. Hamilton nevertheless remains one of the most effective Presidents during the two centuries of the Royal Irish Academy. His tenure is characterised by a more business-like approach to publications and also by the early stages of a real academic interest in Irish cultural studies.

9 DISCOVERY OF QUATERNIONS

"I then and there felt the galvanic circuit of thought close; and the sparks which fell from it were the fundamental equations between i, j, k, exactly such as I have used them ever since."

Hamilton to Tait, October 15, 1858

Just as Hamilton's highly original meditations on the mathematical expression of optics had begun in Trim at an early age, so too did his other equally original reflections on the laws of algebra. In his early studies on the origins of language, those habits instilled by Uncle James had obviously pointed to the great desirability of clarifying the roots of thought. So when he turned to mathematics, after meeting Zerah Colburn in 1819, the same habit of probing basic origins was naturally transferred.

At first, under James' tuition, young William had been content with comparatively minor forays into eastern etymology. But in his mid-teens, these early original essays began to broaden out with startling rapidity. Where he had previously been accustomed to trace the origins of languages, he now began to seek the original sources of mathematics in a similar way.

Geometry, arithmetic and algebra were therefore naturally the three subjects which presented themselves thus to young William's inquiries. Of these the first, geometry, probably seemed most amenable because the evolution from the basic text of Euclid was relatively clear. The other two he would consider later, but only after he had worked out for himself the stages by which Euclid *might* have produced his logical axioms and final synthesis.

Sometime during his eighteenth year, in early 1823, young Hamilton wrote a remarkably imaginative classical dialogue along these lines. In this work, he casts himself as Pappus, who first described the geometry of the beehive some centuries after Euclid's time. Now the pupil is able to question his great master on meeting him in the after-life.[1]

By any standards, this dialogue is a truly remarkable exercise in creative writing, the more so when it is realised that its author was little over eighteen. Graves had the good sense to reproduce all its three thousand words in their entirety, a somewhat abridged version of which is given here.[2] To savour the full flavour of this novel essay into the imaginary realm, readers should of course consult the lengthier version.

The *Dialogue with Euclid* is significant because it sheds considerable light on Hamilton's future creativity. One can almost witness the two halves of

125

his brain alternatively in operation as his critical faculties question the creative. Many of his later mathematical characteristics, such as intuition, beauty, symmetry and the urge to generality — all appear specifically considered for the first time here.

Working out how Euclid might have started therefore prepared William to apply similar lessons to his own later innovations in mathematics. Of these, the most obvious was his possibly mistaken, but still strangely fruitful, search for the origins of algebra. The *Dialogue* is little known nowadays, but still ranks as a classic example of youthful imagination and scientific creativity. It remains remarkable if only for the felicity with which its precepts were followed by its author to great advantage in later years.

The Dialogue with Euclid

The essay begins with Pappus questioning his great forerunner whom he has encountered in the Elysian fields:

Pappus: Inform me what it was that first suggested to your mind the consideration of those Theorems which have come down under your name?
Euclid: It was not unintentionally that I adopted, as the medium of communicating, a Synthesis which presented them under a form the best adapted to excite astonishment, and to disguise the process of discovery.

The Inventor of a curious piece of mechanism does not expose his artifice to the vulgar eye; nor does an architect, when he has erected a magnificent edifice, leave the scaffolding behind.

Yet now I am willing, if such be your desire, to reveal the entire process of discovery.
Pappus: There is nothing which I have more often or more ardently desired. And in the first place, I wish to know ... by what intuition you selected *a priori* all that could be necessary or useful, and nothing besides ... why you began with those Definitions, Postulates and Axioms ...
Euclid: You are not to suppose that they received at once that form in which they now appear. The Definitions arose, some out of the necessity of making my own ideas precise, and of communicating them to others; some were suggested by analogy and others invented afterwards ...

The Postulates were at one time more numerous than they now are. It was not at once that I perceived the smallest number of data that were sufficient to resolve all geometrical problems.
Pappus: Since then you neither began by defining terms before you had contemplated ideas, nor by assuming things easy to be done before you had perceived the use of doing them, nor yet by asserting truths self-evident, I find it difficult to conjecture how you did begin.
Euclid: While yet a boy my imagination had been captivated by the 'Eternal and Immutable Ideas' of my illustrious contemporary (Plato). I sought to

discover what I could fancy to have been in the Divine mind, the archetype of figure; something simple, perfect and one. I found it in the equilateral triangle; and from the contemplation of this figure, Geometry as a Science has arisen.

Pappus: Was not the circle at least equally simple?

Euclid: I might mention the natural basis of the human mind to consider a straight line as in some way emblematic of rectitude, and a curve on the contrary; a remark confirmed, I believe, by the etymological analogy of all languages.

And the character of simplicity obliged me to take the smallest possible number of (straight) sides; and this I soon found to be three.

Besides, the ideas which I entertained of symmetry, and of beauty, induced me to attend only to regular figures, regarding none else as symmetrical or beautiful.

Pappus: From this history of your first problem, and of the definitions, postulates and axioms which it introduced, I can form some idea of the others; but you have not satisfied my curiosity on the subject of the theorems.

Euclid goes on to discuss several theorems in more detail, explaining how the imaginary rotation of figures in space could bring out unexpected similarities. Rotation in space would later form the basis of Hamilton's major discovery of quaternions in 1843. But usually nothing could be expressed in final perfect form initially.

Euclid: All was intuition ... Few of my theorems were at first discovered in all that generality which they now exhibit.

Pappus: You have not succeeded in completely explaining the process of discovery. Difficulties still remain which I may mention at another time. It is however much less mysterious than it was before ...

Metaphysics Intervene

Hamilton was now in a position to transfer the lessons he had learned from contemplating Euclid to other topics. Of these, Algebra provided the most obvious example. Already he was doubtless keenly aware of that subject's lack of known history or indeed of any sound theoretical basis comparable to that possessed by Geometry. This point he mentions in a letter to Cousin Arthur soon afterwards:

> *September 4, 1823:* When my uncle wished me to learn Algebra, he said he was afraid I would not like its uphill work after the smooth and easy path of Geometry. However I became equally fond of Algebra, though I never mastered some parts of the science. Indeed the resources of Algebra have probably not been yet exhausted.[3]

Over the next twelve years, William would continue to pursue this issue at intervals among other researches, finally publishing his conclusions on the subject in 1835. And when he eventually did so, his conclusion would be influenced by the metaphysical studies he had been making in the interval. We know that William was interested in metaphysics from his College undergraduate days, for in the Stanley Papers there is a revealing account of him holding a Berkelian discussion with his listening sisters:

> Two of these properties belong to all bodies, namely extent and impenetrability. And this is what is meant by saying that the body is extended. 'See now', said he, touching his sister's cheek, 'when I touch you here I get a certain sensation, and when I touch you there I get another sensation, but when I put my finger here away from your cheek I don't get any sensation at all. So you are not spread over the whole Universe![4]

Soon afterwards, Hamilton began studying the works of the Edinburgh mathematician and philosopher, Dugald Stewart, and from this basis began to extend his reading during the early Dunsink days. Most notably, Stewart contained an abridged version of Kant's philosophy and Hamilton now determined to lay his hands on the original. Kant was also discussed when he visited Coleridge, whose prose writings had likewise been studied for their metaphysical content.

Hamilton was particularly impressed by one of Coleridge's poems entitled *Time, real and imaginary*, an echo of the philosopher's views on this subject. Much earlier, as a boy, William had been accustomed to dwell on Beattie's poem, *The Minstrel*, a work containing the following intriguing lines:

> And Reason now through Number, Time and Space,
> Darts the keen lustre of her serious eye;
> And learns from facts compared the Laws to trace,
> Whose long progression leads to Deity.

In short, Hamilton's mind was now concerned with the topic of time as well as the origins of algebra. And when he was finally able to study Kant's *Critique of Pure Reason* in the original, the two took final union in his mind. Kant sought to find a bond or union between materialism and idealism. He regarded Space as the form of our external sense, since from it is derived the shape and extension observed in outside objects. Time, on the other hand, seems to be a form of internal experience alone. It may be a form of intuition built into our minds inescapably; we must then experience phenomena as temporal, much as wearing red glasses confers a rosy colour on observed reality.

Kant also suggested that the natural science of space already existed as geometry, the inference being that there was room for a corresponding science of time. He did not however develop this point further. Hamilton had also been thinking about the same issue before reading Kant fully. And now he concluded that time also had its own science already in existence — algebra!

Algebra as the Science of Pure Time

To count, to measure and to order were for Hamilton three very different, though connected, acts of thought.[5] These aspects of nature were already dealt with by three somewhat different branches of science — arithmetic, metrology and algebra. Hamilton thought that in arithmetic, number is best considered as an answer to the question 'How many?' It constitutes a science of multitude found on the relations of more and fewer, or ultimately of the many and the one. Metrology is more concerned with measurement and magnitude, and so essentially different from arithmetic.

In algebra, Hamilton considered the role of number to be radically different again. Here he thought it really answers the question 'How placed in a succession?' If so, it inevitably suggests comparison with temporal order — the everyday experience of time, where we perceive events succeed each other regularly.

The link with time seems strengthened when one considers its three great natural divisions into future, present and past. Algebra too has three very different kinds of number — positive, zero and negative. William considered this similarity too striking to be mere coincidence. Instead, algebra seemed more likely to be the unrealised expression of a science for which there was an obvious need. This was a totally new addition to the scientific repertory, one which nobody seems to have considered in any way previously. In short, Hamilton now began to propose and develop algebra as the Science of Pure Time.

By 'pure' William meant an idealised or mathematical version of reality, one which is purified of the many irrelevancies of everyday experience. Geometry already obviously fulfilled a similar function for ordinary space. In geometry, the point was the simplest or most basic concept; for time and algebra, the moment would serve equally.

Whether or not one agreed with this line of development, there were many inconsistencies in algebra as it stood. To bolster his argument, Hamilton first listed these with unusual clarity and simplicity:

> That a greater magnitude may be subtracted from a less, and that the remainder is less than nothing; that two negative numbers, or numbers denoting magnitude less than nothing, may be multiplied the one by the other, and that the product will be a positive number, or a number denoting a magnitude greater than nothing; and that although the square of a number is therefore always positive, whether the number be positive or negative, yet that numbers called imaginary can be found or conceived or determined ...[6]

Imaginaries are of course those apparently 'impossible' numbers, such as the square root of *minus* unity. Today, the $\sqrt{-1}$ symbol is a fairly simple concept of great utility in algebra, but one which also proved very difficult to interpret for a great many years. Hamilton in 1835 proceeded to explain it in a new and very simple manner. His explanation stemmed directly from his larger idea of algebra as the science of pure time and was in fact the most important advance to have emerged from this source so far. To appreciate the exact nature of Hamilton's contribution, however, requires that we examine briefly the previous history of such issues.

Interpreting the Imaginaries

When Descartes introduced his new or algebraic interpretation of geometry in 1637, the significance of ordinary negative numbers immediately became more clear. Now they could be seen as quantities measured *in an opposite direction* to positive numbers of the same magnitude. Six feet below the ocean surface, for example, could now be seen as a negative amount of altitude and one mile west from a given point could be treated as a negative mile to the east. Similar concepts were found to apply throughout all science, with large gains in understanding and competence.

To transform any number into its negative means, basically, multiplication by negative unity: 6 multiplied by -1 for example turns into -6. On Descartes' system, the same operation is accomplished by a complete reversal of direction about the central point. This necessarily implies turning the original line through 180 degrees. In other words, an eastward line of unit length when multiplied by -1 becomes a *westward* line.

Rotation through 180° however really implies turning through two full quadrants of 90° in sequence. So if *twice* turning through a right angle implies multiplication by negative unity, rotation through just *one* quadrant similarly implies multiplication by the square root of the same quantity. In this manner, the two theoretically possible solutions to the imaginary $\sqrt{-1}$ become represented as north and south lines from the original central point.

All this works well enough for a plane surface and was of course generally accepted before Hamilton was born. Trouble however arises if one tries to extend the same way of thinking into three-dimensional space. Then the operations become so complex that most mathematicians who had attempted it gave up in despair!

In fact it was this great complexity which seems to have motivated Hamilton to seek a wholly new interpretation of the imaginaries quite independent of geometry.[7] And this he was enabled to do through his basic development of algebra as the science of time.

He started by noting that a step in time from one definite moment to another depends only on the relative position or difference between each. Two such steps can differ only in direction (forwards or backwards) and duration (longer or shorter). Direction embraces the ideas of negative and positive, while duration is obviously a reflection of numerical magnitude.

To clarify his ideas on imaginaries, however, he had to go a stage further. It proved insufficient to compare just two 'time-steps' like a and b; instead two *pairs* or *couples* of time-steps needed to be considered. A single couple or pair of time-steps was therefore represented by (a, b) and its value depends on the order of the pair as well as the magnitude of each element. Equally

Hamilton demonstrated that $(-a, -b)$ is the same couple taken negatively, i.e. wholly multiplied by -1.

The imaginary $\sqrt{-1}$ then becomes an operation of a very simple if special kind. It simultaneously makes the elements exchange position, while also effecting a sign change in the first position only! In Hamilton's scheme, to multiply (a, b) by $\sqrt{-1}$ therefore affords $(-b, a)$. And a repetition of this process will obviously give $(-a, -b)$, the same as if the original had been multiplied by negative unity straightaway.

For the non-mathematical reader, Tait gives the following graphic illustration which dramatises these issues:

> If an officer and a private be set upon by thieves, and both be plundered of all they have, this operation may be represented by negative unity. And the imaginary quantity of algebra, or the square root of negative unity, will then be represented by a process which would rob the private only, but at the same time exchange the rank of the two soldiers.
>
> It is obvious that on a repetition of this process both would be robbed, while they would each be left with the same rank as at first.[8]

Hamilton had succeeded in finding a new and wholly algebraic interpretation of imaginaries, one which complemented those earlier geometric ideas. His aim was now to extend the same treatment into three dimensions, a task apparently demanding manipulation of *triplets* instead of the former *couplets*. This however proved a matter of unexpected difficulty and he did not find the answer until his dramatic discovery of quaternions in 1843.

Ironically also the number couples, which he constructed from his basic idea of time-steps, later turned out to have no necessary dependence on time at all! Most have therefore since concluded that Hamilton's grand idea of developing algebra as the 'Science of Pure Time' was mistaken basically. We now accept algebra as a system of formalised logic, a concept clarified in Boole's *Mathematical Analysis of Logic*, published in 1847.

Two years later, Boole came to Cork from Lincoln as the first professor of mathematics at Cork's new Queen's College. There he stayed until his death in 1864; we know that Hamilton at least knew of his existence from occasional references in the archives. Ireland then sheltered during this period the world's two greatest living algebraists and yet, there was little or probably no real fruitful contact between the two!

This may have been because Hamilton after 1849 was already so immersed in quaternions that he had little inclination to consider other algebraic ideas. Such however is mere speculation, so that the lack of contact between Hamilton and Boole remains a minor mystery best left to future scholarship. Indeed it is only one of many such recurring throughout our subject's history.

Finally, it may also be somewhat premature to dismiss totally Hamilton's original idea of a very basic connection between the properties of time and their expression as algebra. For one thing, even now in the latter half of the twentieth century, the proper study of time as a science in its own right has scarcely yet begun.[9]

That a wholly separate science of time will one day develop, with possibly momentous and indeed unimaginable consequences for everybody, now seems increasingly likely. But Hamilton seems to have been the very first scientist to consider this possibility seriously and that an entire century and a half ago.

Personal Affairs

Hamilton's search for the elusive properties of triplets was to occupy him on and off for eight years after he had formally introduced his couplets in 1835. We now know that this search as originally conceived was bound to be unfruitful, because triplets of the required properties simply cannot exist. In the meantime, his Presidency of the RIA and many other matters of more personal interest kept him occupied.

In 1838, his favourite sister, Eliza, suddenly returned from the eastern Mediterranean after giving up her Moravian missionary efforts there. This return seems to have been a somewhat unexpected matter because we find her brother called upon to guarantee her ticket back to Liverpool! On this occasion however, as so often in the past, Cousin Arthur stepped in with the necessary financial aid.[10]

The following year William aided his sister in the publication of a first book of poetry, at her own expense. Scrutiny of this slim little volume affords many clues to her character and a decidedly gloomy one it seems to the present-day reader. Generally, Eliza's poetry reflects the unfulfilled nature of her existence and there is never a hint of romantic love or passion, such as one might expect from a poetess of thirty-two.

One poem, for example, deals with two children, glimpsed in church, who are dressed in mourning; she was obviously reliving the early loss of her own parents here. Another commemorates an American missionary colleague dying of disease in foreign parts. More noble sentiments are evoked at the sight of an obelisk above the Boyne, erected to commemorate King William's victory over the Jacobite army in 1692.[11] Another poem in this book is however more important because it reveals the manner in which William's genius was regarded by his favourite sister:

> Genius, thou art a fearful gift;
> Madness, a broken heart, or early grave,
> These are thy portion ...

The Hamiltons were never a clan to take their talents less than seriously and Eliza could evidently be as needlessly solemn as her famous brother betimes!

Meanwhile, Uncle James was still firmly stuck in his original post as curate at Trim, but now also in unaccustomed dire financial straits. The anti-tithe campaign begun by Catholic tenant farmers in 1831 had effectively decimated the income of many Protestant clergymen by 1835.[12]

Letters from James over this period show signs of an apparent nervous breakdown and in one such letter, the writing tails off into disarray:

> *June 22, 1835:* My brain is a little 'moidered', I believe by the incessant row of a most turbulent mob which has scarcely ever ceased since Monday ...[13]

At first, William seems to have been genuinely unaware of James' predicament because of his preoccupation with more esoteric matters like algebra and time. James, in turn, apparently tried to hide his straits from his nephew, but a timely letter from Dean Butler eventually clarified the true situation. Thereafter William helped out with finance as far as he was able; when he received a Civil Pension in 1843, part of it was made over on a regular basis to James.[14]

Hamilton also tried repeatedly to use his influence with the Establishment to secure a better post for James. The Lord Lieutenant, Dublin Castle and even the Adare family were all petitioned in this regard. None of these efforts was ever in the slightest degree successful until after his uncle died. Then unexpectedly Hamilton succeeded in 1854, securing for James' son a very good living as rector of Loughcrew.[15]

William however was able to meet his uncle's wishes in at least one other field. James, ever mindful of his languages, wrote an etymological essay on the *Punic Passages in Plautus* and this was duly accepted for publication by the RIA in 1834. We can reasonably assume that his famous nephew was not inactive in his assistance and James must have felt proud to have seen his undoubted competence in languages thereby officially recognised.[16]

Hamilton also continued with most of his usual activities during these years, attending the annual meetings of the British Association in England and acting as referee in several scientific disputes. The accession of Queen Victoria in 1837 was marked by official congratulations from the RIA and Hamilton felt sufficiently moved by the occasion to compose one of his customary sonnets:

> ... By thy throne
> Stands Order, vigilant; in holy zone
> Prayers kneel around; arms glitter far away;
> And Chivalry, plume-drooping, hails in thee
> The Symbol of thy Sex's Sovereignty.[17]

The following year, Herschel returned from the Cape after spending five fruitful years observing the southern hemisphere, a period enlivened by the famous American hoax to the effect that he had seen winged humanoids disport themselves on the moon.[18] London scientists held a celebratory banquet in Herschel's honour and Hamilton, now President of the RIA, attended as Ireland's representative. On this occasion, he strengthened a growing friendship with Lord Northampton, then President of the British Association. When Northampton invited him to holiday at his residence of Castle Ashby, William was able to persuade Helen to accompany him. This seems to have been the only time, apart from occasional visits to relatives, when they holidayed together.

Correspondence with Adare on scientific matters continued throughout these years, although the latter was now often busy as a Member of Parliament for a Welsh constituency. Aubrey de Vere too continued to write and sometimes visit, despite Helen's evident antagonism, but he was now growing somewhat solemn and turning towards Catholicism. For a short time, Hamilton even felt tempted to imitate him. But he quickly returned to his customary religious stance, upholding his establishment position from that point on.

In 1841, the Royal Dublin Society fell under official disfavour, a matter of some critical importance since it was in receipt of an annual subvention of £5,300 from the State. Hamilton, in his capacity as President of the RIA, was asked for advice. He recommended continuing support but under a stricter form of constitutional rules.[19]

This was also the year in which Helen was absent with her sister in England and Sydney had to be summoned to restore Dunsink's rapidly disintegrating domestic routine. Hamilton still felt increasingly lonely but now, quite unheralded, a new if distant friendship suddenly materialised. On May 8, 1841, Augustus de Morgan wrote from London requesting some mathematical papers; this was the start of a highly intense correspondence which was to last an amazing twenty-four years. Hamilton and de Morgan wrote to each other about almost everything under the sun as well as mathematics, and the total of their letters would probably fill several large volumes. The Irishman obviously needed such communication more than his correspondent and the latter would prove a wise, witty and stabilising influence on his life henceforward.

In 1842, Robert Graves was asked to write a biographical sketch of Hamilton for the Dublin University Magazine. Cannily, he seized the opportunity to bemoan his friend's still relatively small income of £540 a year. Dublin Castle took up the hint and awarded William an extra £200 in next year's Civil List, the latter immediately apportioning part of his windfall to help Uncle James.[20]

In March 1843, however, a less desirable event took place. The Board visited Dunsink on its annual ritual inspection and some of its members expressed themselves dissatisfied with the running of the observatory. So it was formally suggested that a more public yearly account of its activities would be highly desirable. In addition, there were pointed queries concerning the exact proportion of astronomical calculation carried out by an assistant computist lately reimbursed by the College. Sydney had recently spent her year at Dunsink re-organising the household. But since she was also capable of reducing astronomical data, it was probably the exact nature of her duties that the Board was querying.[21]

These awkward questions were possibly inspired by jealousy at Hamilton's forthcoming pension and equally, may have been part of the general intrigues conducted against him in the Academy at the time. William was able to extricate himself with commendable deftness, but he still felt so hurt by the censures that he began contemplating giving up mathematics.

At this delicate point however, Adare stepped in with a bright solution which seemed to offer an answer to everyone's difficulties. Humphrey Lloyd had just been co-opted Senior Fellow and so resigned as professor of natural philosophy. MacCullagh was professor of mathematics, although really just as much a physicist, so Adare proposed that he move over to Lloyd's vacant Chair. Hamilton could then take up MacCullagh's post and Robinson could transfer from Armagh to superintend Dunsink more professionally.[22]

Surprisingly, the three men most involved were all agreeable to this version of academic musical chairs. But serious legal difficulties immediately arose. Despite all his eminence, William was still not a Fellow of the College and existing Fellows would lose appreciable income if he were to be added to their ranks. Neither would Hamilton now consent to enter the public examination for Fellowship he had so once desired; to do so from his present eminence would entail unacceptable loss of dignity.

This third and final attempt to improve Hamilton's position at Dunsink therefore petered out. It did however gain him the distinct advantage that nobody would bother him further about ordinary observatory routines. Henceforth he could feel free to concentrate on his own interests as much as he pleased.

The Board of course should really have created a special Chair for Hamilton around this period. Then he would not have been so isolated from both potential followers and helpful criticism when his most famed discovery of all came through. This was his sudden realisation of quaternions and the dramatic moment of their revelation was at hand.

The Eureka Moment

Throughout all this time, and especially since his paper on couplets in 1835, Hamilton had continued to ponder the problem of triplets on and off. He wondered about the significance of triads in nature and philosophy, as expressed by Kant and Coleridge; he delved into religion and the special status accorded the Holy Trinity.[23] This interest may reflect the current emerging European interest in triads in theoretical chemistry.

Then one morning in April 1842, all these philosophical aspects suddenly seemed to Hamilton to fall into place. In a titanic outpouring of many thousands of words, he wrote out an entire new philosophy of triads which he sent to Lord Adare. Except for the sheer volume involved, there seems no reason to doubt that it was all dashed off "before breakfast" as he claimed. If so, it evidently represented the typically sudden emergence of long subconscious work.[24]

Hamilton's new philosophy was based on two further tripartite sub-divisions of what he saw as the three primary faculties of Will, Mind and Life respectively. Their further subdivision twice, and interaction with each other, afforded a final total of 27 categories. Temperance, for example, was a triadic subdivision of self-control, the latter in turn being an obvious triadic derivation of one of the three main faculties — Will.

Will was assigned the symbol A in view of its leading position, while self-control was denoted by the lesser symbol a. Temperance, on the lowest step of the hierarchy, obviously rated only y, so that its final codification in Hamilton's scheme was A a y!

The modern reader will doubtless judge that this certainly novel exercise rests on a somewhat shaky foundation to say the least. It does however convey a strong impression of Hamilton's unique enthusiasms and ways of thinking and it also exhibits how deeply he was immersed in triadic speculation around this time.

Hamilton's sudden outburst of triadic philosophy was not of course the answer to his longstanding mathematical problem. There, the difficulty was how triplets might be *multiplied* so as to transform any line or vector into another in three-dimensional space. Triplets could readily be added or subtracted, but multiplication was a more difficult problem by far.[25]

During the autumn of 1843, Hamilton was concentrating on this problem more deeply than usual. Even his two boys, then aged eight and six, became aware of his concerns. Every morning at breakfast, he was questioned eagerly: "Well, Papa, can you multiply triplets?" To which the answer was a sadly negative shake of the head: "No, I can only add and subtract them."

Then quite suddenly and even dramatically, all this was changed. On Monday, October 16, 1843, Hamilton was walking along the Royal Canal about two miles from Dunsink on his way to a meeting of the Royal Irish Academy. Helen was with him, although his thoughts as usual were likely elsewhere in less prosaic realms. As they approached the city in the late autumn twilight, the dramatic flash of inspiration came.

Hamilton suddenly realised that triplets were after all inadequate for his purpose and that what he needed was *four* components instead of *three*! A group of four had long been known in classics as *quaternions*, whence Hamilton's most dramatic discovery took its name.

This instance of sudden creativity, following on long digestion of a problem, is certainly one of the best documented in all science history. Adequate information exists about the general background as well as the precise manner in which sudden inspiration came. As such, it remains an episode of outstanding interest to students of creativity, as well as to scientists generally.

Hankins has gone into the mathematical background with his usual thoroughness. Hamilton himself has left two very similar and therefore corroborative accounts of the precise 'Eureka moment' when he so suddenly saw the truth.[26]

The first of these personal accounts was written to his disciple P. G. Tait some fifteen years after the event:

> *October 15, 1858:* (Quaternions) started into life, or light, full grown, on the 16th of October, 1843, as I was walking with Lady Hamilton to Dublin, and came up to Brougham Bridge ... That is to say, I then and

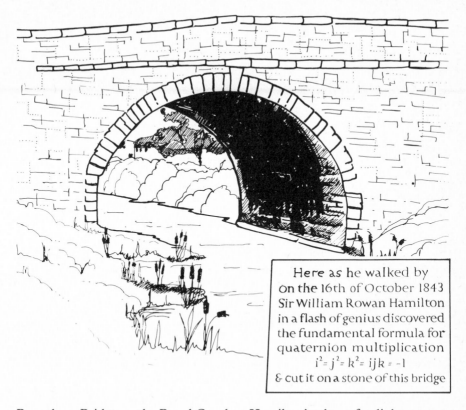

Here as he walked by
on the 16th of October 1843
Sir William Rowan Hamilton
in a flash of genius discovered
the fundamental formula for
quaternion multiplication
$$i^2 = j^2 = k^2 = ijk = -1$$
& cut it on a stone of this bridge

Brougham Bridge on the Royal Canal — Hamilton's place of enlightenment, with the modern plaque that commemorates his famous discovery of quaternions in 1843   *(Drawing M. Caulfield; Plaque, Courtesy P.A. Wayman, Director, Dunsink Observatory)*

there felt the galvanic circuit of thought *close*; and the sparks which fell from it were the *fundamental equations between i, j, k,* exactly such as I have used them ever since.

I pulled out, on the spot, a pocket-book which still exists and made an entry on which, *at that very moment*, I felt that it might be worth my while to expend the labour of at least ten (and it might be fifteen) years to come.[27]

One month before his death, Hamilton again recorded the same event for the benefit of his son Archibald and likely future psychologists. The words now are different, but again the account is essentially similar:[28]

Although (your mother) talked with me now and then, yet an *undercurrent* of thought was going on in my mind, which gave at last a *result*, whereof it is not too much to say that I felt *at once* an importance.

An *electric* circuit seemed to *close*; and a spark flashed forth, the herald (as I *foresaw, immediately*) of màny long years to come of definitely directed thought and work . . .

Nor could I resist the impulse — unphilosophical as it may have been

— to cut with a knife on a stone of Brougham Bridge as we passed it, the fundamental formula with the symbols i, j, k, namely,

$$i^2 = j^2 = k^2 = ijk = -1$$

Hamilton's famous carving on Brougham Bridge has long since been eroded; however, a modern commemorative plaque, erected at the suggestion of Premier Eamon de Valera, now marks the place. But we do not have any record of what, if anything, Lady Hamilton had to say about the event. Probably she did not have time to say much in any case, for Hamilton immediately rushed into the Academy "within the hour" to tell his peers of his new discovery.

The great, if mistaken, project which would occupy him almost obsessively for the last third of his life was thereby launched.

PART III

DECLINE

10 THE STRUGGLE TO EXPRESS

"It is my most sincere and unaffected conviction that a gentleman of good general education . . . is likely to be able to advance a good way in the reading of my volume: and . . . will be agreeably surprised to find it almost light reading."
Hamilton to Rev. M. O'Sullivan, August 1853

The sudden flash of inspiration which struck Hamilton on his famous walk along the Royal Canal was certainly eye-opening in scope. For him, it immediately revealed great vistas extending over a whole new continent of mathematical knowledge, an almost limitless terrain reaching out to far horizons which nobody had even glimpsed before.

Hamilton's last twenty-two years were therefore to be spent exploring, describing, and to a large extent creating, this previously unknown area of mathematics. These labours were also to be carried out almost entirely on his own. Given this striking isolation in his researches, it is hardly surprising to find that he ended up discussing highly abstruse issues which were then intelligible to very few except himself. Even today, they are regarded as of but limited importance! Hamilton had never been a good communicator, but now with quaternions this weakness was to diminish his effectiveness almost totally.

Before discussing these aspects in more detail, it is obviously important that we should try to form a clearer idea of what quaternions involved. They were the journalist's favourite example of scientific incomprehensibility in the half-century before relativity. Nowadays however, they may be somewhat easier to understand. But that is merely because they are in essence the first theoretical expression of the working principle behind the familiar Rubik cube!

For many years, Hamilton had been trying unsuccessfully to extend his earlier algebraic method of couplets which described the imaginary square roots of unity or $\sqrt{-1}$. This method complemented the geometric or Cartesian convention of describing these same imaginaries as a northward or a southward line. Both descriptions worked well enough when confined to the two dimensions of a plane surface, as discussed earlier in Chapter 9.

The next step was obviously to extend the same ways of thinking into the more complex area of solid or three-dimensional geometry. The cube is an obvious example of the latter, but here all previous attempts to extend the Cartesian or geometric convention had failed. In effect, the procedures

Diagram illustrating geometric
representation of square roots

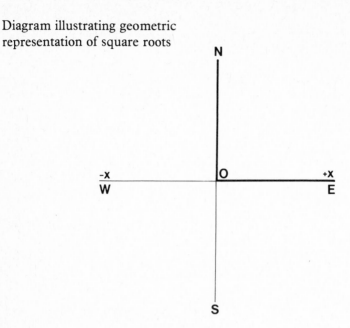

To convert +x into –x involves multiplying by –1 or rotation through 180°.
The same end is achieved by multiplying *twice* by the imaginary $\sqrt{-1}$ or by two
consecutive rotations through 90°.
The northward and southward lines can therefore be equated in this sense with
the two imaginary square roots of unity.

became too complex or indeterminate once mathematicians tried to apply
them to anything beyond the plane.

Hamilton therefore determined to seek a primarily algebraic solution and
thus bypass this difficulty. Essentially this meant extending his couplets
(which worked so well for two dimensions) into triplets (which should work
for three). One half of the couplet always involved the imaginary or $\sqrt{-1}$
quantity. Therefore it seemed only natural that the triplets should contain
two imaginaries.

But the dramatic revelation at Brougham Bridge changed all this utterly.
Suddenly Hamilton realised that his purpose required four numbers
(quaternions) instead of three! And since the fruitless triplets would have
involved two imaginaries, it followed naturally that the quaternions would
require three different extensions of the $\sqrt{-1}$ idea.

Quaternions then suddenly evolved as a very special set of four related
numbers or geometric elements. Three of these numbers were imaginary
and one was real. The three imaginaries were all a direct development of the
existing convention that a northward (or southward) line depicts negative
unity. Alternately, such a line may represent the operation of rotation
through one right angle, as with the Rubik cube.

In the original convention, however, the imaginary two square roots of negative unity had been depicted by the north-south axis alone. Hamilton now took the additional step of making the east-west and up-down axes similarly imaginary. Quaternions therefore emerged with three separate square roots of negative unity — equivalent to the three main axes of space or solid geometry.[1]

To assign an equal imaginary character to all three space dimensions may be considered another way of stating that all are also equally real. In any case, Hamilton now assigned the symbol i to the eastward line, with $-i$ naturally being its westward counterpart; j represents the northward line similarly and $-j$ its southward opposite. The last in the trio is k and $-k$, depicting upward and downward directions.

As previously the symbols i, j, k may now depict either the unit lines themselves or the operation of turning through a right angle. When such a line is used as an operator (multiplying factor) on any of the others, it means a rotation through one right angle about its own direction. And it is very important that the operator be written *first* when such a transformation is described mathematically.

To turn the northward line about the eastward one and leftward through 90°, however, obviously results in the former becoming the upward line. This geometric operation can equally be expressed more concisely algebraically as:

$$ij = k$$

If the same operation is now continued through a further 90°, one naturally multiplies by i again. Now however, the original northward line j, which had turned into upward k, becomes transformed into the southward line, i.e. $-j$. Or again to put the matter algebraically:

$$iij = ik = -j$$

Cancelling out the j on either side of the two end terms then leaves:

$$i^2 = -1$$

a result reflecting the original assigned role of i as a square root of negative unity.

The element -1 was of course the fourth and indeed only real number in the group of four symbols which constitutes quaternions; i, j and k were all imaginary. But since the latter were also essentially similar if not quite equal, we can now begin to appreciate the key equation which Hamilton so excitedly scratched on Brougham Bridge:

$$i^2 = j^2 = k^2 = i\,j\,k = -1$$

Hamilton had therefore now successfully combined geometry with algebra in an altogether more extensive fashion than in his former works. For while to add (or subtract) had previously meant motion forward (or backward), to multiply henceforth meant rotation around any of the axes in three-dimensional space.

Obviously this was a radical new way of looking at things, with many potential applications where rotation or translation were concerned. Quaternions for example could be applied to the problem of transforming

The relation of Quaternions to the Rubik Cube mechanism

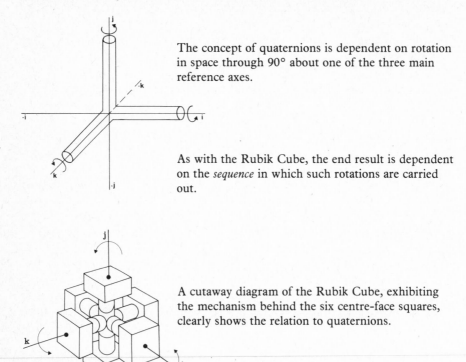

The concept of quaternions is dependent on rotation in space through 90° about one of the three main reference axes.

As with the Rubik Cube, the end result is dependent on the *sequence* in which such rotations are carried out.

A cutaway diagram of the Rubik Cube, exhibiting the mechanism behind the six centre-face squares, clearly shows the relation to quaternions.

any directed line in space into any other of differing length and direction. Such lines Hamilton now called vectors, a term he was first to apply in its modern meaning.[2]

Again the essential requirement of four operations or a quaternion emerges here. To change one side of a triangle into another, for example, demands four quantities to be specified. Two are required for specification of the original axes of one side (e.g. north and east). A third number specifies the amount of rotation necessary to superimpose the second line. Finally, a fourth number is needed to lengthen or shorten it as appropriate.

Hamilton's sudden insight into all this now made him realise that he had invented a whole new way of contemplating mathematics generally. Quaternions were perfectly capable of replacing many existing methods with an entirely new notation or mathematical language. And once he had realised that such was possible, he immediately assumed that it was desirable that it should come about.

This however was not necessarily so. To see that something is possible does not necessarily imply that it should be equally desirable. Quaternions then stood in relation to the rest of mathematics much as Esperanto does to the English language today. It is indeed perfectly feasible to replace the latter by the former, but few see any really compelling reasons for such a change. This was also the attitude of most mathematicians where quaternions were concerned!

The Commutative Law

If most of his fellow-scientists then proved notably hesitant about adopting quaternions as Hamilton envisaged, they were however unanimous about the great significance of an associated development. For the initial steps of quaternions proved quite definitely that a principle, previously accepted as obvious, need not always hold. This was the famous Commutative Law. It was one of those things apparently so natural that everybody, before Hamilton, had assumed that it must be always true. Basically, the Commutative Law merely formalised the seemingly obvious truth that 3×2 must always equal 2×3. This means that the *order* of multiplication can be changed or commuted without affecting the result. Whether you start with 2 or 3 had always seemed immaterial, a principle built into the very foundations of algebra as the Commutative Law.

In quaternions, however, it now emerged that the order of multiplication matters very much indeed. Remembering that multiplication is equivalent to rotation in these matters, one can again appreciate this issue in the solution of the Rubik cube puzzle. There the challenge is to get the order or sequence of rotation (multiplication) absolutely right.

A century and a half ago, Hamilton was the first to appreciate this issue mathematically. Suppose for example that you rotate the northward line about the eastward line as previously. Then the appropriate algebraic statement is:

$$ij = k$$

If however you now alter the sequence in the first part of this equation, a very different result is obtained. Since j is written first this time, it now becomes the operator round which i is rotated. In other words, the eastward line, i, is turned about the northward one, j. And since such rotation is always leftward in our convention, the end position of the former is obviously downward, or denoted by $-k$. Expressed algebraically, we then have:

$$ji = -k$$

a result obviously different from the previous one.

For once Hamilton himself was able to give a clear description of this fundamental difference, a point which must have been difficult to convey to the non-mathematical in pre-Rubik days. He did so while discussing quaternions with Lady Rosse during a visit to the great Birr telescope in 1848:[3]

> By taking from my pocket a penknife and partly opening it in a horizontal posture (i.e. knife and blade horizontal), whereof for the moment we may agree to call the handle i and the blade j, I showed that by operating on j with i, by turning the blade though a quadrant with a

screwing (i.e. from left to right) motion, that blade was made to point *upward*.

Whereas on the contrary when I operated on *i* with *j*, or used the blade as the axis of the screwing motion, the handle was made to point *downwards*, thus justifying in the sense in which I employ it, my fundamental . . . and paradoxical formula *ij = −ji*.

Hamilton would obviously have been delighted by having a Rubik cube to dramatise these principles even better and so it becomes a matter of some interest to determine why he never went on to invent the same. This point becomes even more pressing in view of his attempted commercialisation of graph network theory with his Icosian Game which was actually marketed around 1859. (See Chapter 12.)

Several reasons suggest themselves. Of these, the first is that Hamilton was not really practical even with the Icosian Game, since it was John Graves who first suggested he should market it. Secondly, William could hardly distinguish green from blue and so was probably not very colour conscious. (Further proof of the latter emerges from the fact that he passed up the chance to investigate the famed four-colour map problem presented to him by de Morgan in 1852.[3a]) His range would therefore hardly have extended to coding each of the cube's six faces in a different colour as Rubik eventually did. Finally, and perhaps most important, the advanced plastic technology required for creating the Rubik cube's movement mechanism was simply not available in Hamilton's day.

That much granted however, it still seems a pity that Hamilton was never able to capitalise on what he regarded as his greatest discovery. Eventually quaternions were almost to impoverish him, whereas their application in a popular puzzle a century later proved exceedingly remunerative!

Meanwhile, in pure mathematics, the real significance of quaternions turned out to rest on their rejection of the Commutative Law. As such, they stand forever as the very first of the 'new' algebras, those which differ in some vital principle from that conventional algebra which schoolchildren learn. Once it had been shown that some accepted principle in this conventional algebra could be abandoned without great loss, mathematicians found themselves free to create further new algebraic systems almost at will.

Hamilton however never seems to have realised that some of these new systems were almost bound to be superior to his own original one. Because of this, he allowed his vision of quaternions to drive him relentlessly as long as life remained. Yet he should have been conscious of the general principle of inventive obsolescence, there being examples all around him such as the steam engine and the telescope. To be first does not imply being best, by any means.

A Vision of Greatness

Until the advent of quaternions, Hamilton probably saw himself as a scientist of the first rank, but still not quite the immortal he had aimed for during early days. To be hailed by his peers at the British Association meetings as their greatest living mathematician must have been very gratifying, to be sure. But to have radically changed all scientific thought, as Newton did, obviously belonged to a higher and still unattained plane.

Newton of course was the scientist to whom young William had been compared in public by the likes of Brinkley during his undergraduate days. But in the years leading up to 1843, Hamilton must have been deeply conscious that such early promise had all too clearly not yet been fulfilled.

His sudden discovery of quaternions however had now changed all this irrevocably. Hamilton realised that here he had a wholly new method of mathematical notation, a discovery which was, potentially at least, the equal of Newton's calculus. So if scientists generally could be persuaded to use it, his chance of joining the few really great scientific immortals would be enhanced. This therefore was the aim which William set out to achieve with vast energy, if not always wisdom, over the next twenty-two years.

Several of Hamilton's acquaintances also quickly grasped the potential of the new notation system. But instead of following him, they set out immediately to invent others of their own. Since Hamilton had achieved so much by scrapping the previously sacrosanct Commutative Rule, they began to experiment by dropping other hitherto accepted algebraic laws.

Within two months, for example, John Graves had produced an even more complex *System of Octaves* to rival quaternions. Very generously, Hamilton offered to publicise them for him, but unfortunately then forgot about them for a couple of months or so; in the interval, Arthur Cayley published the same discovery. William could only apologise for his carelessness. But the *Octaves*, first described by Graves, henceforth became associated with Cayley's name.[4]

Other researchers, like Charles Graves and de Morgan, also began to search anew for the triplets which Hamilton had so dramatically abandoned in favour of quaternions. Charles thought he had finally found them while half-awake at three o'clock in the morning of November 21, 1844; he got out of bed to record his discovery and deposited it in a sealed envelope with the RIA the same day. When however this envelope was opened three weeks later at the regular meeting, the 'discovery' by Graves proved to be no real advance at all! Charles must have felt humiliated for having created so much ado about nothing, but at the meeting Hamilton moved in smoothly to prevent embarrassment.[5] The truth, in any case, was that all such efforts were inevitably doomed to failure, simply because the long-sought triplets just cannot exist!

MacCullagh also joined in the general excitement following Hamilton's announcement of quaternions. But characteristically, it was again with a claim to his own priority. This time, the paranoid mathematician imagined that the idea of quaternions was embodied in a question he had proposed for the Fellowship Examination of 1842. Hamilton duly noted this claim to priority, but assured all concerned that MacCullagh's question had not really inspired him.[6] By now, in any case, most people were sensibly aware of MacCullagh's unstable temperament and Humphrey Lloyd summed up the matter admirably: "Dear MacCullagh! I really believe he finds it difficult to persuade himself that he did not build the Magnetic Observatory."[7]

This latter observatory was a neo-classical style laboratory, which Lloyd had designed and erected in the Fellows' Garden in 1837. Composed entirely of non-magnetic materials, it has lately been donated to University College, Dublin, for reconstruction on the Belfield campus.[8]

Hamilton, in any case, held steadfast to his original conception, refusing to be diverted by any of these attempts to improve upon quaternions or to confuse their origins. Rather, the outline of all his future efforts now began to assume shape. Vectors and scalars were defined by him in their modern sense; in general, informed manipulation of such symbols promised a radical new method in solid geometry. He now visualised quaternions being utilised in questions involving spherical conics, rotation and various other problems in dynamics. He foresaw innumerable applications in physics, astronomy, crystallography, electrical dynamics — in short, any area where motion or translation in three-dimensional space applied.

And he also expected that totally unforeseen discoveries might well follow from this new way of contemplating things:

> You might, without offence to me, consider that I abused the license of hope, which may be indulged to an inventor, if I were to confess that I expect Quaternions to supply hereafter, not merely *mathematical methods*, but also physical suggestions ... It is impossible to estimate the *chances* given, or opened up, by any *new way of looking* at things; especially when that way admits of being intimately combined ... with calculation of a most rigorous kind.[9]

Hamilton also was confident that quaternions would eventually prove superior to those Cartesian methods whose application by him to optics had launched his scientific career:

> *July 14, 1848:* This new symbolical geometry ... appears to me to be entirely distinct, in its conception and its processes, from the important and celebrated Cartesian geometry ... I feel that I hazard nothing in expressing my conviction that the new method is essentially more powerful than the old; and that only the co-operation of other persons is necessary, in order to manifest that intrinsic superiority of Quaternions over Co-ordinates, which may well remain a matter of doubt so long as the subject is left entirely in my own hands.[10]

Five years after his first dramatic insight, Hamilton was now confident enough to voice opinions of this kind. Between 1844 and 1850, he published a long series of eighteen papers on quaternions in the *Philosophical Magazine*. A related series of ten papers on symbolical geometry appeared in the *Cambridge and Dublin Mathematical Journal* between 1846 and 1849. Over this first six years, Hamilton was therefore publishing a fresh paper on his new method every three months or so. We can thus assume that the method which had taken him so long to discover was by now almost second nature to his thinking.

Such, however, was very far from being the case where others less proficient were concerned. Most mathematicians realised the large novelty in quaternions and few saw any real objections to the method theoretically. But fewer still rushed to take the topic up. For one thing, there did not seem to be much hope of unearthing any really new aspects which Hamilton's fertile imagination had not already conceived. For another, most people found the quaternion way of thinking very difficult. So there was never any real rush to follow the explorer into the new continent of knowledge which he had discovered.

This striking stasis in the early history of quaternions is well illustrated by the British Association meeting at Oxford in 1847. William read a paper on quaternions applied to lunar theory and he was able to answer some weak criticisms from the audience readily enough. Herschel earnestly advised his listeners to take up quaternions, describing them as "a perfect cornucopia, which turn it on which side you will, something rich and valuable was sure to drop out".[11]

Airy however fulfilled his usual role of negative critic and did not agree. To him, the new method's main recommendation so far were those rather limited results which were in accord with earlier findings. But he also advised that all potential disciples should exercise extreme caution, mainly because the new expressions could be so difficult to interpret geometrically.

Here, Airy certainly had a very telling point. Even Hamilton himself at this stage was far from certain what the fourth or 'real' unit in quaternions might mean physically. To hazard that it might denote the single axis of time (as distinct from the three similar axes of space) seemed little more than a metaphysical speculation where critics were concerned.

Hamilton had often pondered on this tricky aspect, as for example in an earlier letter to Uncle James:

> *January 11, 1845:* My letter related to a certain synthesis of the notions of Time and Space, or in their greatest abstraction, of Uno-dimensional and Tri-dimensional Progression, the result being a Quaterno-dimensional Progression, or what I call a Quaternion.[12]

Reading these lines nowadays conveys a curious and almost eerie sense of prescience, as indeed do several others written by Hamilton. One can almost sense him blindly reaching out to grasp the idea of relativity and its four-dimensional world. But that would have to await the advance of knowledge by another half-century, and also the advent of a similar genius in the person of Einstein.

The renowned mathematical physicist, Cornelius Lanczos, has put this aspect quite unequivocally:[13]

> It is astonishing to see how the quaternions of Hamilton foreshadowed our four-dimensional world, in which space and time are united into a single entity, the 'space-time world' of Einstein's Relativity. Today we are inclined to call d the 'time-part' and $ai + bj + ck$ the 'space-part' of the quaternion q.

Lanczos goes further in suggesting that quaternions provide the exact tool nowadays for all problems involving some kind of rotation in the four-dimensional world. Hamilton would doubtless have delighted in showing their utility in this way. His problem was that he lived a full two generations before the discovery of the Minkowski or 'space-time' world.[14]

So all that he could really do in the 1840s was to continue developing his ideas in the light of current physics knowledge, highlighting the various areas where quaternions might substitute for existing methods.

A Book too complex

Obviously one way to clarify his ideas and spread the message more effectively would be through the medium of a book. In June 1848, Hamilton gave a short series of four lectures for the College Fellows and a natural development was the suggestion that these be expanded slightly into a suitable student textbook.

The idea of a book was especially advocated by Charles Graves, who was already planning to introduce quaternions into the College mathematics course. He wanted an elementary text which might be ready by the autumn, one suitable for his own students first and then hopefully others elsewhere. The Board weighed in with a printing grant of £50 and Hamilton began with typical enthusiasm in July.

By now at last, he was at least partly conscious of his own inability to explain things in a simple manner — a fact which emerges clearly in an earlier letter to Herschel:

> *September 1, 1847:* Now I aspire to a method which can be taught, a calculus which can be used by others, and nothing would be more conducive to such a result than the timely questions and criticisms of a judicious friend.[15]

Herschel duly responded with sage advice once the book had started in the following year; his wisdom must be regarded as none the less valuable despite the distressing fact that it would be almost totally ignored:

> *October 27, 1848:* As you go on, let me just suggest that it will be well for a long way forward not to use your own highly abstract language and terms without translating them ...
>
> People *must* be familiarised by degrees to high abstractions; and if at any time they perceive their ideas get bewildered, they will begin at the same time to lose their appetite for further prosecution of the project.
>
> Depend upon it, in the present stage of the introduction of quaternions into general use (the best plan) is, *as far as is practicable*, to use common language, and to introduce the new phrases as strong meat given gradually to babies.[16]

Hamilton however never really took such wise and often repeated counsels to heart. His notorious habit of diverging into sudden flights of fancy in other directions apparently went unchecked as the book progressed. Nevertheless, he still retained a touching faith that the end product would be as readily intelligible to others as to himself. Hamilton therefore completely underestimated the very great difficulty which any new mode of thinking (and especially in abstract mathematical concerns) presents to the uninitiated mind.

The simple treatise, which Graves had requested for his students in June 1848, finally emerged as a massive tome of some seven hundred pages, five years afterwards. *Lectures on Quaternions* had cost the Board £300, exactly six times the originally agreed subsidy. There was also a sum of £20 which Hamilton paid out of his own pocket. This was a financial history notable mainly for the great felicity with which it was to be repeated with his second book a decade afterwards!

Sadly, the *Lectures* also proved largely unreadable for nearly everyone. Herschel for example gave up after just three chapters on his first attempt, nor did he get much further when he tackled it again in 1859. His cry of distress on this second occasion was obviously sincere:

> Do pray think of this. At the risk of offending, I will venture to say you will not have done yourself justice if you do not give the world some clue that a lower class of thinkers can unravel than those who alone can hope to master that book.[17]

Hamilton nevertheless refused to consider his book as it must have appeared to outside eyes. He therefore gave presentation copies to all whom he thought might benefit, including Prince Albert and the Lord Lieutenant, Cavendish. Graves reports that Hamilton was much struck by the intelligent comprehension which the former displayed for the subject.[18] The Lord Lieutenant however, in contrast, was honest enough to doubt his own capabilities:

> *April 19, 1856:* I have great doubt whether I have sufficient mathematical capacity to master the method.[19]

Hamilton also gave presentation copies of the *Lectures* to less exalted personages, friends like his schoolboy chum, Dr. Thomas Fitzpatrick, or his clergyman acquaintance, Rev. Mortimer O'Sullivan. To the latter, he was ingenuous enough to express his opinion on the book's readability:

> *August 4, 1853:* But it is my most sincere and unaffected conviction that a gentleman of good general education, who has once had and used the benefit of the scientific training furnished by a university such as ours, although science may not have been his adopted line of study . . . is likely to be able to advance a good way in the reading of my volume: and that if he consents to take it up *as a study*, he will be agreeably surprised to find it almost light reading.[20]

In another letter to Robert Graves somewhat later, Hamilton also reveals his deep belief that in writing his book he had been making history:

> *July 18, 1855:* I may indulge the hope, at moments, that . . . my own volume may survive even several centuries — nay that, as the earliest work in its own department, it may exist 'till books shall be no more. But it deeply presses on my reflection how much wiser a book is Tennyson's *Princess* than my *Quaternions*.[21]

In this, as well as in his judgement on general readability, William was of course wide of the mark. Although the *Lectures* only cost five shillings, hardly a single copy seems to have been purchased in Dublin during its first year. Evidently, the intended student market never materialised. In the words of Lanczos a century later, it would have been a good textbook had it been confined to just 70 pages instead of the 700 eventually attained![22]

Where Hamilton Failed

Hamilton's first major attempt to spread the message of quaternions must then be seen as almost total failure and it is instructive to consider why such was so. 'To see, relate and express' are the three sequential tasks of the discoverer in science and each of these can profitably be considered in turn.

First, Hamilton saw the basic idea of quaternions in striking entirety during his famous walk along the Royal Canal. This episode may usefully be compared with Darwin's not-quite-so-sudden realisation of the evolution principle on the Galapagos Islands. In each case, the incident was similarly total, a novel act of intellectual illumination embracing large future possibilities.

Darwin however would hardly have made much impact had he simply gone home to announce the principle of evolution as a fact. Neither would Hamilton had he abandoned quaternions after his initial address to the RIA on October 13, 1843. In both cases, the new mode of thinking required to be *related* to all pertinent existing science to demonstrate its relevance. It is this demanding labour of relating which the discoverer must next undertake, a task which occupied both Hamilton and Darwin for many years.

And finally, the inventor must *express* his new coherent body of knowledge in a manner acceptable to most of his fellow scientists. If he can do this with results which still provide an advance on previous methods, the higher status of *innovator* has been attained.

The discoverer has now progressed from being the mere *inventor* of a bright idea and is transformed naturally into an *innovator*, about to impose new ways of thinking on his world. Darwin's *Origin of Species* was eminently successful at this final stage: equally clearly, Hamilton's *Lectures on Quaternions* was not.

That quaternions eventually did not turn out to be the superior method of mathematical notation which Hamilton envisaged is not really the main point here. The point is rather that his first major work, to express the idea, could certainly have been cast in a more effective form. The inventor would thereby have attained a wider audience capable of testing the scope of his thinking more effectively.

We are forced to conclude that Hamilton badly needed a determined editor and more realistic criticism in everyday conversation from suitably qualified confidants. This would have served him better than the constant flattery bestowed on him by unqualified acquaintances such as Adare and de Vere!

11 TROUBLED TIMES

"Kneeling, I offered to her the Book which represented the scientific labours of my life. Rising, I received, or took as my reward . . . a kiss, nay many kisses . . ."

Hamilton to de Vere, August 7, 1855

The years during which quaternions were conceived and first developed were naturally trying times for Hamilton. To propound a really radical idea, upsetting all previous conventions, is always a stressful experience for even the boldest innovator. Internally, the ego comes under strain as long accepted foundational beliefs fragment in the new intellectual earthquake. Externally, anxiety is generated as the novel construction erected in their stead becomes subject to the repeated aftershocks of criticism and test.

In Hamilton's case, these normal stresses were exacerbated by various traumas at a more personal level. We have earlier noted the striking change in his formerly cheerful personality from about 1839 onwards. This was the period when his wife deserted him for over a year. Coping with her at a distance was obviously difficult for William, not to mention care of the infants as well as the perennial servant problem at Dunsink.

Many of those relatives who had served so effectively in various practical matters were now also naturally beginning to die away. His mother's sister, Aunt Mary Hutton, passed away in 1837, leaving the sisters a total of £1,000 in her will. But at the same time, her death removed a stable source of financial security to which the family could always turn in time of need.

The death of Cousin Arthur in December 1840 was an even keener loss. The wise old counsellor had always served as a source of worldly wisdom to guide William in his rather less practical ways of thinking. In effect, he served as a second father to the family. It is perhaps significant that Hamilton's drinking habits became more pronounced and public after Cousin Arthur died, gradually escalating until his disgrace at the Geological Society dinner in February 1846.

Arthur's house at 18 South Cumberland Street had also served as a second home for the Hamiltons. There the sisters could always reside anytime they wished, when not otherwise employed. Grace in particular was mostly there as housekeeper except for the early Dunsink years, the domestic role having fallen to her naturally as the eldest sister after their mother died.

MacCullagh

Bust of James MacCullagh in the Common Room of Trinity College,
Dublin   (*Courtesy Trinity College, Dublin*)

Once the doors of Cumberland Street were finally closed forever, Grace appears to have gone into a long slow decline. Henceforth the sisters would be ageing spinster ladies, supported by their own devices or William's generosity. When not employed as governesses or lady companions, they stayed in lodgings around their native North Dublin area at his expense. And it was under such far from cheerful conditions that Grace was first to die, at the age of 44 in June 1846.

The epitaph for Grace seems best supplied by her sister Sydney who was in attendance during her last days:

> In short, she was everything (to the family). My brother once said of her
> 'I think that if I were told that the house was on fire, I should say, well,
> tell Grace'.[1]

Just before Grace died, William had resolved on a regime of total abstinence, at the same time resigning as President of the RIA. The following year however, two other important figures among his relatives also passed away. At Trim, Uncle James died in July at the respectable age of 71, that early mentor to whom, more than any other, Hamilton owed his present intellectual eminence.

James died poor as ever and still curate of Trim as he had started half a century before. Significantly, his tombstone is a very modest slate half-hidden at the back of the church where he had served a lifetime, a striking contrast to the many, far more ostentatious, minor mausoleums toward the front. In death as in life, the many merits of James Hamilton and his ideas remained unrecognised.

Three months later, in October, William's other clerical uncle died. He was the Rev. John Willey, that Moravian minister who had taken care of the sisters back in 1817 when their mother died. John Willey also encouraged young William in his early boyish astronomical pursuits. Later he was always greatly proud of his nephew's official position at Dunsink and many letters in the archives testify to his striking neatness and precision in matters astronomical.[2]

No sooner was John Willey buried than Hamilton was stricken by a far more unexpected death much nearer home. This was the suicide of his frequent rival MacCullagh, in late October 1847. The latter apparently destroyed most of his current research papers in a manic outburst and then killed himself in his College rooms.[3]

This dramatic and tragic event may have been occasioned by MacCullagh's recent defeat in an election where he had hoped to represent Trinity in the nationalist interest. He was however also a chronic hypochondriac, subject to dyspepsia, and his health had deteriorated markedly of late. But his solitary existence, fevered temperament and ceaseless mental activity (sometimes expressed as paranoia) all doubtless contributed to the final act.

The archives also contain several notes to Hamilton written shortly beforehand; they show that even MacCullagh realised he was pushing himself too far:

What with various things, I scarcely know whither to turn myself; I
cannot think of going out to the observatory. Some other time perhaps I
may be able to pay you a visit. A walk or a ride before breakfast would
be the best thing in the world for me . . .[4]

MacCullagh's tragic end sent shockwaves of horror through Dublin
intellectual circles, the more so because suicide was still widely believed to
incur the penalty of eternal hell. The College nevertheless honoured him
with an official funeral service before the body was sent north by the new
railway for burial in his native parish of Bodoney, near Strabane. Hamilton
with others thereafter successfully petitioned for an official pension for his
relatives.

William was also moved by the solemnity of this event to express his
thoughts in the customary poem, in which he refers to MacCullagh's almost
successful attempt to build a mechanical ether model:

Great, good, unhappy! for his country's fame
Too hard he toiled; from too unresting brain
His arachnaean web of thought he wove.
The planet-form he loved, the crystal's frame
Through which he taught to trace light's tremulous frame,
Shall be his symbols in the cypress grove.[5]

Over the following years, several other formative influences in the life of
Hamilton also naturally passed away. Maria Edgeworth died in 1849, still
sprightly until near the end; Wordsworth joined her the following year.
Although his recent correspondence with Hamilton had not been as
frequent as formerly, the sage had undoubtedly performed a signal service
in steering the younger man away from his earlier inclinations towards a
serious poetic career.

One year later, Hamilton was again shaken by another literary loss. This
time it was his favourite poetess sister Eliza, best loved and most educated of
all the girls in the family. Eliza, like Grace, had long been ailing in a general
decline, undoubtedly not helped by her unfulfilled lifestyle; like Grace too,
she died in lodgings at the probably significant age of 44. Her last rooms
were at 12 Upper Dorset Street, close to the Bethesda Church to which she
was so attached; again the redoubtable Sydney was in attendance during her
last days.

Eliza had long realised that she was dying and her final poem "written on
her last birthday, April 3, 1851, contained a most express and pathetic
farewell to earth".[6] When she died on May 14, William was at her bedside;
he records that her moment of passing was apparently quite painless,
"literally a falling asleep, as we fully believe, in the Lord". And immediately
after death, her countenance assumed a *"beautiful* expression" — details
which comforted William greatly.

Like all her predecessors, Eliza was buried in the old family churchyard
of St. Mary's, not far from the original shop in Jervis Street. And there
William now arranged a suitable tombstone in full expectation that he too
would be laid beside her and his parents eventually.[7]

Hamilton's feelings and continuing financial support for his favourite sister may have been entirely praiseworthy, but he also deserves censure for a somewhat priggish act committed three years later. It was only then that he could bring himself to inspect his departed sister's papers, discovering among them a diary in which Eliza had recorded her impressions of the many famous visitors to Dunsink, twenty years before.

One might have expected William, with his great regard for records, to preserve this diary faithfully as a matter of historical interest. Eliza's account of Wordsworth which survives from other sources proves that she could be lively and accurate in her descriptions. We can guess that Adare, Airy, Anglesey and Mrs. Hemans, as well as the entire Board of Visitors, were other subjects who were recorded in her diary with equal accuracy. Hamilton however now judged that his sister had described some of these important personages "too freely" and so he consigned Eliza's journal to the flames!

Although this is a very common occurrence in family circles, it seems more like an act of petty censorship, given Hamilton's perpetual great regard for leaving records. In the case of Eliza's journal, William's decision is exacerbated by his feeble attempt at self-excuse. In a letter to Lady Dunraven, he depicts his act as a sacrifice because "(the journal), I am convinced, would have brought me in some hundreds of pounds if I could have borne to publish it..." This still does not explain why he could not have simply preserved the document with his many others for posterity.[8] Obviously Hamilton could be as hypocritical and self-righteous as any other middle-class Victorian when he felt that the social proprieties were being breached.

The catalogue of mortality among Hamilton's immediate relatives ends with the death of his youngest sister Archianna in 1860. Again she died around the age of 44, a curious coincidence suggesting some medical or psychological common factor among the Hamilton sisters. Archianna was always retarded in at least some faculties and, like her two predecessors, she died in Dublin lodging rooms with the redoubtable Sydney in attendance.

The death of her last dependent sister now left Sydney free of all ties, in her fiftieth year. She therefore soon embarked on a foreign venture to Nicaragua and, when this failed, after several years embarked again for New Zealand! She was always the toughest in the Hamilton family and would eventually outlive her brother by a full two dozen years.

Old Love Revives

Hamilton during the 1840s was also much disturbed by the partial return into his life of Catherine Disney, his first and often proclaimed greatest love. But now, his rigid social conservatism left him unable to seize the opportunity — as a more flexible or less scrupulous individual like Dionysius Lardner would have done.[9] In short, he never made any move to consummate that passion so frequently declared in his many poems over the decades and this despite the fact that the lady was now obviously trying to make herself available.

The early intense feelings evoked by Catherine had never really deserted Hamilton, even though he had scarce seen her since their last meeting in the dome of Armagh Observatory in 1830. Then he had written that poem which describes her with two children from her marriage four years earlier. Now these same sons were in their late teens, seeking suitable careers, and they were the means whereby William and Catherine met again.

One of these boys was James William Barlow and he entered Trinity aged about sixteen in 1842. Hamilton soon took a special interest in this son of his lost love and it was probably concerning this that her brother, the Rev. Thomas Disney, took Catherine out to Dunsink in 1845.

This was likely the first non-accidental meeting between the two in sixteen years, but the unquenched flame of former mutual attraction apparently started to flare up immediately. Nevertheless, there seems to have been no further contact between the two for several years.

Meantime, Catherine's son was progressing through Trinity with creditable distinction and Hamilton apparently now started coaching him with more intensity to gain a Fellowship. In this, the pair did not succeed on their first attempt, but Catherine still wrote to William in July 1848, thanking him for his aid. An accelerating exchange of letters followed for about six weeks, with one which made clear for the first time that Catherine had always equally loved William![10]

Both sides however felt equally guilty about their sinful feelings, torn between the attraction of illicit romance and the sterner dictates of ingrained religion. Finally, Catherine could stand the increasing tension no longer and decided to confess everything to her clergyman husband! The latter had always, of course, been aware of the attraction between Hamilton and his wife, who was about fifteen years younger than himself. Now he wrote to William, remonstrating in a half-defensive manner, the latter replying in formal tones that he was sure the episode could now be considered closed.

By this time however Catherine was in the throes of a nervous breakdown and, early in September, she took an overdose of laudanum. This attempt at suicide was not quite successful, but it did have several important outcomes. One was that she left her elderly husband, more or less completely to stay with her mother and various brothers around Dublin for the next five years. Another was that she seems to have abandoned her former strong faith in religion, once clear of her husband's constant preaching ways.[11]

The third important outcome of Catherine's attempted suicide was its effect on Hamilton. He was at Birr Castle with Airy during the height of the crisis; a combination of challenge from the latter and worry about his true love now weakened his vow of abstinence, taken two years before. William therefore started drinking once again, nor would he make any further attempt to desist permanently from that point on.

Catherine was now relatively free and seldom more than a few miles away. William's stronger sense of religion and duty however still kept him from meeting her. But this did not stop him from proclaiming his continuing interest at second-hand. So much is obvious when he writes to his old acquaintance Anglesey, now Master-General of the Ordnance. In this letter, William is seeking a post for another of Catherine's sons:

> *November 15, 1848:* Among my very oldest and dearest friends — though not otherwise connected with me — are the maternal relatives of a young gentleman called Brabazon Barlow; and I know that they have for a good while looked forward to his procuring, at some time or another, a small office in the department of the public service, which is honoured by having your Lordship at its head ...
>
> My main motive for thus presuming to trouble your Lordship is my old and warm friendship for those maternal relatives of his to whom I have already alluded ...[12]

Hamilton also persevered in his efforts to coach young J. W. Barlow into a Fellowship and these efforts were finally successful in May 1850. He helped his protégé with quaternions, while supplying the same information to Charles Graves, responsible for questions on the subject in the Fellowship examination.[13] With help of this order, it would have been difficult for Catherine's son to fail!

Having now largely shed the conventions of an unhappy marriage, Catherine was obviously the bolder of the two. She continued to declare her interest by various little hints and stratagems, presenting Hamilton with a Bible and Prayer Book as well as a later presentation note. Perhaps she felt these gifts to be in fitting tone with a long poem of high moral content which Hamilton had sent her through her relatives:

> O suffering saint! and too severely tried,
> But that thy God unseen, is at thy side...
> Thyself to blame, by Him acquitted be,
> Such is the present lot assigned to thee.
> But thou shalt see thy Saviour face to face,
> The dark vale issuing in a sunny place ...[25]

This is a poem which strikingly resembles Eliza at her most sanctimonious and one cannot help wondering what Catherine must have felt when she received these dark foreboding lines. Possibly she was at last beginning to realise the folly of thinking that William could ever act boldly, in accordance with his earlier grandiloquent poetic declarations.

Three years later however, another and more open invitation arrived, one which even the ineffectual Hamilton could not ignore. In mid-October 1853, she sent him a pencil case bearing the inscription: "From one whom you must never forget, nor think unkindly of, and who would have died more contented if we had once more met." The implication was that death was in the offing and this was the factor which finally proved sufficient to break William's curiously vacillating code of morality!

Hamilton now immediately hurried round to Robert Disney's house in Donnybrook where Catherine was staying and there, he was invited to return for dinner later in the day. His agitation in the interval can only be imagined, but in any case he had resolved on a suitable parting gift. This was his recently published *Lectures on Quaternions*, a book which even the most eminent mathematicians could scarcely read!

William found Catherine languid and wasting, quite possibly dying from a general decline precipitated by prolonged despair. She was resting on a sofa by the fire in a room to which she had been carried so that they could at last have total privacy. In the almost obligatory poem written after the event, Hamilton leaves a highly dramatic picture of this almost last scene:

> Do you remember, I enquired,
> Some incident of long ago?
> For unforgotten thoughts desired,
> Their image in her heart to know.
> Then do I! with sad voice she said,
> While clothes propped up her languid head;
> And then, as if her fond and faithful love,
> All doubts of her remembrance would remove,
> She roused herself to murmur over again
> A long lost fragment of a boyish strain,
> Which in her heart and sacred recollection,
> Had lingered from those days of young affection;
> For thrice ten years it lay enshrined,
> Within the casket of her mind . . .[15]

What happened next Hamilton also describes in a letter to his perennial marital consultant, de Vere:

> Kneeling, I offered to her the Book (*Lectures on Quaternions*) which represented the scientific labours of my life. Rising, I received, or took as my reward, all that she could lawfully give — a kiss, nay many kisses — for the *known* and *near* approach of *death* made such communion holy. It could not be indeed, without *agitation* on both sides, that for the first time in our *lives*, our lips then met . . .[16]

William saw Catherine just once again before her death, a fortnight afterwards in late October 1853. As soon as she died, he hurried over to the house; her ever-loyal family gave back to him all their secret correspondence which was found within her bed.

The same relations later gave Hamilton those many mementoes of Catherine which he was to collect with compulsive obsession over the next few years. Journals, books and a lock of her once-blonde hair were all locked away in his cluttered desk at the observatory; there too resided a couple of miniature portraits which he would take out to gaze upon daily for many years.

Hamilton furthermore became obsessed with the very story of his life-long 'romance' with Catherine. Afterwards, he would delight in retelling it to suitably appreciative audiences who could be trusted to remain sympathetic but discreet. Aubrey de Vere was naturally most favoured among such confidants, even though now at the age of forty, he himself still showed little signs of marrying. Catherine's surviving relatives formed another favoured audience and, as such, sometimes received letters grieving over their dead sister twice a day!

The long attachment between William and Catherine is certainly at least a minor classic in the tradition of romantic love; as such, it may in future become more widely known. Its psychological interest lies in the role of an inspirational Other, as perceived by a genius whose romantic aspirations remained unfulfilled. The story also exemplifies the rigid inhibitions and constraints which Victorian morality and religion could impose on even its greatest thinkers. And finally, it sheds strong light on the surprising degree to which behaviour can be governed by current prevalent concepts of love.

Hamilton was of course steeped in the Romantic tradition where such matters were concerned. There the most frequent themes are those of true love, foiled by external circumstances, condemned to remain unrequited, at least temporarily, or maybe even doomed to be finally unfulfilled. It is a pattern or script which probably began with the mediaeval troubadours and their natural requirement to sustain audience interest as long as possible.

It was also a pattern which Hamilton was conditioned to follow faithfully right to the bitter end. Then he would have a real romance to ponder over instead of just another commonplace illicit affair. It would also still be a respectable story, one which he could relive guiltlessly by telling it over and over again to any listeners whom he deemed worthy. We are forced to conclude that William lived more for the telling than the doing, a failing perhaps understandable in one whose entire being was oriented more towards the mental rather than the physical!

Those final scenes by the dying Catherine's bedside did however produce at least one positive consequence. When all was over, Hamilton seems to have shed at least some of his former major inhibitions where women were concerned. From then on, we find him flirting more openly with various females, sometimes even going so far as to kiss them in the Meridian Room.[17] Catherine's first and last tragic embraces therefore did at least have the effect of breaking down some inhibition barriers for her beloved Hamilton!

The romance of William and Catherine also resulted in another happy outcome many years after both were dead. Her son and his protégé, James William Barlow, rose steadily through the College hierarchy after Hamilton had coached him into a Fellowship in 1850. Ten years later he became professor of Modern History and eventually Vice-Provost in 1899; his college career is now commemorated by a memorial tablet just inside the present Chapel door. We can assume that William and Catherine would have been gratified could they but have known.

Religion Intensified

During the 1840s, Hamilton had a great many pressures — moral, intellectual and domestic — with which to contend. There were family problems, bereavements and above all his unresolved feelings about Catherine, all of which must have seriously interfered with his new ambition: to develop quaternions and spread their message far and wide. It is therefore quite understandable that he should have felt himself under strain occasionally and equally that he should seek solace now and then in alcohol.

Early in the decade, the cumulative effect of such factors became apparent to his friends in the form of a dangerously overactive mind. The three Graves brothers in particular began to fear that he might suffer a breakdown under the strain. Writing to his brother, Robert, about this time, John Graves describes William's symptoms with typical clarity:

> *November 25, 1844:* While I was lately in Dublin ... I could not help thinking that Hamilton was overstraining his mind by incessant exertion in mathematics. The way in which he went on orally with abstruse calculations seemed to me to indicate the morbid activity of brain resulting from overwork. The evil of such exertion was manifest to me in the *painful exertion* of his face ... and in a certain nervous irritability of temperament.[18]

The same could obviously be said of MacCullagh during these years, but we have no record of similar remarks concerning him. In any case, John Graves recommended that Hamilton should take a holiday when his current paper on quaternions was finished, a piece of sound advice which of course was not acted upon. Hamilton stayed on at Dunsink, continuing to pour out letters and mathematics, so that other friends too began to worry about his general well-being.

In June of the following year, for example, Robert Graves met him during the British Association meeting at Cambridge. He judged him "less calm than he was wont to be, exhibiting symptoms of an overactive mind, of a brain too easily excitable".[19] On this occasion, Hamilton suddenly confessed to his old clerical friend that he was growing too fond of alcohol and desired to kneel down on the spot so that he might be granted absolution for his sins!

Robert did not think the occasion a fitting one on which to grant William's quite possibly bibulous request immediately. But the Graves brothers were prominent again the following February when Hamilton had disgraced himself with alcohol. Now Charles and Robert both visited Dunsink and extracted from him a pledge of total abstinence; the penitent resolved to contribute one shilling weekly to the Society for the Propagation of the Gospel in Foreign Parts as long as he kept to his teetotal regime!

This weekly donation to the Gospel Society was just one instance of Hamilton's heightened interest in religion during these years. Robert Graves found this interest unhealthily excessive; we can deduce that it may have been partly due to over-compensation for inner guilt concerning Catherine and alcohol. At all events, this was at once the most traumatic period of Hamilton's life and also his most religious.

Part of William's enhanced interest in religious matters also found outlet in long calculations on Christian chronology. This was a topic in which he had been interested since his early days at Trim. As an undergraduate, young Hamilton had successfully passed the dreaded examiner Kennedy, by connecting the biblical story of solar stasis to the Greek legend of the darkness preceding the birth of Hercules. Now he could use his own great knowledge of astronomy to clarify some of the more obscure corners of Christian chronology.

Early in 1842, for example, he calculated the exact date of the Council of Nicaea in 325 AD — a chronological exercise duly published by the RIA.[20] This can be considered a typical example of his lifelong interest in exact dates and in numerology. His range extended from the dating of the Hegira to checking Rober's discovery of a regular heptagon inscribed within a circle in the outline of the ancient Egyptian temple of Edfu.[21] The latter he found to be accurate to within one part in eight hundred thousand of the diameter.

A somewhat more revealing composition was the letter which Hamilton published during his 'most chronological' period, around 1842. Here he was greatly concerned with the ten days which elapsed between Christ's Ascension into Heaven and his subsequent despatch of the Holy Ghost at Pentecost. He starts by noting how the Gospels record that the Apostles could at first easily watch Christ's gradual ascent, rather like a modern moon-rocket at take-off.[22] Naturally Hamilton then begins to wonder about the subsequent journey:

> But how long was it subsequent? We dare not, by mere reasoning, attempt to decide this question. That place to which the Saviour has been exalted ... may well be thought to be inconceivably remote from the whole astronomical universe; no eye, no telescope, we may suppose, has pierced the mighty interspace; light may not yet have been able to spread from thence to us, if such an effluence be suffered thence to radiate.

Apart from this oddly prophetic vision of Heaven as likely the earliest scientific reference to a black hole, Hamilton eventually concluded that Christ may have spent the entire ten days between Ascension Thursday and Pentecost on a triumphal journey to the Heavenly Throne. Indeed quite possibly, He had visited many other inhabited planets along the way:

> May not the transit from the cloud to the throne have been but one continued passage, in long triumphal pomp, through powers and principalities made subject ... while the Universe beheld its God and all the angels worshipped Him?

The modern reader may be forgiven for taking these speculations as a kind of pseudo-scientific parody. But for Hamilton such issues were genuine and real. Probably his reflections on such matters were now starting to indicate a slight decline in faith, a decline which did not really surface until near his last days. Then, for the first time, he would grudgingly admit that his earliest education had perhaps taken the Bible chronology too literally.[23]

Hamilton's keen interest in religion during the 1840s was also much stimulated by the great doctrinal controversies then raging in the Established Church. The Church of Ireland, to which he belonged, was really the local branch of the Established Church in England. It was also a

Church which had been well embedded in privilege and patronage, in contrast to the Catholic and Presbyterian Churches whose members made up most of Ireland's population. During Hamilton's lifetime, this privileged position was gradually eroded and was diminished considerably by the abolition of tithes (1840) and the Church Disestablishment Act (1869).

For a time Hamilton seemed attracted to the Oxford Movement, which began in 1833 as a somewhat radical theological crusade; indeed in 1841, one of its leaders, Nathaniel Pusey, visited him at Dunsink. Four years later, one of the Movement's most famous figures, John Henry Newman, converted to Catholicism. Aubrey de Vere and many others followed in due course. It was at one time possible that Hamilton just might have followed them as well.

William however soon recoiled from such a significant move and thereafter reasserted his firm attachment to the Church of Ireland. Obviously, his religious concerns of 1842 can also be considered in this light. The following year he was prominent in his support for Stackallan College, a Church school founded as a sort of Irish Eton for the ruling class.

In 1851, Hamilton was also elected as one of the two churchwardens of his local church at Castleknock. In this role he became embroiled in a minor theological dispute with his old rival, Archbishop Richard Whately, now otherwise a firm friend. The dispute concerned a magnificent commemorative stained-glass window, installed by Mrs. Elinor Turner in memory of her late husband. The window had some features to which the Archbishop objected, notably the dangerous heretical symbols of the dove, the lamb and the pelican.[24]

The Archbishop demanded that the offending window be removed, a demand resisted by the donor and her supporter, Hamilton. Eventually after much tedious correspondence, it was agreed that the window would remain and that the offending symbols would be covered over! This compromise must have been revoked at some point afterwards because the window still survives in its original glory as the east window of the chancel in Castleknock Church. And there the modern visitor can readily inspect it, an interesting relic of those trivial concerns with which genius can often get itself embroiled.

The period 1845-1848 was also of course marked in Ireland by the terrible Great Famine, in which one-sixth of the entire population died.[25] Most of the casualties were among the poorer section of the population, the Catholics, and occurred along the west coast, safely far from Dublin's gaze. These deaths were caused by failure of the potato crop and related epidemics. Some well-meaning landlords, like the de Veres and Edgeworths, did their best for the starving peasantry by organising such relief measures as they could.

On Hamilton, however, the heart-rending scenes of human misery, occurring less than a hundred miles away, had little or no effect of any kind. Indeed, they touched him about as little as if they had been occurring on the far side of the moon; likely he might have taken more interest had they been

happening there! With Kane and the rest of the Irish scientific establishment, he did next to nothing for his starving countrymen, an horrendous
failure of the intellectuals which still seems difficult to explain.[26]

It now seems surely obvious that the mind which, in 1842, could compute
the date of Nicaea could easily have suggested more efficient methods of
famine relief four years later on. But the truth is that Hamilton contributed
nothing worthwhile, if at all, to the famine relief effort. Indeed little
awareness of the scale of the tragedy emerges from the occasional references
in his letters during this period.

That Hamilton however realised himself to be wanting during this
episode seems also true. In one letter to de Morgan, he quotes the opinion of
some friends who advised him that his best Famine Contribution would be
to work even harder at quaternions for the greater glory of Ireland! But, as
with his burning of Eliza's journal, this only seems self-exculpation of the
weakest kind.

Further insight into Hamilton's highly selective feelings about matters
Irish also occurs in his poetry of this time. In 1842 for example, his poetry
mourned a distant British defeat in the Khyber Pass.[27] In 1846, he could
compose yet another fulsome sonnet as his paddle-steamer from England
approached the Irish coast:

My native land, appear! these eyes await
Impatiently thy rising over the bare
Expanse of waters; fondly searching where
Thy fair but hidden form lingers so late...
In thee my homeward thoughts still claim their share,
My heart, my life, to thee are dedicate.[28]

This poem proceeds to compare Ireland to the classic Queen of Beauty,
apparently quite oblivious of the fact that up to half the population was now
approaching desperate famine straits. Of the fate of these hapless millions
there is scarcely a word in Hamilton's voluminous correspondence — and
not even a mention in one solitary line of all his many poems.

If the historian were to rely solely on Hamilton's wide-ranging writings as
a source for the social history of nineteenth-century Ireland, he would
encounter almost no indication that the Famine had ever occurred at all!

Hamilton the man

There were then some very striking anomalies and even contradictions in
Hamilton's personality. It therefore becomes a matter of some consequence
to seek a clear idea of his image, the way in which he was regarded by
himself and also by his friends in relation to his world. Much can be gleaned
about such matters from his correspondence and more from various other
writings in which he records his own views.

A primary and important fact is that absolutely nobody ever doubted
Hamilton's great genius or unusual cerebral power. His unusual intelligence

in matters academic had been apparent from an early age and his own consciousness of this was constantly reinforced by praise from his elders during childhood. Later similar praise would flow almost continuously from many fellow scientists and also from friends and flatterers such as de Vere.

This same consciousness of his unusual mental powers in turn led Hamilton to preserve a very full account of the many workings of his divergent mind. This probably started in the early years with Uncle James' theory that he could create genius more or less to order. Some such thinking may have lain behind the preservation of Aunt Sydney's letters, recording young William's progress through childhood.

In later years friends, like Aubrey de Vere, took up the same theme, frequently urging him to record his mental workings as totally as possible. The result is therefore that Hamilton's thoughts are as fully documented (albeit in haphazard fashion) as even the most investigative biographer could wish.

This strongly felt obligation — to document for posterity — led Hamilton to detail major events such as the famous 'Eureka moment' when he suddenly discovered quaternions near Brougham Bridge. But he also details other lesser events such as his youthful invention of a semaphore. If one includes his poetry and reflections on symmetry and beauty, Hamilton has left enough material to satisfy the demands of several sizeable doctoral theses on creativity.

Ironically, however, the same urges which drove Hamilton to reduce the apparent chaos of nature to greater order never extended to the more mundane level of his own papers. These were in large disorder, a growing mass of confusion which inevitably became more jumbled as the years went on. In the next chapter, we will include an account of an eye-witness who described the rather incredible scene presented by Hamilton's apparently chaotic study. Here it is sufficient to surmise that his notoriously poor office procedure may have begun with the example of Uncle James who was similarly careless.[29]

If however Hamilton was rightly regarded as a scientist of the first rank in matters mathematical, nobody thought of him as half so competent in everyday affairs. Various legends grew up around his lack of ordinary common-sense in everyday matters. Some of these he seems to have encouraged, in accordance with his image of the absent-minded professor writ large. On occasions he could even make fun of himself in this respect:

> October 11, 1833: The picture by Theodore Lane of the Mathematician boiling his watch and holding an egg in his hand while reading Euclid has amused all my country friends, whom I have assured it is a portrait of myself . . .[30]

And yet Hamilton showed himself competent enough always in his various administrative functions, apart from the actual routine observations at Dunsink. He was for instance a very good President of the RIA. And he was also at various times executor to several estates of deceased relatives, duties which he seems to have performed quite satisfactorily. Whenever his obligations concerned others, Hamilton then seems to have been notably scrupulous and competent, indeed so much so that it is hard to think of him ever in a mischievous context. The same can be seen in the care and courtesy with which he always answered the many, and sometimes foolish, questions which flowed into Dunsink from the general public.

Hamilton's great courtesy and general amiability were in fact almost legendary. He seems to have treated high and low with equal good manners, while still sharply conscious of social differences. Once in the troubled thirties, some burglars were apprehended at Dunsink. And while they were awaiting removal to prison, Hamilton gravely enquired of them whether they would have milk and sugar with their tea!

Ladies invariably found him charming and also apparently attractive because of his obvious intelligence. One even professed herself to be of the opinion that he would bow to a cat if the occasion arose.[31] Hamilton was in fact always notably kind to animals, a trait which can again be traced back to the days of many household pets at Trim. The hound, called Smoke, which came to Dunsink in the early days with his sisters, was apparently thrashed just once during its relatively long life. That was because William had caught it engaged in chewing up the family Bible.[32]

Animals similarly appear to have reciprocated Hamilton's sense of fellow-being, as on the occasion when a strange dog suddenly arose and kissed him in Catherine Disney's old mansion at Summerhill.[33]

Hamilton also often liked to write or walk with a family cat on his shoulders. And it is recorded that a dove flew in through an open window to sit awhile on his shoulder while he was leading the family at morning prayers.[34] It may be difficult for the modern urbanised mind to accept such stories in their entirety; but in truth, they may record a certain former empathy between man and nature, which has been banished by the generally harsher environment of modern times.

Hamilton also saw himself as a patriotic Irishman, although as we have seen this vision could be inexcusably limited at times. He always felt that his work was directed towards the greater glory of his country and that his achievements would give it an imperishable name in the history of science, just as Greece was glorious in philosophy. But Hamilton's idea of Ireland was always as one of many separate states within the greater unity of the Empire. So it certainly did not reflect that status of total independence to which most of his fellows in the large Catholic majority would eventually aspire.

Self-Analysis

William's lack of concern about the great Famine tragedy becomes all the more striking when we consider that he was generally interested in diverse happenings of every kind. Politics, religion and literature all interested him;

Hamilton and one of his sons, *circa* 1845   *(Courtesy Royal Irish Academy)*

so too did natural curiosities like thunderstorms, cloud patterns, hypnotism, coincidence and ghosts.[35]

In matters such as these, Hamilton expressed occasional interest in fringe phenomena, although always very clearly refraining from commitment in the absence of convincing proof. One of these fringe sciences in which he expressed a more than usual interest was phrenology, quite probably because his unusually wide brow would in such terms have been equated with large intelligence.

In any case, the phrenological fashion then current afforded Hamilton the requisite framework for a very revealing exercise in self-analysis. Dated February 21, 1838, this document contains an attempt by Hamilton to characterise the various facets of his personality as seen by himself. The terminology in which he did so is now inevitably dated, but the entire exercise is such a patently honest attempt to seek the truth that it is worth considering in more modern form here.[36]

Physically, Hamilton then saw himself as average or unimpressive, probably below middle height and already running to slight overweight. He tended to move about at a moderate pace and none of his senses were especially acute. His eyesight would soon require the aid of spectacles and the bronchial complaint which had plagued him from childhood could still flare up occasionally.

Hamilton also could hardly discern green from blue and would develop curious symptoms of double vision in later years. Nor had he any memory for music, although much affected by good passages when he heard them; this lack of ability in music he found surprising because of his great regard for poetry and rhythm.

William also regarded his piety, faith and veneration as only moderate. This is an assessment which the modern reader may find surprising but which was nevertheless probably accurate relative to the general climate of his times.

On the other hand, Hamilton saw himself as strong in passion or what was then called 'amativeness'. Oblique hints by Graves elsewhere confirm William's amatory qualities. He seems to have been a strongly sexed personality whom women often found attractive, but he would have preferred lasting attachments to indiscriminate affairs. The great length of his attachment to Catherine Disney, as well as his continuing devotion to his hopeless wife Helen, certainly prove this point well.

Hamilton saw himself as a moderately good parent, "fond of children but not disposed to have them constantly with me". He also liked to observe and record their behaviour while still in the infant stage; here we can discern a hopeful echo of his own childhood when William's nascent genius was so fondly chronicled by his mentors at Trim. Early letters to his colleagues are full of hopeful indications of further future genius among his family by the optimistic parent of Dunsink. Gradually this theme turns to wearied concern as his family matures and shows increasing signs of striking general inability.

Hamilton also had an unusually clear picture of himself as a somewhat impractical individual, "usually too abstracted to observe much; yet when stimulated, I can remember individual persons and things". This same perpetual abstraction often made him lose his way round Dublin and tended to make him unpunctual; typically enough, the theorist who liked to speculate on time was often late for his appointments. He was similarly aware of the contrast between his enjoyment of order in the abstract and his general disorder in daily routines.

Concentration was also another point in which William was quite clear on his abilities, recording himself as having a "strong great power of abstraction, a disposition to study one subject only". But again, he recognises a nature in general impractical, with "a fondness for constructing theories, but nothing else". Maybe his lack of practicality stemmed from the fact he had only slight liking for actual experiment, while at the same time being generally interested in diverse facts and anecdotes of all kinds. In these matters also, echoes of the early schoolboy days at Trim persist.

Neither did Hamilton ever really like to criticise the work of others as Airy did, perhaps because he recognised his own need for approbation as being very strong. His own theorising he recognised as rooted in his general urge to Ideality, augmented by the fact that imitation of the works of others did not greatly attract him. The capacity to invent he found was helped by his conscientious attitude and very strong sense of self-esteem, and also by his occasional habit of working right through the night without a break.

In more personal life, Hamilton regarded himself as moderately acquisitive. But his perpetual overdraft, and the many creditors forced to make the long trek out to Dunsink, suggest that he was hardly very successful in this sphere!

Perhaps such frequent visitors influenced William's spirit of hope, one which he describes as variable — sometimes sanguine, sometimes depressed. He may indeed have fitted the classic manic-depressive profile, now soaring to feverish activity when stimulated, now sunk into lethargy when lacking company or inspirational ideas.

Hamilton felt isolation rather keenly because he always enjoyed good talk and company. And on the social level his listeners seem to have been equally fascinated by him. He describes himself as of strong congruity (the ability to relate in company), enjoying wit in others while still carefully observant of their habits and manners. But he also regarded himself as provocative in talk and ideas, one with "a great fondness for argument, but not a disposition to quarrel".

Overall, however, he classified himself as generally benevolent, a judgement for which there is indeed abundant corroborative testimony. Indeed it is hard to think of even a single nasty, malicious or spiteful remark ever made by Hamilton about anybody — a truly notable record befitting his public reputation as the perfect gentleman.

Finally, concerning his natural gifts and aptitudes, William regarded his facility with numbers and calculation as "very great". His linguistic capabilities he found not at all so striking; there he credits himself with "facility and pleasure in acquiring foreign languages so far as to read them; but not in learning to speak or write them". So much for the fabled thirteen languages which were supposedly at his command!

Equally, however, he was confident of his large competence in English spiced with suitable classical allusions, the latter no doubt influencing his "disposition to speak oratorically".

Elsewhere Hamilton expresses his wish to be most remembered by the classical Plutarchian epitaph of a "labour- and truth-loving man". Of his labours there can be absolutely no doubt; his urge to seek truth despite lapses emerges very strongly in the painfully honest exercise in self-analysis described here.

Hamilton sought in his mathematical research to describe the natural world in his own new language of quaternions; he likewise tried to describe his personal strengths and failings with similar felicity!

12 THE LAST DECADE

"His diligence of late was even excessive – interfering with his sleep, his meals, his exercise, his social enjoyments. It was, I believe, fatally injurious to his health."

Charles Graves, November 1865

Although Hamilton was ultimately to become almost totally obsessed with quaternions to the exclusion of most other things, this did not happen until his last years. During the 1850s, for example, he continued to make new contacts and hold occasional parties at Dunsink and this despite the loss of Catherine Disney earlier in the decade.

Lady Hamilton never seems to have been present on such occasions or, if she was, it was certainly in a very minor role. Some of Hamilton's foreign friends, encountered at the British Association meetings, never realised that he had a wife at all. Even Romney Robinson was moved to speculate that Helen was nothing more than "an abstract idea" — the reason being that he had never met her in all the thirty years he had known Hamilton.[1]

William's continued public involvement during these years is typified by his active role in the national committee, convened in 1852, to erect a statue to the recently deceased poet Thomas Moore. This committee was launched with a large public meeting in the Rotunda, at which Hamilton gave the customary speech:

> Obscurely toiling, as I habitually do, in the deep recesses of science ... (and) having no hope of winning that electric sympathy which it is the prerogative of the poet to excite, it might have been wiser for me ... to have been wholly silent on a theme on which I have so few pretensions to speak.[2]

Hamilton was nevertheless still deeply interested in poetry, as well as many other things, and poets continued to figure among the many new acquaintances he made. One such was the future Lady Wilde, who as 'Speranza' was renowned for her fervent nationalist verses in the *Nation* newspaper. Despite the obvious gulf in political sentiment, Hamilton apparently recognised a kindred spirit and in a letter to de Morgan he describes her as "quite a genius".

Then he goes on to relate an incident which later turned out to be a curious minor quirk in literary history:

May 9, 1855: A very odd and original lady has also lately had a baby; such things, as you know, will happen . . . (Recently) when I met her for the first time in my life, she told me of this young Pagan as she called him. And she asked me to be a godfather, perhaps because she is an admirer of Wordsworth. However I declined.[3]

The 'young Pagan' mentioned here, of course, grew up in due time to be the famous Oscar Wilde, a writer of great ability as well as public notoriety. Could Hamilton have glimpsed this slice of the future, it remains an interesting speculation what he might have done. He might certainly have liked to stand as godfather because of the future literary connection, but on the other hand Wilde's sexual peccadilloes would probably have made him refuse even more decidedly! Lady Wilde in any case became a firm friend and, as such, one of the favoured circle in whom William liked to confide the tale of Catherine's romantic end.

Another lady who came back into Hamilton's life with some prominence in these years was Louisa Disney Reid. Around 1827, Hamilton had briefly contemplated marrying her as a substitute for her sister Catherine, despite the fact that Louisa was then just fourteen to his twenty-two years.[4] Now however, each realised the truth about William's earlier intentions and indeed felt so free with each other as to even exchange kisses in the Meridian Room.[5]

For a year or two also, around 1858, Hamilton conducted an intensive correspondence with Mrs. Mary Ward of Booterstown. She was a cousin of the Earl of Rosse and also a successful popular science writer. In an era of general self-improvement, her book on the microscope was selling very well. So now Hamilton acted as her adviser for a similar publication on astronomy. Unfortunately she was killed in a coach crash soon afterwards, so that a developing friendship, as well as a promising career, was thereby cut off.

In 1857, the British Association meeting came round again to Dublin and this time Hamilton acted as Vice-President. In this role he seems to have very effectively assisted his old friend Humphrey Lloyd, who was in overall charge. Indeed all went so well that Mrs. Lloyd thanked Hamilton personally in a very emotional display of gratitude. But this was to be one of the last of those great public occasions on which William could hold an entire audience spellbound.[6]

The following year, Hamilton held a literary gathering at Dunsink and here, its former glories as an intellectual salon were briefly revived. Leading literary lights of the day were present, among them Lady Wilde and the poet Dennis Florence MacCarthy. So too was his old friend Aubrey de Vere, now a leading Catholic intellectual and inclined to become intensely boring about his new concerns. William and Aubrey took a final stroll among the beeches along the Tolka where they had often walked and talked so earnestly of old. By now however, their former great affinity had obviously been eroded beyond any hope of salvage and Hamilton regarded Aubrey's new enthusiasms as undesirable for himself:

No beauty of Nature seemed able to win him, for even a minute, from
his intense contemplation of what he regards as the 'Glories of Mary';
and I confess that I parted from him with a feeling of fatigue.[7]

Thus ended a friendship which began under such peculiar circumstances,
when Aubrey had so strongly opposed William's intentions towards his
sister Ellen twenty-six years before.

Hamilton was struck off the Council of the RIA for non-attendance in
1858, a common occurrence in the Academy. He was, however, reinstated
the following year. His last attendance at a British Association meeting was
at the Manchester gathering in 1861. And his final venture into academic
politics came in 1863, when the RIA was in danger of being swallowed up
by the rival Royal Dublin Society (RDS).

Here Hamilton for the last time exerted himself, with some of the old
vigour, to save the Academy with which he had been associated for so long.
He noted the odd reversal of that previous occasion, back in 1843, when he
had saved the RDS, then threatened by withdrawal of government support.
Eventually, the new threat to the RIA was successfully warded off, but
really by this time Hamilton was deep into his final great obsession with
quaternions.[8]

The Icosian Game

Hamilton's widely divergent range of active interests in so many spheres
continued until almost the end. Proof of his continuing creativity is also
evident from his invention of the hodograph in 1846 and from his very
different discovery of the Icosian calculus in 1856.

William was at the British Association meeting in Cheltenham during
August of that year and, before returning to Dublin, spent a very productive
two weeks with John Graves who lived nearby. The stay was fruitful largely
because it afforded Hamilton his first real opportunity of browsing through
Graves' unrivalled collection of mathematical books.[9] From these evolved
his new idea of an Icosian calculus, a discovery which Hankins describes for
the mathematical specialist with his usual clarity.[10]

Here it is sufficient to note that Hamilton's work was originally based on
the classical twenty-sided solid — the icosahedron. Its twenty regular faces,
each an equilateral triangle, have a total of sixty edges. Sixty similar edges
however are also possessed by the next lowest regular solid — the
dodecahedron. It has twelve regular and similar faces, each of which is a
pentagon. Twelve faces, with five edges each, afford the same total as twenty
triangles, each with three.

The lower solid, or dodecahedron, however is much simpler to depict in
flattened or two-dimensional form. It was therefore on such a projection of
the dodecahedron that all Hamilton's development was ultimately carried
out.

Considered in this way, Hamilton's new reflections really become an

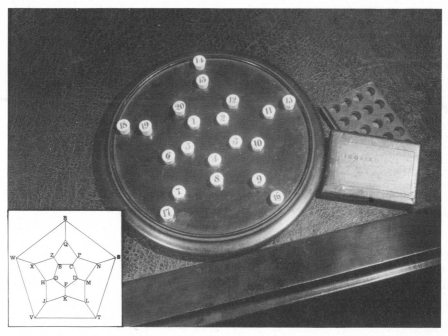

The Icosian Diagram and the Game   *(after Graves; Courtesy Royal Irish Academy)*

exercise in what we now term 'graph theory'. Another manifestation at a simpler level occurs in those children's puzzles sometimes presented with matchsticks. Essentially, one tries to trace a path traversing all points or edges *without recrossing*, until one ends up back at the starting point.

Hamilton's new discovery was really a method for the solution of such a problem, couched in mathematical terms. He developed a system of symbols and operators involved with the various roots of unity, somewhat as in quaternions. When such equations are so expressed that they end up equal to unity, they depict a complete circuit of the figure involving every point just once. A path like this, involving every vertex of a figure just once only, is therefore now known as a Hamilton Circuit.

Hamilton was involved with his friend and correspondent, T. P. Kirkman, in the development of these ideas. And between them they succeeded in focussing fresh interest on what had previously been a rather neglected area. But now, in addition, Graves conceived the idea that the Icosian diagram could be marketed as a commercial puzzle board, supplied with twenty wooden pegs to mark out selected routes. Hence arose the idea of expressing Hamilton's reflections on the mathematics of graph theory as the Icosian Game.

Graves contacted a London games' manufacturer called John Jacques who finally offered £25 for the idea. Hamilton also got six free copies of the puzzle in return for a suitable set of instructions and finally Graves got £3 for his legal fees.[11]

As might be predicted, Hamilton at first proved more eager to expound his mathematics than to set out the rules of the game for potential customers. He wished to start the instructions with a mathematical explanation of the game, so that all buyers would have to read it first! Mr. Jacques naturally felt that this would detract from the commercial appeal of his product. And ultimately, William was grudgingly forced to agree that his mathematical theory should go in at the end.[12]

Hamilton's finances were now far from healthy and so he entertained strong hopes that his invention might sell well. This alas did not occur, partly because the puzzle was really too easy to solve in practice. Here William seems to have been misled by the ingenuity of his mathematical solution into concluding that a non-theoretical or practical solution should be equally difficult. He placed one of his free copies of the puzzle in the Fellows' Room at Trinity; there it was generally derided as too simple and even children found the practical solution not too difficult.

This curious difference, between expectation and reality, again sheds further light on Hamilton's basically impractical mind. Because Icosian theory was undoubtedly a matter of considerable innovation and difficulty, he never realised that practical methods might solve the puzzle readily. This was of course the exact opposite to his expectations for quaternions. There, he expected that everybody should find the subject as easy as he did, whereas of course most people found quaternions very difficult!

William however had gained the sum of £25, before expenses, from his new invention — a figure equal to a fortnight's salary. His bankers professed themselves delighted at this somewhat tardy proof of the financial worth of genius in the marketplace.[13] In practice, however, this remained the only sum that Hamilton ever earned directly as the result of all those labours from his ever-restless mind!

The de Morgan Correspondence

Hamilton then remained mathematically creative, as well as socially active, until his final great obsession with quaternions started after 1859. Indeed he was never quite the solitary genius toiling alone in his study whom Bell has depicted in his ill-conceived work.[14] So much is obvious from the continuing, and sometimes very intense, correspondence which William conducted with the London mathematician de Morgan over these years.

The latter was well known for his researches into the origins of algebra and kindred matters, and it was this which originally led him to open the correspondence:

> *May 8, 1841:* I hardly know whether you remember that we made a little personal acquaintance some twelve years ago when you were in London ...
>
> I shall be very glad to see the *Theory of Triplets* pointed out in your paper on algebra; time-triplets or space-triplets, I don't care which.[15]

William responded with unusual alacrity and thereby one of the most fascinating and revealing correspondences in all science history was begun. The total volume of writing between these two eminent mathematicians probably runs to half a million words. Graves saw fit to print 400 pages of it at the end of his biography, but this is still far from the overall total.[16] Sometimes there were long interludes between letters but more often, it was by return post. Often the postman who ferried Hamilton's replies down from Dunsink was bribed by endless cups of tea while the composer was feverishly finishing his correspondence upstairs!

In many cases also Hamilton was so eager to cram in an afterthought that he wrote on the space inside the upright flap just before sealing the envelope.[17] In fact, as at various other points, there seems to have been something almost too fevered about William's writings here. Their repeated underscoring and superfluous exclamation marks seem remarkably evocative of certain types of mental disorder — states wherein the sufferer experiences great difficulty in expressing feelings adequately.

In the same context, Hamilton's almost unnatural disregard for time and appointments may be construed in terms of mild schizophrenia. His son records that "he was almost invariably late for church, dinners and public meetings of all kinds." He might answer a letter a day, or a month, or even a year, after he received it; even then, he sometimes omitted to post the answer after his writing was done! All this is what one might expect of an other-worldly genius, but the experienced may also recognise the characteristic symptoms of near dysfunction here.

In any case, and in this sometimes odd manner, William and de Morgan corresponded about almost everything under the sun. Less than half their writings are strictly mathematical; the rest concern politics, religion, women, race and general happenings of the day. Family matters are interspersed with humorous stories or just plain gossip; there are discussions on ghosts, coincidence, scandals, royalty and personages encountered on both sides.[18]

Overall, however, the most abiding impression is that of de Morgan's letters acting as a calm stabilising influence on Hamilton's sometimes overheated mind. Clearly, the latter was sorely in need of an everyday confidant with whom he could converse at his own level. Such opportunities at Dunsink being few and far between, the role of de Morgan as a distant substitute was crucial.

As might be expected, a goodly portion of the correspondence also concerns the various upheavals in the established order then taking place in Ireland. Both correspondents were united in their deep prejudice against the growing influence of Roman Catholicism. Hamilton was especially critical of the new generation of uncultured Catholic clergymen with which Maynooth was then supplying the countryside. For him, they would never have the same educated appreciation of culture as Uncle James and other alumni of the old Trinity school.[19]

In 1858, Hamilton also joined forces with de Morgan and William Thomson (later Lord Kelvin) in a concerted attempt to decimalise the currency. Hamilton even made sets of cardboard money and toured the local schools explaining to the children the easier calculations which would result! He also drafted a legal bill for submission to Parliament and had it printed at his own expense. But he likewise thought that the natural unit of his new currency should be the *mil* or tenth of a penny — a touching example of scientific innocence in pre-Keynesian days.[20] Many British scientists, including Herschel, Babbage and Airy, sided with Hamilton and de Morgan in this effort. Eventually the political powers of the day decided otherwise and decimalisation of the currency had to wait for another century before it came to pass.

Above all else however, William corresponded with de Morgan about the nature, history and progress of his beloved quaternions. The latter was therefore one of the prime influences who aided Hamilton to his last great decision that a new book was required on the subject. Henceforth, his life would be dominated (and perhaps shortened) by this decision, finally taken about the middle of 1858.

A Final Masterpiece

A new exposition was obviously required because William's *Lectures on Quaternions*, published in 1853, had not succeeded as he had hoped. Hardly a single copy of the book was bought in Dublin and few of the Trinity Fellows seemed really interested. Most were agreed on the unique nature of Hamilton's contribution, but this was far from sharing his greater vision of quaternions — as a better mathematical method to describe the world.

This issue is neatly summed up in a remark by the future Provost, George Salmon, then a Fellow and a very distinguished algebraic geometer, whom Hamilton had hoped would become a disciple during the 1850s:

> But when he asked me whether I thought his new method was billed to supersede the older ones, I was obliged to say in candour that I did not think so.[21]

What Hamilton really required at this stage was a competent populariser, capable of explaining his ideas in a simpler manner than he himself could. And such a person finally appeared in August 1858. He was 27-year-old Peter Guthrie Tait, just then beginning his career as professor of mathematics at the new Queen's College in Belfast.

Tait quickly won his way into Hamilton's regard by showing an obvious acquaintance with quaternions, while still seeking the master's guidance at more difficult parts. The younger man was now also beginning a formidable career as a very able science publicist and quaternions seemed an obvious subject for his pen. He thought that practical applications were more important so that people could grasp how useful quaternions really were — a point not readily obvious from the highly theoretical *Lectures*.

Unfortunately, Hamilton himself had now come round to the same way of thinking and wanted to write a practical work of his own! While therefore agreeing that his new, and indeed only, disciple should write a simple and practical exposition of quaternions, he also requested that publication be held up until his own work along the same lines might first appear! This book of his own was now already underway and planned to run to three hundred pages at the most. Herschel strongly approved of its apparent simplicity and the Trinity Board had voted a publication grant of £100. William confidently projected that it would be available within two years.

Tait took these intentions of Hamilton quite literally and, with a somewhat touching simplicity, laid his own publication plans accordingly. In late 1859, the Macmillian Publishing Company therefore advertised his *Introductory Treatise on Quaternions* as forthcoming soon. Hamilton saw a copy of this advance publicity and concluded that his pupil was trying to beat him to the publication date!

Tait, in fact, never had any such intentions, having merely taken Hamilton's initial publication schedule at face value. A distinct chill set in for awhile, which Tait eventually resolved by coming out to Dunsink in June 1861. There the master told him that his own work might be out by August, so that his disciple could decently publish in 1862. By now however, the latter had obviously grown wise to Hamilton's almost schizophrenic lack of time-sense and so decided that his own work would have to lie dormant until whenever the inventor would eventually publish.

William's same striking lack of time-sense also cost him a further great opportunity to publicise quaternions in 1863. Tait was now at Edinburgh and co-operating with Thomson at Glasgow on their great joint *Natural Philosophy* — probably the best physics textbook of Victorian times. Thomson was an out-and-out mechanist and so disliked quaternions. But still, he was persuaded to allow space for a dozen pages on them in the appendix. Tait sent these pages off to Hamilton in August, with an urgent request for comments and correction. By December, they still had not arrived back complete and so eventually the text was forced to go ahead without any reference to quaternions.[22]

Again there seems something more than merely the common practical limitations of genius in this episode. It strongly suggests a mental condition bordering on the pathological, a matter perhaps for future scholars to investigate somewhat more exhaustively.

Meantime the book which Hamilton had originally begun as a simple manual had grown to much larger significance in the writer's mind. Numerous applications to solid geometry, mechanics, astronomy and optics were now to be added in. All these would demonstrate the vast utility of the new mathematical notation which Hamilton had conceived entirely on his own.

William now therefore saw himself as writing for posterity, composing what he foresaw as one of the greatest mathematical treatises of all time. He would create an historical textbook for Ireland, just as Newton had enhanced England's glory with the *Principia* two centuries before! Thus did his last titanic effort seek to achieve the ambition of perpetual fame which the boy at Trim had set himself almost half a century before.

It is of course a matter of history that this last great vision turned out to be almost disastrously misconceived. When Hamilton's *Elements of Quaternions* was eventually published posthumously, it proved sadly as unreadable as the earlier *Lectures*. Only 500 copies were ever published at £1 apiece and even many of these were given away as presentation copies.

Ultimately Tait became the most effective expositor of quaternions. His long-deferred *Elementary Treatise on Quaternions* appeared in 1867, there being two further editions in 1873 and 1890. He also wrote a more formal *Introduction to Quaternions* in 1873, again with two further editions in 1881 and 1894.

These works meant that quaternions attracted large attention from leading physicists like James Clerk Maxwell for a time. Soon however they were replaced by vector analysis, which was a much simpler method derived from Hamilton's original idea. Indeed the very term 'vector' was first employed in its modern sense by Hamilton and Hankins graphically describes vector analysis as "quaternions for the practical man".[23]

Quaternions, as Hamilton conceived them, therefore never quite turned out to be the new magical key to the universe as he had dreamed. It is of course always possible that they may yet do so. But this seems increasingly unlikely as science advances ever further beyond the knowledge and methodology of a century ago. Hamilton therefore was basically mistaken in his deep conviction that he was creating an everlasting masterpiece of mathematics during his last seven years.

Decline at Dunsink

In any case, the sheer titanic mental effort involved in such a project inevitably exerted an increasing toll. The work intended to be finished in less than three hundred pages by 1860 was half as long again by mid-1863! Neither was there any prospect of an end in sight. For William, completion of the *Elements* now began to assume the character of some distant desert mirage, always elusive and far-off as ever despite vast effort expended on trying to catch up with it.

A work of this nature was also very difficult to print because of its many different symbols and obviously supporting finance was required. The Board had awarded £100 for the simple manual proposed in 1858, advancing a similar sum in 1862 when the work was expanding so drastically. But this second amount would not be paid until the work was finished and any further expense would have to be borne by Hamilton himself.[24]

William eventually did pay £50 (about one month's income) out of his own pocket. But as the book expanded, so did the original printing estimates. The costs piled up far beyond even the revised estimates as page proofs came back from the printers. Worry over this mounting debt was a growing torment during Hamilton's last days. Inevitably also it began to affect the never very stable Dunsink household regime.

William's three children were by now in their twenties, but all of them far from exhibiting any signs of future genius as their father had once fondly hoped. The eldest, William Edwin, seemed destined to be a drifter always, even though his father had once paid out a startling half-year's salary to place him with an engineering firm. His brother, Archibald, was an ordained curate, but one of such extraordinary incompetence that nobody seemed prepared to offer him a steady place.[25] Even in their late twenties, both these men were then still dependent on their father for occasional handouts and the records contain various references to such 'loans' which never seem to have been repaid.[26]

Hamilton's daughter, Helen Eliza, was therefore likely to have been his greatest comfort during these last years. Effectively abandoned by her mother during the first two years after her birth in 1840, she grew up thereafter with a noticeable if slight eccentricity. A shy lonely girl much interested in flowers and kind to animals, she often accompanied Hamilton on visits to local beauty spots in his final years.

Meantime, William's never-tidy study degenerated into something akin to an intellectual rubbish dump during these last years. Letters recently received were liable to land on top of a growing stack of papers into which they duly sank to be forgotten. With luck they might re-emerge many months later and then be answered as if received yesterday! Sometimes however, the newly written replies suffered the same fate and there are many joking references to such happenings in the de Morgan correspondence.

But if the ageing Hamilton was so inordinately untidy about his papers as to be grossly inefficient, he still retained that early sense of humour which often enabled him to laugh at his own deficiencies. Perhaps, however, the most vivid picture of Hamilton, at work on his last great misconceived masterpiece, comes from the pen of Sir Robert Ball, who served at Dunsink during the years 1874-92:

> In the study where he wrote, books, papers and letters were buried together in indescribable confusion. They overflowed from the bookcases and shelves on to the floor. They were not only piled in corners, but they spread over the room in an ever-deepening mass, until his study (as I was told by a nephew of the great man) presented a most extraordinary appearance.
>
> There was a kind of laneway from the door to his writing table, on either side of which papers, books, letters and mathematical manuscripts were heaped together to a depth of two or three feet. Visits of the housemaid to this sanctum were rigidly interdicted.
>
> Soaring aloft in mathematical speculation, Sir William was utterly oblivious to the sound of the dinner bell. When at last nature did make some food necessary, a chop would be handed in on a plate at the door.
>
> The nephew above declared to me that, when he visited this room, he saw many of these plates with the chop bones on them, thrown about on the piles of manuscripts.[27]

Other references however indicate that Hamilton's study may not have

Hamilton at the age of fifty-four *(after Graves)*

seemed quite so chaotic from the owner's viewpoint. He could for example immediately detect if any paper had been moved even an inch or so from the top of its pile — the inference being that there really was some sort of filing system decodeable by himself alone.[28]

Lady Hamilton had largely opted out of household management for many years; other legends suggest that the servants then ran the house more or less as they pleased. That this may well be true is supported by a curious note in the archives, wherein Hamilton apparently works out his reasons for sacking an employee called Milmou:

> You are charging me constantly more and more and bringing me in less and less. You are continuously year after year harrying me to buy new leads and not (reuse) old ones. You never or very rarely give me in any satisfactory or indeed intelligible account of what is going on here as regards expense or gain.
>
> I therefore wish (you) to try in the Spring of this year whether you cannot get some other employment in England or elsewhere.
>
> And in the meantime, I must insist upon your reducing next week's bill below this week's![29]

During these years, Hamilton had a mounting overdraft which eventually ran up to over £300, or six months' salary. Since he was then accustomed to delay settling bills as long as possible, duns were frequent visitors to Dunsink. Their advent never seems to have bothered him in the slightest and indeed he often pressed them into service to carry back letters for the city post![30]

All these were of course peripheral matters compared with the growing demands of William's ever-expanding *magnum opus*. But taken in conjunction, they must have meant that Dunsink was a highly tense and also disorganised household over his last few years. As such, it inevitably presents a saddening contrast to the cheerful enthusiasm and boundless optimism with which William and his sisters had first arrived there, almost forty years before.

Final Days

Hamilton's health had never been exactly robust and there are constant references to bronchial troubles going back to his earliest school days. Later he was obviously partial to alcohol and possibly unduly so. His son records that he liked to take occasional sips of porter to forestall fatigue while working at his papers, admitting also that his father had a "constitutional proclivity" towards alcohol.[31]

On the other hand, the popular legend of Hamilton as a hopeless alcoholic during his final years is almost certainly inaccurate. His physician, Dr. Wyse, records that he had never encountered his patient in an inebriated state. He then goes on to make the obvious point that a permanent dipsomaniac could hardly have completed the laborious calculations and development of his last great work.[32]

The truth is likely that a combination of overwork and worry, operating on a constitution already somewhat weakened by alcohol, finally proved fatal for Hamilton.

Gout is another consequence of over-indulgence in alcohol and William began to suffer from it increasingly during his last ten years. We know from his letters to de Morgan that other disorders, like defective vision and occasional epileptic seizures, were now also manifesting themselves.[33] But gout and bronchitis seemingly were the main elements in his final fatal illness, which began in May 1865.

Before its sad conclusion, however, a final and most pleasing scientific honour was bestowed on Hamilton. Across the Atlantic, quaternions had always been held in high esteem. And when the new National Academy of Sciences (NAS) was founded in America, one of its first acts was to elect Hamilton as first on the list of foreign associates. Effectively this meant that the Americans now recognised him as the greatest foreign scientist anywhere in the world!

The NAS election took place on January 9, 1865, but news of the honour was delayed in the post. William therefore did not hear about it until he received a second confirmation on June 12, 1865. Receipt of the news seems to have rallied him somewhat and, for a month or so, he was again able to resume his correspondence and continue with the still unfinished book.[34]

However, it was becoming all too obvious that Hamilton was no longer equal to such labour, a matter apparent in a letter from his son William Edwin around this time:

> He feels in many ways that he is quite equal to continue his most difficult Quaternion investigations — but when he makes the attempt, he then finds either that physical exhaustion soon stops him or that, if he does go on working, a worse reaction follows. He feels this and most painfully, though he will not admit it, or rest from mathematical work for an hour of his own free will.[35]

A few weeks earlier, Hamilton had received a bill from the printer for £145, one which he obviously could not pay. His reaction now was to stop signing cheques of any kind and nobody at Dunsink therefore had any money to pay the grocer or the doctor. Lady Hamilton was ill as usual in a house that now had to be kept in total silence; their son Archibald and his sister Helen were absent in Clogher a hundred miles away. This left the remaining son, William Edwin, in charge of the hushed observatory on the hilltop and, given the circumstances, he seems to have managed with commendable efficiency.

Robert Graves went out to visit his old friend on July 16 and found him happy that the final pages of the book were now almost at last complete. Together, they spent four hours discussing religion, metaphysics and all the usual topics that interested William. Hamilton's mind seemed as clear and powerful as ever, but he looked emaciated and very feeble physically.

Graves came out again in response to an urgent message on September 2 and this time found William fully conscious that his end was nigh. Again there was a lucid exchange on topics of a suitably religious nature, but this time terminated by a formal last farewell.

Hamilton died at 2.30 pm on the same day and Graves' account of his final moments is noteworthy:

> ... he breathed his last, having first, as I learned the following day, solemnly stretched himself at full length upon his bed, and symmetrically disposed his arms and hands, thus calmly to await his death.[36]

As in the earlier case of Eliza's death, Hankins disputes this account because of the Victorian predilection for impressive last moments. Others, more familiar with ancient custom and the Irish way of death, are likely to be less sceptical. In my opinion, Graves' accounts of both events seem to be characteristically true.

The College establishment gave Hamilton a splendid funeral, well-reported in the newspapers of the day. The body, encased in a triple suite of coffins, was brought from Dunsink to the College Chapel on September 7, 1865. After a funeral service there, a public procession followed the hearse through the city, led by the secretary of the RIA, with the Academic Mace veiled in mourning for their former President.

Hamilton was buried on the north side of the new Mount Jerome Cemetery, where his tombstone remains accessible for inspection still. He was not laid to rest beside Eliza and the other members of his family as he had often contemplated formerly. This was because the old family churchyard of St. Mary's had been closed to funerals a few years earlier; it is now a pleasant public park in modern Jervis Street.

Aftermath

William Edwin remained in charge of family matters after the funeral, winding up his father's untidy affairs with very commendable efficiency. It was he who made the final publication arrangements for the near completed *Elements of Quaternions* — the book on which Hamilton had laboured so unceasingly for his last seven years. The Board, very generously, assumed responsibility for all sums outstanding, thereby expending a total of more than £400 in addition to the £50 Hamilton had already paid. The copyright was left with the family in return for donation of all Hamilton's papers to the College archives, there being some hope for a time that the book might even bring in profitable royalties.

Elements of Quaternions however turned out to be a mighty tome of some eight hundred pages, a volume every bit as generally indigestible as the earlier *Lectures*. Those few who could read it found the content turgid and over-developed; probably it would have been a better presentation had William restricted it to one hundred and sixty pages at the most. Only 500 copies of the *Elements* were therefore ever printed, even though this limitation meant that there was soon a brisk trade in second-hand copies.[37]

William Edwin also arranged with Robert Graves to write the authorised biography, that massive work to which the modern scholar must remain so indebted. Graves collected as much as he could of Hamilton's correspondence, in addition to the formidable total already present at the observatory. His three-part work, of some eight hundred thousand words, appeared between 1882 and 1891 and is now available again in a modern edition.[38]

Graves was thorough, fair and highly illuminating in his vast labour of bringing some order into Hamilton's chaotic papers. He was almost eighty when he finished and he received an honorary doctorate from Dublin University for his work of twenty years. Trinity College supported the publication with a minor subsidy, so that its generosity towards Hamilton did not end with the *Elements*.

Hamilton's civil pension of £200 was transferred to his wife and daughter equally. The former retired to a cottage in nearby Drumcondra and died as a blind, total recluse in 1869. If she had taken her duties as a wife more seriously, Hamilton would likely have lived for many more years.

Their daughter, Helen Eliza, married in the same year that her mother died. Her husband was the Rev. John O'Regan, long a local friend of the family. She was 29 and he was 52 at the time of their marriage, but both were evidently very happy together for just one short year. Then Helen died from complications following the birth of their son John, a boy of fine intellect who eventually grew up as Hamilton's only known grandchild.[39] From him is descended the O'Regan family of Marlborough, England — the source of many further Hamilton letters which were recently added to the Trinity College archives.[40]

William Edwin eventually emigrated to Canada after he had wound up his father's affairs so effectively. There he is last heard of in 1891, as an advertising entrepeneur and editorial contributor to the *Planet* newspaper in Chatham, Ontario.[41] Whether he ever married remains unknown, so that there is an obvious need for local scholars to round off this part of the Hamilton family history.

Archibald never succeeded in holding down a permanent job as a curate and some of his surviving letters reveal clear signs of growing mental instability.[42] As with Helen and William Edwin, Hankins has traced his life as far as possible.[43] Effectively he remained dependent on the O'Regan family for support, an eccentric old clergyman, greatly beloved by children, around Clogher until his death in 1914.

The redoubtable Sydney proved herself by far the toughest and most realistic of the original family. After the death of Archianna in 1860, she decided to emigrate to Nicaragua in a bid for a new life at the age of 51. She went there on a venture scheme, promoted by the fraudulent Dr. Cullen, to cut a canal across the Isthmus of Darien. She also had hopes that she could secure an appointment to reorganise the derelict observatory at Bogota, high in the mountains four hundred miles southeast.[44] Hamilton's youthful dream of creating an astronomer from one of his sisters, in the manner of Caroline Herschel, therefore evidently was still not entirely dead.

Sydney took her unemployed nephew, William Edwin, along with her on this expedition, but conditions proved so tough that he soon returned home. For about a decade, she supported herself somehow in Central America until William's wife and daughter were both dead. Then the Irish scientific establishment tried unsuccessfully to get the annual civil pension of £200 extended on Sydney's behalf. Meantime the prospects for Bogota Observatory had proven every bit as chimerical as Cullen's mythical canal.

Around 1872, Sydney returned to Ireland but then, aged over 60, she set out again for foreign parts. This time, she travelled to New Zealand, possibly as a governess or nanny to some emigrating Irish family. In any case, Sydney's second emigration venture proved unexpectedly more fortunate than her first. The Governor of New Zealand was Sir George Grey, a much travelled colonial administrator who also happened to be a great devotee of quaternions! As soon as he heard that their inventor's sister was now in the locality, he sent for her officially.[45]

Grey had served for a time in Ireland with the British Army during Hamilton's early Dunsink days. He was also a friend of Babbage and of other British Association members and so likely had met William personally. Doubtless his influence now helped Sydney to gain a new post as matron of Auckland Asylum for the Insane.[46]

Although this employment provided free accommodation together with £66 annually, working conditions were apparently far from satisfactory. The staff were severely overworked and the new matron was seldom able to leave her post. And a report by the Inspector during 1874 regrets "to say that I have witnessed very unseemly disputes and altercations between the Matron and some of the female attendants."[47]

By 1878, this state of affairs had evidently deteriorated and in September of that year, Sydney resigned along with the superintendent, Dr. Aickin. She then went to live as a paying guest and general companion to a Mrs. Robertson, whose brother had known William in Ireland. Her income came in the form of cheques from the ever-loyal O'Regans and Sir George Grey also evidently continued to help out in various ways.

In her last extant letter of April 1888, Sydney thanks the Governor for his continuing kindness. She apologises for being unable to receive him on his latest social call because of illness and, in a sentence oddly reminiscent of her famous brother, explains that the state of her bedroom "is not fit to bring any stranger into."[48]

Sydney also gave Sir George the presentation copy of Hamilton's biography which Robert Graves sent to her. When she finally died at the age of 79 on March 3, 1889, she was buried in Auckland Public Cemetry between the Aickin and Robertson family plots. Graves sent out a tombstone recording her connection with her famous brother; thus was the last of the family, so tragically orphaned in 1819, finally laid to rest.[49]

13 HAMILTON IN PERSPECTIVE

"My childish acquaintance with various languages may, as I have often since thought, have assisted me in my maturer study of mathematical symbols, and even in my attempts to enlarge the limits of mathematical expression."

Hamilton to de Morgan, April 16, 1852

Apart from the many fascinating characteristics of his private personality, the story of William Rowan Hamilton presents at least four general aspects which are of especial interest. He was an astronomer, who rarely pursued his official vocation after the early days, and also a first-rate scientist, who probably never carried out one real practical experiment. He was a poet who probably considered himself to be better than he really was. And finally his life and achievements provide an excellent case history in the study of genius or creativity.

In this final chapter, it seems therefore fitting to establish an overall perspective on each of these four fields in turn.

The Astronomer

Ireland had four major or continuously operating observatories during Hamilton's lifetime. These were at Dunsink, Armagh, Markree and Birr.[1] None of the last three enjoyed Dunsink's distinct advantage as official home of the Astronomer Royal nor its close connection with the country's major university.

Considering Birr first as the most important, it was there that the world's largest telescope was produced during Hamilton's middle years. William Parsons, later the third Earl of Rosse, had the great advantage in his scientific endeavours of a family castle and a large fortune. His real contribution was to extend the difficult art of casting speculum metal alloy to the point where he could produce a six-foot mirror by 1845. When this was mounted in the great Birr telescope, its unprecedented resolving power enabled the spiral nature of the nebulae to be established immediately.[2]

Hamilton called at Birr frequently to inspect these wonders at various times from 1833 onwards. But he never sought to apply his new theoretical approach to optics to any of the practical problems encountered in the Rosse design. This was probably because he always regarded himself as a very 'pure' applied mathematician. Still, the paradox remains that Ireland produced both the most advanced system of theoretical optics and the world's greatest telescope within fifteen years of each other, without any fruitful interaction between the two.

Armagh naturally follows Birr in the list of achievements in Irish astronomy. There, around 1845, Romney Robinson invented the familiar spinning-cup anemometer, an instrument so efficient at measuring wind speeds that it is still in worldwide use. Robinson was also an assiduous and meticulous observer, and the great Armagh Catalogue of 1859 records the location of 5,345 stars. Twenty years later, the location of another thousand stars was published by the Royal Dublin Society.

Despite the fact that Robinson and Hamilton were always firm personal friends, official co-operation between Dunsink and Armagh was at best fitful. The only real joint experiment took place in 1838, when rockets fired from the summit of Slieve Gullion, northwest of Dundalk, were noted by both observatories. As might be expected, Robinson was the main inspiration and organiser but, even so, Hamilton seems to have neglected some of Dunsink's half of the observational schedule.[3]

Ireland's third observatory was at Markree in County Sligo. There, on his family estate, the remarkable Edward Joshua Cooper seems to have been stimulated by the Birr Castle developments. At any rate, his ample private means enabled him to buy in about 1831 the world's largest refractor lens — a suitable rival to the record reflector Rosse was trying to build.

Cooper proved even more assiduous than Robinson at identifying and recording new stars. Over 60,000 were located at Markree and their listing published at government expense in 1851, of which only about 9,000 were already known. Three years earlier, Markree had located an asteroid or minor planet dubbed Metis and this became known as the 'Irish Planet' for a time. Such was Cooper's enthusiasm in general that Markree was widely regarded as one of the most richly furnished of all private observatories.[4]

Compared with these dazzling achievements, the record of Dunsink under Hamilton seems almost dismal. Earlier, Brinkley had caused a worthwhile if mistaken stir with his supposed discovery of stellar parallax, the end result of which was a general tightening of observational routines. Nothing of a similar nature or practical interest ever emerged during his successor's reign.[5]

This is readily understandable, however, when one realises that observatory work at this period was almost entirely a matter of collecting new data patiently. Nor was there ever much likelihood of any new scientific laws or sweeping generalisations emerging from such work. For it was science mainly at the lowest possible level of data collection and, as such, quite unsuited to Hamilton's soaring mind and strongly imaginative tendencies.

Dunsink then remained a rather mediocre institution throughout Hamilton's stewardship, at once the most official but also least productive of Ireland's four main observatories. Hamilton could never remain long committed to the sheer drudgery involved in much of stellar observation; in this sense, Brinkley was quite correct when he cautioned his former protégé against accepting the post at the inexperienced age of twenty-two.

The Scientist

If Hamilton was then a total failure as a practising astronomer, he was of course at the same time universally recognised as the greatest English-speaking mathematician of his epoch. And while his fellow astronomers recognised well this disparity, they were still thankful for his presence. To them, a mathematician of such ability was obviously more valuable than just another cataloguer of the stars.[6]

Trinity College too was proud of his eminence, while still sometimes deploring his failure in practical observatory routines. That the Board soon recognised their initial error in his appointment is proved by the three abortive attempts to transfer him to a more suitable post within the College structure. But they should have created a special Chair of Mathematics for William, the better to nurture his undoubted and unceasing productivity.[7]

Dunsink however was still not entirely a hindrance to the development of Hamilton. Anybody who knows its eminent site and the woody paths along the neighbouring Tolka can hardly doubt that it must have helped to inspire genius a century and a half ago. Even now, a certain sense of peace and tranquility still envelops the area and it is easy to understand how this must have played a role in Hamilton's thinking when he inhabited the locality.

On the other hand, Dunsink was also relatively distant from Trinity, about five miles away. There Hamilton's academic duties required little more than the statutory twelve annual lectures on astronomy. So isolation was a major disadvantage during the last third of his life, when he was almost entirely alone in his development of quaternions.

Had Hamilton for example been more in daily contact with fellow scholars and with questioning pupils during this stage, his two large books on quaternions could hardly have wandered off into general incomprehensibility. A student audience might have provided sufficient feedback to enable him to realise how difficult others found ideas which were instantly obvious to him. So a new school of quaternionists could have developed round the master, with eager disciples branching out to spread the message more effectively.

Although it has been customary to term Hamilton a mathematician, he might perhaps equally be termed a mathematical physicist nowadays. This is because his aim was often to express the existing laws of physics in a superior or more elegant form. Such, for example, was his achievement in his early novel algebraic approach to optics and equally in his extension of the same treatment to dynamics in 1834.

The latter is of course now regarded as Hamilton's single greatest achievement. This is because it was found to be so remarkably suited to the modern mathematical investigation of atomic structure according to the quantum or wave-particle idea. Atomic fission, chemical bonds and laser beams are among the modern developments now irrevocably grounded in these same mathematics. In fact, no hour passes but some scientist somewhere uses Hamilton's mathematics to investigate such phenomena. It is therefore easy to understand Schrödinger's conclusion that Hamilton was possibly one of the greatest scientists who ever lived.[8]

William himself however could have known nothing of all this when he died in 1865, still struggling to finish his epic second book on quaternions. Ironically, therefore, he was blind to the real source of his future fame, while yet concentrating vainly to further an even greater dream which the rest of science eventually refused to share. To Hamilton, quaternions represented a completely new method of mathematical notation, one capable of displacing all previous methods including Cartesian geometry. This indeed they were entirely capable of doing; that such never happened was simply because most people found them far too difficult.

William Thomson (later Lord Kelvin), for example, could never find any instance where quaternions were superior to existing methods which had served well enough previously. That they were novel and different was obvious. But that they were more effective or superior was not.

Ironically, Hamilton never seems to have understood this properly. Once his own mind grew rapidly acclimatised to thinking in the new quaternion mode, he genuinely believed that others should find his method equally simple. Friends like Herschel and de Morgan tried to warn him repeatedly but with little effect, presumably because Hamilton really required more constant feedback and criticism at the level of everyday contact.

The final great irony in quaternions also passed entirely unrecognised by their obsessed discoverer. He never realised that once he had invented them as the first new or unconventional algebra, many other different new systems would also become feasible. Inevitably some of these systems proved simpler to work with than the very first method realised by Hamilton. So the primary key to the new continent which he had discovered soon proved to be obsolescent.[9]

Although this state of affairs may always change again as science develops further, quaternions at present seem to be mainly of historical interest.[10] They are important as the first developed system of unconventional algebra, obeying laws other than those in the algebra people learnt at school. Likewise, their four elements foreshadow almost eerily the later concept of space-time in relativity, the twentieth-century revolution by which Einstein finally displaced Newton.[11]

Hamilton would have found it very difficult to develop the modern space-time concept given the limited physical ideas of his era. That he was however groping towards something similar seems obvious, most simply as expressed in his poem *The Tetractys*, written for Herschel in 1846:

> And how the One of Time, of Space the Three,
> Might, in the Chain of Symbol, girdled be.[12]

It therefore becomes easier, in overall perspective, for us to appreciate Synge's description of Hamilton as a really extraordinary man — an early Victorian figure who belonged to the previous century while still writing for our own.[13]

Hamilton's prolonged metaphysical speculations on time and algebra may also have had another concrete result which has not been emphasised previously. His 1835 paper on this topic must have been among the earliest, if not indeed the first, wherein any scientist anywhere seriously proposed that time deserves to be dealt with as a separate science on its own.[14] There matters largely rested until a revival of interest in the possibility of such a science arose with relativity in the early part of the present century.

Our present interest in time did not, however, come to a fruitful focal point until G. J. Whitrow published his famous *Natural Philosophy of Time* in 1961. In the introduction to this work, Whitrow acknowledges that his work had been antedated by J. L. Synge's plea for more interest in time as a separate scientific discipline — a plea which had appeared in the *New Scientist* two years earlier.[15]

J. L. Synge had been Professor of Natural Philosophy at Dublin University between 1925 and 1930, and during this period made the first catalogue of Hamilton's voluminous notebooks from a mathematical viewpoint.[16] References to a possible science of time (which Hamilton of course equated with algebra) are frequent throughout these notebooks and in the subsequent catalogue. The link, from Hamilton through Synge to the modern interest in time as a wholly separate science in its own right, seems therefore obvious. That Hamilton appears to have been the very first to raise the possibility of time as a separate science seems equally clear.

The Poet

Hamilton of course also devoted great thought to poetry and approximately one hundred and fifty of his poems have survived. Some of these are inevitably more striking than others and nearly all of them now seem to be very dated in style. Accepting these constraints, much of Hamilton's poetry still seems acceptable and accomplished, at least to me. His verses are far from the banal compositions sometimes unknowingly proposed.

One reason why Hamilton devoted such time to poetry is that he regarded it as one of the highest possible expression of creativity. Naturally it ranked below religion and metaphysics in his scale of creative values. But it still ranked equal to mathematics when he assigned importance to the rank of things.[16a]

We can perhaps even surmise that William would have preferred to have been a poet rather than a mathematician, a preference inherent in a rather wistful observation he made to Robert Graves when aged fifty:

> *July 18, 1855* . . . But it deeply presses on my reflections how much wiser is Tennyson's *Princess* than my *Quaternions*.[17]

In any case, Hamilton's poems are inevitably of lasting interest because of all they tell us about the man. The topics which he thought worth writing about are in themselves revealing clues to his interests and character, and the manner and frequency with which he wrote about them even more so. His habit of verse composition at important moments may nowadays seem unusual, but it was a common practice among the educated in Victorian times.

Curiously enough, very few of Hamilton's poems treat of mathematics, either indirectly or explicitly. Indeed the only example that comes readily to mind is his 1846 poem, *The Tetractys*, quoted earlier — a sonnet wherein he fancifully connects quaternions with ancient Pythagorean lore.[17a]

Otherwise Hamilton probably felt that mathematics and poetry were best kept separate as expressions of his creativity. For us the important thing about his poetry is that it affords a reliable guide to his non-mathematical thinking and personal interests.

Without the evidence of his many poems about his lost love, we would then know less of Hamilton's lifelong infatuation with Catherine Disney. His early great drive towards scientific fame comes across more clearly in all those verses to Catherine than in his prose writings. So too does his habitual regard for natural beauty as expressed in his verses about the Dargle and Tolka streams.[18]

Hamilton was also of course stirred by the major historical happenings of his era. And these form a considerable segment of his poems. The accession of Queen Victoria in 1837 and her arrival in Dublin in 1851 were both celebrated by sonnets full of loyal sentiment; a military setback in the Khyber during 1842 was also commemorated in suitably dolorous lines. But we have also seen how the saddest event in the entire history of his native land — the cataclysmic famine of 1845-48 — passes by totally unversified. This omission of course provides a remarkable insight into Hamilton's psyche. Somewhat like his mathematics and his romantic longings, Hamilton's poetry offers a highly idealised and selective interpretation of reality. As such, it expresses a viewpoint not always in total harmony with the real world.

Finally it should be noticed that not all of Hamilton's many poems were in a solemn, serious or morbid vein. Unlike his sister Eliza, he possessed the invaluable gift of being able to laugh sometimes at his own solemnity. A good example is contained in his account of a celebratory dinner attended by him in his forty-sixth year:

> I helped the soup without any splashing,
> And also the salmon without much mashing;
> Cut up the fowls in morsels nice,
> And served about the melting ice;

> And seeking every taste to please,
> Scooped out the ripe and rotten cheese . . .[19]

Here, almost for the last time, emerges an echo of that younger Hamilton, the cheerful radiant character whose very presence could light up a party room. The cares of a disastrous marriage, which stamp his later portraits with such heavy solemnity, had evidently not yet entirely effaced that earlier and far more cheerful personality.

Let us then be duly grateful that Hamilton saw fit to reveal so much of himself through his many poems; without them, we would obviously know far less about his remarkable personality and character.

The Prodigy

Almost from infancy, Hamilton was of course well recognised as a prodigy — a person of such extraordinary attainment as to inspire wonder. Child prodigies of one sort or another are really not all that unusual, but it is not too often that they grow up to fulfil their early promise as young William duly did.

In addition however, Hamilton was always greatly conscious of what he regarded as his duty to leave an adequate record of his mental workings for posterity. This may have started with Uncle James and his theory that genius was largely a matter of cultivation, given suitable material. If so, there was an obvious need to keep due records of the experiment as it developed, a requirement from which Hamilton's great regard for keeping records of all sorts may initially have stemmed. In any case, the result is that we now have an unusually complete development record for one of the greatest minds of the nineteenth century — a fascinating case history for serious students of creativity.

Apart from being naturally quick and alert, young William was also notably positive, enthusiastic, energetic and wise. He seems to have leaped to his early lessons and was soon ahead of them with very little urging; there was never any question of having to force him to study as can sometimes occur with bright but negative children.

Praise from his elders was probably the main factor in this striking urge towards early achievement. Coevals like his sisters seem to have been typically more disparaging, although what other youngsters around Trim thought of him we simply do not know. Certainly however there are no signs of rejection by his peers or classmates, but instead ample evidence of many friendships from about his fourteenth year.

All in all, the boyhood of young William then seems to have been a happy and favoured one and this despite the fact that he had lost both parents by fourteen. His early separation from his mother and the later loss of Aunt Sydney must however have affected his psyche deeply. Taken in conjunction with his later loss of Catherine Disney at a crucial stage, we can see how his apparent and pronounced inferiority complex *vis-à-vis* the opposite sex naturally came to be.

His early ready obedience to his elders however also left young William worldly wise in other ways. They were never slow in urging him to self-promotion, as with his famous call on the Persian Ambassador or his first visit to Brinkley at Dunsink. Indeed the same canny attitudes persisted during all his life, with Hamilton always quick to ingratiate himself with people who might be of advantage later on. As well as being naturally clever and hard-working, Hamilton then had a large amount of career wisdom — a quality perhaps not always apparent in the highly creative.

To cap these qualities, Hamilton was always deeply ambitious, not so much in worldly matters as in his constant pursuit of ever-greater fame. Knighthood at the age of thirty probably only spurred him further, his real ambition being to become a second Newton as Brinkley had prophesied when he was just eighteen.

This was the chance which he really foresaw as soon as he grasped the essence of quaternions in the famous episode at Brougham Bridge. To create an entire new mathematical language, capable of superseding many existing notational schemes across all mathematics, would obviously have been an achievement sufficient for even Hamilton's idea of everlasting fame. His weakness lay in his refusal to recognise that the new language of his creation was not necessarily any better than the old.

That Hamilton was nevertheless always a genuine prodigy in mathematics stemmed also in part from his truly prodigious working ways. No calculation was ever too involved for him. Nor would he hesitate to pursue a laborious problem in arithmetic to the tenth decimal place.[20] One cannot help thinking that, in such matters, he would have benefitted greatly from even the cheapest modern pocket calculator!

On the other hand, the many hours Hamilton spent in such arithmetical drudgery probably conferred an unusual degree of familiarity with whatever problem was in hand. The same applied to his repeated drafts of important papers in the effort to achieve ultimate elegance and economy of style. Indeed it was precisely because of such characteristic absolute attention to detail that he was enabled to discover the conical refraction phenomenon in 1832.

Hamilton was also naturally optimistic and self-confident; he seems to have possessed a genuine power of inspiration which enabled him to divine intuitively the direction in which progress might be made. Once he had grasped this true direction, mighty labours of calculation and development would remain. Such, for example, was his immediate realisation of the years of work which stretched ahead of him after his first sudden formulation of quaternions.

Obviously Hamilton's subconscious had long been busy before such ideas surfaced into consciousness. Often he speaks of long periods of apparent inactivity, followed by a sudden burst of activity which might occupy him for twelve hours at a stretch. The sudden new philosophy of triads (which he dashed off to Adare in a single morning) provides an excellent example here.

Finally, a prodigy is hardly ever total greatness; those habits which confer large distinction in some parts inevitably imply a corresponding weakness in other areas. William for example was clearly eminent in mathematics. Yet the same creative urges which made him so involved a certain carelessness in everyday finance. He therefore died in debt and worried about it and this although his Dunsink income should have been more than adequate for a normally prudent man.

A more serious weakness was his consistent refusal to explain his highly advanced thinking in terms which would be comprehensible to his intended audience. His very first paper *On Caustics*, refused by the RIA, exhibited this weakness; so also did his final two large works on quaternions, which very few could read. Well-meaning friends repeatedly warned him about these failings with no obvious result.

In this as in so many other aspects, Hamilton adhered rigidly to his sometimes unproductive habits right up to the end.

Aspects of Genius

One may then conclude that a detailed study of Hamilton affords various lessons relevant to the greater question of genius in general. To elucidate these at the detailed level of specialist psychology would require investigation beyond the scope of the present work, so that only a few very general conclusions, made in a tentative manner, seem appropriate here.

The first of these conclusions naturally concerns our understanding of what genius is normally taken to be. It has been defined as "superior power of understanding" — an unusual intellectual ability which affords new conceptual connections not previously understood. In short, the genius sees further and deeper into the nature of things than more ordinary minds.

This was obviously true of Hamilton in great degree. Whether he was making his dramatic prediction of conical refraction, employing his Characteristic Function or discovering quaternions, one common factor always stood out. At such times, he saw further and more clearly than other men.

Discovery on this plane naturally implies a high degree of specialised intelligence. From this it does not follow that the opposite must be true. For it has long been realised that high intelligence does not at all imply a corresponding degree of innovative or creative ability. This is a sometimes distressing fact of which groups like Mensa have long been painfully aware.

Neither does high intelligence necessarily function in every manifestation of the individual's personality. Hamilton, for example, excelled in mathematics beyond nearly everybody of his time. And yet in social episodes like his courtship of Ellen de Vere or Catherine Disney, we find him acting almost stupidly. The conclusion is that William's social intelligence — the ability to understand and utilise those unspoken rules which really govern society — was far below his scientific competence.

Hamilton also exhibits strong characteristics of both divergence and convergence, according to Hudson's terms.[21] Broadly, the diverger is a person of very wide interests and concerns, free-ranging in thought in the manner often popularly associated with creative artists. The converger, in contrast, seems a rather narrow-minded individual, a steady reliable person of tidy habits who might readily make a good bureaucrat.

Such personality differences can also be associated with overall levels of creativity. A diverger who can never converge seems likely to remain a sort of intellectual grasshopper, a mere purveyor of bright ideas who cannot settle to the task of developing any of them. A converger, on the other hand, seems unlikely ever to have any new ideas at all! A steady output of creative genius may imply the ability to switch at will between the two contrasting personality profiles.

Hamilton seems to fit this pattern rather well. In retrospect, his strong interests in matters like the Holy Trinity seem not unconnected with his other considerations of the basic mathematical symbols — minus, zero, plus. These in turn he sought to relate to the three great temporal classifications of future, present and past. And all of this thinking would eventually lead him to his most highly regarded discovery which was quaternions.

Equally, however, Hamilton never lacked the very essential elements of discipline and energy with which to labour over the further development of such ideas. The huge mass of mathematical calculations in his manuscripts is abundant testimony to his ability to converge when necessary. They also imply that, like Newton, he must have been 'thinking into' such problems more or less continuously.

The case of Airy forms an interesting contrast here. He comes across very strongly as a converger — a tidy-minded scientific bureaucrat whose strong tendency to file everything eventually became a joke among his peers. Airy seems to have been inherently resistant to new ideas and often expressed his opposition to Hamilton's metaphysical divergencies.

Novel ideas themselves of course are not all of equal merit or importance; it can be helpful to classify them in four ascending levels of creativity. Each of these levels is apparent in the case of Hamilton and so it becomes instructive to consider each of them in turn.

The first or lowest level of creativity can then find expression in some minor improvement to an existing concept or mechanism. Basically, this is therefore the 'better mousetrap' level. Hamilton attained it with the hodograph and also with the improved semaphore designed during his schooldays at Trim.

A somewhat higher level of creativity may be required for production of some new phenomenon. In technology, inventions like the jet engine or hovercraft are obviously more creative than a new can-opener. So they exemplify this second level. With Hamilton, we can assign the discovery of conical refraction to a similar plane.

A third and much rarer level of creativity seems present when somebody advances a new scientific law. If this new law is a major one, its discoverer joins the ranks of the top few hundred scientists of all time. Boyle, Stokes, Avogadro and many other such names familiar to science all showed creativity to this unusual degree. So too undisputably did Hamilton with his optical-mechanical analogy, so widely used today.

The fourth and highest level of creativity, however, may change all future thought in the widest possible manner for evermore. An educated person can now hardly think of motion without being influenced by Newton and Einstein nor can he get far in biology without considering Darwin. These great household names are in the ranks of the top few dozen of all thinkers ever and they are the real immortals whom young William so ardently made up his mind to join.

This topmost pinnacle Hamilton never quite attained. Had quaternions really turned out to be an acceptable new key to the universe as he expected, then he might well be regarded on the Newton plane today. In practice, of course, quaternions have never become established (at least so far) and so he failed in his bid to join the real scientific immortals by the narrowest of margins.

Hamilton's failed hopes for quaternions also exemplify another curious conclusion. For the genius may not properly recognise which of his various achievements will eventually turn out to be most important in the end. Hamilton's obstinate belief in the importance of quaternions is strongly reminiscent of Newton's great faith in his own alchemist research. With Newton, optics seem to have been regarded as almost a secondary matter; so too it was with Hamilton and his main discovery of the optical-mechanical analogy.

William's ever-persistent urge to fame also illustrates the great extent to which early ambition can form the guiding force of future years. Darwin has stated somewhere that if a young man forms an ambition with sufficient purpose, then the necessary skills will gradually accrue to him like bloom which gathers on the vine. This statement seems supported throughout the life of Hamilton, there being almost a certain inevitability about his progress once the commitment to mathematics was begun.

In this progress, his highly cultured family background proved to be an invaluable asset. The infant William obviously possessed superior intellectual potential. But his subsequent development was clearly facilitated by the stimulating environment and ambitious elders among whom he lived. Had he for example been born into some Eskimo tribe, or even a remote Irish village of the same era, his path to achievement would certainly have been more difficult by far. And these same elders were socially skilful to a marked degree in furthering the interests of their prodigy. Young William's early call on the Persian Ambassador and his later visits to Brinkley shared a common serious purpose. His guardians had evidently inculcated the desirability of getting himself known in important circles and this too was yet another precept which he followed conscientiously throughout his days.

There is even a close existing parallel which highlights this point very well. This is the sad career of Robert Murphy, that other Irish prodigy of apparently similar potential born in 1809. He was born into poor circumstances in Mallow, but at the age of fifteen suddenly emerged self-educated in mathematics, after illness had kept him in bed for a year. In fact young Murphy now proved so impressive that a public subscription was raised to send him off to Cambridge; de Morgan records the general interest caused around 1825 by the fact that there were then two mathematical prodigies from Ireland.[22]

Murphy soon published several highly original papers in mathematics, so that he was likely near the level of Hamilton or at least MacCullagh. He won a Fellowship in 1829 and was a dean in Caius College within two years. Soon however he "had fallen into dissipated habits", so that his creditors forced him to leave College in 1832. After seeking temporary refuge in Ireland, he tried to make a comeback four years later, but this was terminated by his early death in 1843.

Murphy then seems to have resembled MacCullagh in that both likely found their lowly origins to have been a handicap in the nineteenth-century university milieu. But no such drawback ever hindered Hamilton, accustomed as he was to move in the proper circles from the earliest years.

Most of these few conclusions on genius as manifested by William seem generally applicable to others of similar intellect in any age. There is however one final and very striking aspect of Hamilton's story which may be less widely applicable. This is the great extent to which his intellect was deliberately shaped, and almost perhaps created, during his first eighteen years under Uncle James at Trim.

The Jesuits have been reputed to hold that the dominant adult patterns are established by late childhood. This seems eminently obvious in William's case, notably in the great felicity with which he persevered in various personal habits picked up during early days. That this aspect may be less obvious in the case of others could easily be ascribed to lack of comparable documentation on their early lives.

Uncle James evidently believed that genius could be created more or less to order from suitable starting material. Whether or not such is indeed true must still remain a question beyond the bounds of present knowledge. Perhaps it will emerge eventually that there are several distinct routes to intellectual eminence; Hamilton may then be classified as one of those geniuses who are deliberately made as much as born.

Earlier controversies between the relative merits of nature and nurture seem notably misconceived in this context. Both elements obviously have a part to play. For genius at first resembles some rare and delicate seed of uncertain origin, one which is only capable of attaining full potential with the aid of certain necessary nutrients. Nature and nurture are therefore both essential — a conclusion eminently obvious throughout the life of William Rowan Hamilton.

SOURCES AND REFERENCES

The main body of Hamilton papers, lodged in the Manuscript Library of Trinity College, Dublin, contains his mathematical papers and notebooks, his correspondence and miscellaneous items, together with further papers and letters acquired from the O'Regan and Graves families. These various items are catalogued and where referred to here will be identified as TCD Ms. x/y. The first of the numerals refers to the manuscript collection and the second to the serial number of the item referred to. The other principal sources utilised are the biographies by Graves and Hankins:

> R. P. Graves, *Life of Sir William Rowan Hamilton.* Dublin: Hodges Figgis, 1882-1891.

> T. L. Hankins, *Sir William Rowan Hamilton.* Baltimore: Johns Hopkins U.P., 1980.

After initial references, these biographies are referenced as follows: Graves, *Life,* p. x. and Hankins, p. x.

After initial references, the National Library of Ireland and the Dictionary of National Biography are referenced in abbreviated form, NLI and DNB respectively.

PREFACE

1. C. Holborn, A New Visibility for Gifted Children, *Science*, Vol. 210, November 1980, p. 879.

2. J. L. Synge, *Scripta Mathematica*, Vol. 2. New York, 1945, p. 18.

3. R. P. Graves, *Life of Sir William Rowan Hamilton.* Dublin: Hodges Figgis, 1882-1891.

4. T. L. Hankins, *Sir William Rowan Hamilton.* Baltimore: Johns Hopkins U.P., 1980.

5. The Einstein archives, for example, contain over forty thousand documents; cf. J. Walsh on this topic, *Science*, Vol. 213, July 1981, p. 309.

CHAPTER 1

1. Letter to de Morgan, July 26, 1852. TCD Ms. 1493/626. See also TCD Ms. 5123/33-2136 for tentative family tree back to 1617.

2. G.T. Black, *Surnames of Scotland*. New York Public Library, 1962.

3. D. Douglas, *Scottish Peerage*, Vol. 4. Edinburgh, 1907.

4. *Dictionary of National Biography*, Vol. 7. London, 1882, p. 1068.

5. *The Book of Trinity College Dublin 1591-1891*. Dublin: Hodges Figgis, 1892.

6. DNB, Vol. 7, p. 1107.

7. *ibid*. Vol. 7, p. 1070; cf. also Patrick Moore, *Armagh Observatory*. Armagh, 1967, p. 7.

8. DNB, Vol. 7, p. 1031.

9. *ibid*. Vol. 7, p. 1071.

10. *ibid*. Vol. 17, p. 332; cf. also Harold Nicolson, *The Desire to Please*. London: Constable, 1943, p. 170 *et seq*.

11. Since Hamilton was born on August 3-4, 1805, the important time would have been ca. November 1, 1804, when however A. H. Rowan was in London under strict banishment.

12. Graves, *Life*. Vol. 1, p. 3 *et seq*.

13. H. Nicolson, *The Desire to Please*. London: Constable, 1943, p. 35.

14. Collection of Dublin Street Directories, 1750-1800, National Library of Ireland, Dublin.

15. This was the annual sum which accrued to A. H. Rowan in her will.

16. Graves, *Life*. Vol. 1, p. 8. This birth date and also that of another brother Arthur, given in the family tree constructed by Graves, does not agree with the parish records of St. Mary's Church.

17. *Parish Records of St.Patrick's Church, Dublin*. NLI.

17a. P.G.Tait, Tribute to Hamilton, *North British Review*. September 1866.

18. Arthur was the cousin of James and Archibald and therefore really a distant uncle to WRH. He was also known as 'Counsellor', a common legal nickname in Ireland then.

19. Notes on family history by Eliza (undated). TCD Ms. 5123/33-1773.

20. Graves, *Life*. Vol. 1, p. 5; Hankins, p. 400.

21. There were two local churches of St. Mary's with which the Dublin Hamiltons were associated. One was the old parish church in Jervis Street which still survives. The other was the Moravian Church of St. Mary's in Bethesda Place one mile to the north, a derelict cinema in 1982!

22. This time was recorded by Archibald, not always wholly reliable in such matters! For the significance of the midnight birth, cf. F. Manuel, *Portrait of Newton*. London: Muller, 1980, p. 29.

CHAPTER 2

1. Graves, *Life*. Vol. 1, pp. 29-30.

2. Trade Directories suggest that Archibald's practice was expanding greatly between 1800 and 1809.

3. The purchasing power of £1 during William Rowan Hamilton's lifetime may be taken as twenty or twenty-five times its 1982 value. Cf. Prof. Ivor Pearce, *Sunday Telegraph*, April 11, 1982.

4. Graves, *Life*. Vol. 1, p. 13; Nicholson, *The Desire to Please*. p. 176 *et seq*.

5. Plea for the sect of Seceders by A. Hamilton, March 1812(?). TCD Ms. 7762/72-15.

6. Graves, *Life*. Vol. 1, p. 53.

7. E. T. Bell, *Men of Mathematics*. London: Penguin, 1953, p. 373.

8. Family reminiscences. TCD Ms. 5123/33-1922.

9. Michael Quene, *Ríocht na Mídhe*. 1971, Vol. 1, p. 40. This article is the source of most of our extra knowledge about Uncle James and the Diocesan School of Trim.

10. Sermon by Rev. James Hamilton. NLI, p. 1958.

11. E. Evans, *The Ruins of Trim*. Dublin, 1886.

12. Unreferenced quotations in this chapter can be found in Graves, *Life*. Vol. 1, pp. 29-43. Others are numbered as necessary. As with most quotations henceforth, these have been subdivided into paragraphs where appropriate.

13. TCD Ms. 5123/33-2139; the next quote of January 4, 1811, is from the same source.

14. TCD Ms. 7762/72-12

15. *ibid* — 13

16. *ibid* — 9

17. Graves, *Life*. Vol. 1, p. 45.

18. *ibid*. p. 47.

19. Hankins, p. 13.

20. This legend started with P. G. Tait's obituary in the *North British Review* 45, 1866, pp. 37-74. It then became strengthened through language accretion starting with the subsequent edition of *Encyclopaedia Britannica*.

21. E. T. Bell, *Men of Mathematics*. London: Penguin, 1953, p. 374.

22. *Dictionary of Scientists*. London: Chambers, 1966, p. 106. Other works quote fifteen, and one author even credits Hamilton with *fifty* languages, e.g. Bryan Morgan, *Men and Discoveries in Mathematics*. London, 1972.

23. TCD Ms. 5123/33-2028.

24. Sanskrit alphabet copied out by WRH. TCD Ms. 5123/33-2084; minor Sanskrit translation by WRH, TCD Ms. 5123/33-2281.

25. Letter from WRH to Aunt Mary Hutton, September 16, 1822; Graves, *Life*. Vol. 1, p. 113.

26. WRH to Aubrey de Vere, September 24, 1832; Graves, *Life*. Vol. 1, p. 614.

27. WRH to de Morgan, January 3, 1855; Graves, *Life*. Vol. 3, p. 491.

28. C. Holden, A New Visibility for Gifted Children, *Science*, Vol. 210, November 1980, p. 879.

29. These stages of mathematical achievement are recorded in Graves, *Life*. Vol. 1, pp. 46-77.

CHAPTER 3

1. E.T.Bell, *Men of Mathematics*. p. 374.

2. Michael Quene, *Ríocht na Mídhe*. Vol. 1, p. 40.

3. Sermon by Rev. James Hamilton. NLI, p. 1958.

4. S. Lewis, *Topographical Dictionary of Ireland*. 1837, Vol. 2, p. 643.

5. There seems to be growing evidence of late that children may readily be educated to a much higher level than generally believed. Cf. the recent case of Ruth Lawrence, aged 11, who beat all 528 other candidates in the 1981 entrance examination for Oxford University. Cf. *Daily Telegraph*, May 17, 1982 *et seq.*

6. TCD Ms. 7762/72-19.

7. Graves, *Life*. Vol. 1, p. 76.

8. Rudimentary Oriental language exercises. TCD Ms. 5123/33-2082 *et seq.*

9. Graves, *Life*. Vol. 1, p. 55; TCD Ms. 5123/33-48.

10. Graves, *Life*. Vol. 1, p. 14.

11. *ibid*. p. 53

12. WRH to Archibald, March 4, 1819. TCD Ms. 5123/33-27; Graves, *Life*. Vol. 1, p. 55.

13. Family Reminiscences. TCD Ms. 5123/33-1922; Graves, *Life*. Vol. 3, p. 153.

14. Archibald to WRH, March 16, 1819. TCD Ms. 5123/33-28; Archibald to WRH, May 20, 1819; Graves, *Life*. Vol. 1, p. 57.

15. *ibid*. Vol. 2, p. 594. Of Archianna he writes: "though possessed of some faculties in at least average degree, (she) was deficient in practical ability."

16. TCD Ms. 5123/33-36; Graves, *Life*. Vol. 1, p. 61.

17. WRH to Eliza, July 17, 1819. TCD Ms. 5123/33-37; Graves, *Life*. Vol. 1, p. 62.

18. *ibid*. Vol. 1, p. 72.

19. Notes on family history by Eliza. TCD Ms. 5123/33-1773; Graves, *Life*. Vol. 3, p. 110.

20. E.T. Bell, *Men of Mathematics*. p. 373.

21. WRH to Eliza, January 1820. TCD Ms. 1493-1; Graves, *Life*. Vol. 1, p. 75.

22. *ibid*. Vol. 2, p. 198; Vol. 3, p. 83.

23. Cf. Chapter 9, this volume 'Discovery of Quaternions'.

24. Graves, *Life*. Vol.1, p. 95.

25. *ibid*. Vol. 1, p. 120.

26. *ibid*. Vol. 1, p. 139.

27. *ibid*. Vol. 1, p. 104.

28. TCD Ms. 5123/33-23.

29. The Edgeworth semaphore had four twenty-foot triangles, four circles and eight pointures. Manipulation of these afforded a total of some 7,000 combinations intended to be looked up in a special code book!

30. WRH to Robert Graves, July 21, 1841. TCD Ms. 5123/33-816.

31. WRH to Cousin Arthur, July 11, 1843. TCD Ms. 5123/33-68.

32. DNB, Vol. 2, p. 1255.

33. Graves, *Life*. Vol. 1, p. 102; Essay on Value of 0/0, March 13, 1822. TCD Ms. 5123/33-50.

34. Graves, *Life*. Vol. 1, p. 111.

35. *ibid*. Vol. 1, p. 117.

CHAPTER 4

1. WRH to Cousin Arthur, May 31, 1823. TCD Ms. 5123/33-64; Graves, *Life*. Vol. 1, p. 181.

2. This institution furthered 'alternative' education in association with the Royal Dublin Society.

3. Graves, *Life*. Vol. 1, p. 109.

4. Collection of Dublin Street Directories, 1750-1850. NLI.

5. Hankins, p. 30.

6. WRH to Eliza, October 9, 1822; Graves, *Life*. Vol. 1, p. 115.

7. WRH to Cousin Arthur, October 12, 1822; Graves, *Life*. Vol. 1, p. 117.

8. WRH to Cousin Arthur, May 31, 1823; Graves, *Life*. Vol. 1, p. 141.

9. Gordon L. Davies, *The Story of Science in Trinity College*. Dublin: Trinity College, 1977.

9a. T. G. Paterson, *Irish Astronomical Journal*, 1959, Vol. 5, p. 6.

10. A. J. McConnell, "The Dublin Mathematical School in the First Half of the Nineteenth Century", *Proceedings R.I.A.*, 1945, 50, 6, p. 755.

11. *The Book of Trinity College, 1591-1891*.

12. Graves, *Life*. Vol. 3, p. 216.

13. *ibid*. Vol. 1, p. 148; TCD Ms. 5123/33-82.

14. Graves, *Life*. Vol.1, p. 161.

15. *ibid.* Vol.1, p. 167.

16. *ibid.* Vol.1, p. 166.

17. *ibid.* Vol.1, p. 181; TCD Ms. 5123/33-100.

18. Graves, *Life.* Vol. 1, p. 129.

19. Burke's *Guide to Irish Country Houses,* p. 158.

20. Hankins, pp. 347-358.

21. Cf. Chapter 11, this volume, 'Old Love Revives'.

22. Graves, *Life.* Vol.1, p. 174.

23. WRH to P. G. Tait, October 6, 1858. TCD Ms. 1492, Notebook 146, p. 59.

24. Graves, *Life.* Vol.1, p. 183.

25. *ibid.* Vol. 1. p. 110.

26. The Wellington Monument in Trim was erected in an incomplete state around 1819.

27. WRH to Archibald, March 29, 1818. TCD Ms. 5123/33-25.

28. Graves, *Life.* Vol.1, p. 114. Hankins notes that Hamilton had just finished reading Brewster's *Life of Newton* at this point; cf. p. 403, note 19.

29. The mathematically proficient should consult Hankins (pp. 61-87) for more specialist detail here.

30. An essay of ca. ten thousand words on *Right Lines,* acknowledged by WRH in 1834 as the direct ancestor of his *Systems of Rays.* TCD Ms. 5123/33-52.

31. Graves, *Life.* Vol. 1, p. 114.

32. *ibid.* Vol. 1, p. 141.

33. *ibid.* Vol. 1, p. 592.

34. Hankins, p. 67.

35. Graves, *Life.* Vol. 1, p. 228.

CHAPTER 5

1. Patrick Moore, *Armagh Observatory.* p. 5.

2. Séan O'Donnell, Famous Irish Scientists. *Technology Ireland,* September 1977, p. 47.

3. G. L. Davies, *The Story of Science in Trinity College,* 1977.

4. *Trans. Royal Irish Academy,* 1786, Vol. 1, p. 1.

5. *The Book of Trinity College,* p. 152.

6. Patrick Moore, *Armagh Observatory,* p. 152.

7. DNB. Vol. 4, p. 1067.

8. *ibid*. Vol. 2, p. 1255.

9. Hankins, pp. 44-45.

10. Graves, *Life*. Vol. 1, p. 233; Uncle James to WRH. TCD Ms. 1493-11F.

11. DNB. Vol. 1, p. 23.

12. Graves, *Life*. Vol. 1, p. 239; TCD Ms. 5123/33-121, -128.

13. DNB. Vol. 13, p. 512. Nimmo built many piers and harbours along the western coast as public works projects and one such in Galway City is still known as Nimmo's Pier.

14. WRH to Eliza, August 30, 1827; Graves, *Life*. Vol. 1, p. 253.

15. WRH to Eliza, September 16, 1827; Graves, *Life*. Vol. 1, p. 264.

16. Graves, *Life*. Vol. 1, p. 264.

17. *ibid*. Vol. 1, p. 266.

18. TCD Ms. 5123/33-1890.

19. WRH to R. P. Graves, July 25, 1846. TCD Ms. 1493-357.

20. Metaphysical discussions with the sisters. TCD Ms. 5123/33-2088.

21. Graves, *Life*. Vol. 1, p. 272. The same theme is repeated elsewhere, e.g. TCD Ms. 5123/33-143 or TCD Ms. 1493-25,-31,-41.

22. Hankins, p. 47.

23. Patrick Wayman, *Irish Astronomical Journal*, December 1971, p. 135.

24. Graves, *Life*. Vol. 2, p. 266.

25. See Chapter 11, this volume, 'Religion Intensified'.

26. Graves, *Life*. Vol. 1, p. 294.

27. *ibid*. Vol. 1. p. 311.

28. WRH to J. Herschel, May 8, 1829. TCD Ms. 1493-48.

CHAPTER 6

1. Graves, *Life*. Vol. 1, p. 497.

2. *ibid*. Vol. 1, pp. 501-503.

2a. TCD Ms. 5123/33-1394.

3. Hankins, pp. xvi-xix.

4. A. Friendly, *Beaufort of the Admiralty*. London: Hutchinson, 1977.

5. Graves, *Life*. Vol. 1, p. 309.

6. R. Robinson to WRH, May 14, 1831. TCD Ms. 1493-71.

7. TCD Ms. 1492, Notebook 103.5, p. 277.

8. Graves, *Life*. Vol.1, p. 361.

9. This book was published by Hodges and Smith, Dublin, at Eliza's own expense in 1838-9. WRH's annotated copy is now with the National Library in Dublin. Cf. TCD Ms. 5123/33-805.

10. WRH to Wordsworth, February 2, 1831; Graves, *Life*. Vol. 1, p. 426.

11. Graves, *Life*. Vol. 1, p. 443.

12. DNB. Vol. 4, p. 873.

13. Graves, *Life*. Vol. 1, p. 455.

14. *ibid*. Vol. 1, p. 459 *et seq*.

15. *ibid*. Vol.1, p. 518.

16. Hankins, p. 109.

17. *Dublin University Magazine*. February 1843, p. 199.

18. Adare to WRH, June 30, 1834; Graves, *Life*. Vol. 2, p. 94.

19. Graves, *Life*. Vol. 1, p. 564; Hankins, p. 112.

20. Graves, *Life*. Vol. 1, p. 622.

21. *ibid*. Vol. 2, pp. 4-5. These two pages contain four love poems written by WRH to Helen between November 6 and 12, 1832.

22. *ibid*. Vol. 2, pp. 6-10. These pages contain a further six love poems written between November 17 and 23, 1832.

23. Uncle James to WRH, January 13, 1832. TCD Ms. 5123/33-255.

24. Letters between WRH and Sydney, May 1833. TCD Ms. 5123/33-361,-363.

25. No portrait of Hamilton's wife is known to have survived. The supposed likeness reproduced by Hankins (on page 123) really depicts WRH and his daughter then aged nineteen. This picture was taken at the Fulneck Moravian Settlement near Leeds in September 1859. Cf. Graves, *Life*. Vol. 3, p. 119.

CHAPTER 7

1. Sir Joseph Larmor, *Mathematical and Physical Papers*. Cambridge U.P., Vol. 1, p. 640.

2. DNB. Vol. 1, p. 23.

3. Sir W. R. Hamilton, *The Mathematical Papers*. Cambridge U.P., 1931, 1940, 1967, plus a fourth volume now in preparation.

4. See for example, Hankins, pp. 70-81, 184-196, etc.

5. Séan O'Donnell, The Science of Time. *Technology Ireland*, February 1975, p. 27.

6. C. Lanczos, *University Review of N.U.I.*, Vol. IV, 2, 1967, pp. 151-166.

7. J. L. Synge, *Scripta Mathematica*, Vol. 2. New York, 1945, p. 16.

8. A. Schuster, *An Introduction to the Theory of Optics*. London: Arnold, 1920, pp. 179-190.

9. Graves, *Life*. Vol. 1, p. 632. Hamilton predicted an angular deviation of 1° 55′ in one case and Lloyd found it to be 1° 52′.

10. Graves, *Life*. Vol. 2, p. 532.

11. *ibid*. Vol. 1, p. 632.

12. *ibid*. Vol. 1, pp. 686-689.

13. *ibid*. Vol. 1, p. 637, quoting Airy in *London and Edinburgh Philosophical Magazine*, June 1833, p. 420.

13a. E.T.Bell, *Men of Mathematics*. p. 384.

14. Graves, *Life*. Vol. 2, p. 289.

15. *ibid*. Vol. 2, p. 73.

16. Hankins, pp. 181-198.

17. J. Herschel to WRH, June 13, 1835. TCD Ms. 1493-109; Graves, *Life*. Vol. 2, p. 127.

18. J. L. Synge, *Scripta Mathematica*, Vol. 2. 1945, p. 17.

19. P. G. Tait, *North British Review*, 1866, 45, p. 50.

20. E. Schrödinger, *Scripta Mathematica*, Vol. 2. 1945, p. 82.

CHAPTER 8

1. Graves, *Life*. Vol. 1, p. 570.

2. *ibid*. Vol. 2, p. 122.

3. *ibid*. Vol. 2, p. 154.

4. W. R. Wilde, *Dean Swift's Life*. Dublin: Hodges and Smith, 1849, p. 53 *et seq.*

5. G. L. Davies, *The Story of Science in Trinity College*. Dublin: Trinity College, 1977.

6. WRH was born August 4, 1805, and died September 2, 1865. His chronological midpoint was therefore August 18, 1835.

7. TCD Ms. 7762/72-497.

8. Sir W. R. Hamilton, *Lectures on Quaternions*. Dublin: Hodges and Smith, 1853.

9. TCD Ms. 7762/72-498.

10. WRH to Col. Sabine, May 14, 1847; Graves, *Life*. Vol. 2, p. 570. The plea of poverty was accepted by de Morgan in his *Budget of Paradoxes*, London, 1872, p. 22.

11. Clibborn to WRH, July 4, 1840. TCD Ms. 1493-185a.

12. Graves, *Life*. Vol. 1, p. 578.

13. *ibid*. Vol. 2, p. 172.

14. *ibid*. Vol. 2, pp. 212-221.

15. *ibid.* Vol. 2, p. 234; TCD Ms. 4015-88.

16. *ibid.* Vol. 2, p. 237.

17. *ibid.* Vol. 2, p. 280. Mary Sommerville had been very successful in popularising Laplace's *Mécanique Céleste* for the Society for the Diffusion of Useful Knowledge.

18. *Proceedings of the R.I.A.*, Vol. IV, p. 574.

19. Graves, *Life.* Vol. 2, p. 268.

20. *ibid.* Vol. 2, p. 341.

21. Pamphlet by WRH, July 14, 1836. TCD Ms. 7762/72 -537.

22. Pamphlet about Presidency of R.I.A., February 1840. TCD Ms. 1493-1427.

23. WRH to Grace, September 12, 1839. TCD Ms. 7762/72-721.

24. Graves, *Life.* Vol. 2, p. 506.

CHAPTER 9

1. Euclid lived around 300 BC and Pappus was one of the last great classical geometers six centuries afterwards.

2. Graves, *Life.* Vol. 1, pp. 662-671.

3. *ibid.* Vol. 1, p. 111.

4. TCD Ms. 5123/33-2088.

5. This theme appears in a great many writings by WRH over the years. *See* Letter to Adare, TCD Ms. 5123/33-450 and TCD Ms. 1493-429.

6. *Transactions R.I.A.* 1837, pp. 293-295.

7. P. G. Tait, *North British Review*, 1866, 45, pp. 37-74.

8. *ibid.* p. 56.

9. Séan O'Donnell, The Science of Time. *Technology Ireland*, February 1975.

10. Eliza had gone out to Turkey with her Willey cousins and this experience of foreign missionary work is commemorated in several of her poems.

11. Letter from her publishers to Eliza Hamilton, April 29, 1841. TCD Ms. 5123/33-805.

12. G. Ó Tuathaigh, *Ireland Before the Famine.* Dublin: Gill and Macmillan, 1979, p. 177.

13. Uncle James to WRH, June 22, 1835. TCD Ms. 5123/33-440.

14. WRH to R. P. Graves, August 25, 1846. TCD Ms. 1493/360.

15. Correspondence on behalf of nephew James. TCD Ms. 5123/33-1272. Cf. Graves, *Life.* Vol. 3, p. 6.

16. Graves, *Life.* Vol. 2, p. 147.

17. *ibid.* Vol. 2, p. 204.

18. Cf. *Sky and Telescope*. October 1981.

19. Graves, *Life*. Vol. 2, p. 339.

20. *ibid*. Vol. 2, pp. 447-449.

21. Patrick Wayman, *Irish Astronomical Journal*, December 1971, p. 135.

22. Graves, *Life*. Vol. 2, p. 421.

23. *ibid*. Vol. 1, p. 547.

24. *ibid*. Vol. 2, pp. 363-375.

25. We now know this to be impossible.

26. Hankins, pp. 283-325.

27. Graves, *Life*. Vol. 2, p. 435.

28. *ibid*. Vol. 2, p. 434. WRH to son Archibald, August 5, 1865. TCD Ms. 5123/33-669.

CHAPTER 10

1. P. G. Tait, *North British Review*, 1866, p. 57 *et seq.*

2. Hankins, p. 321.

3. WRH to Rev. M. O'Sullivan, August 4, 1853. TCD Ms. 1493/1214; Graves, *Life*. Vol. 2, p. 683.

3a. Hankins, p. 347.

4. *ibid*. p. 304.

5. Charles Graves, On Algebraic Triplets. *Proceedings R.I.A.*, 1847, 3, pp. 51-108.

6. Hankins, p.306; Graves, *Life*. Vol. 2, pp. 463-472.

7. *ibid*. Vol. 2, p. 471.

8. G. L. Davies, *The Story of Science in Trinity College*. 1977.

9. See also Graves, *Life*. Vol. 2, p. 588; Vol. 3, pp. 77, 138.

10. Graves, *Life*. Vol. 2, p. 607.

11. *Athaneum*, July 1847, p. 711.

12. Graves, *Life*. Vol. 2, p. 478.

13. C. Lanczos, *University Review of N.U.I.*, IV, 2, 1967, p. 160.

14. H. Minkowski worked out the mathematics of relativity in very fruitful form.

15. TCD Ms. 1493/408.

16. Graves, *Life*. Vol. 2, p. 633.

17. J. Herschel to WRH, November 18, 1859. TCD Ms. 5123/33-1460.

18. Graves, *Life*. Vol. 2, p. 687.

19. Lord Lieutenant to WRH, April 19, 1856. TCD Ms. 5123/33-1309.

20. WRH to M. O'Sullivan, August 4, 1853. TCD Ms. 5123/33-1219.

21. Graves, *Life*. Vol. 3, p. 189; TCD Ms. 1493-831.

22. C. Lanczos, *op. cit.*

CHAPTER 11

1. Graves, *Life*. Vol. 2, p. 523.

2. Letters to WRH from John Willey. TCD Ms. 5123/33-174,-271.

3. DNB. Vol. 12, p. 454.

4. MacCullagh to WRH (undated). TCD Ms. 1493/1972.

5. Graves, *Life*. Vol. 2, p. 596.

6. *ibid*. Vol. 2, pp. 668-670.

7. WRH to R. P. Graves, June 16, 1851. TCD Ms. 5123/33-1158.

8. Graves, *Life*. Vol. 3, p. 27.

9. DNB. Vol. 11, p.586. Lardner separated from his wife in 1820 and, at the age of 47 in 1840, eloped with another married lady.

10. NLI. 905, p. 85.

11. TCD Ms. 1492/129.5, pp.123 *et seq.*

12. WRH to Anglesey, November 15, 1848. TCD Ms. 5123/33-1085.

13. WRH to J. Barlow, January 1849. TCD Ms. 5123/33-1099. WRH to Eliza, August 19, 1850. TCD Ms. 5123/33-1129.

14. Graves, *Life*. Vol. 2, p. 652.

15. TCD Ms. 5123/33-2201.

16. NLI. 905, p. 88.

17. TCD Ms. 1492, Notebook 123.5, p. 15.

18. Graves, *Life*. Vol. 2, p. 462.

19. *ibid*. Vol. 2, p. 491.

20. *Proceedings R.I.A.*, May 9, 1842.

21. Graves, *Life*. Vol. 3, p. 142.

22. *Irish Ecclesiastical Journal*, May 1842.

23. Graves, *Life*. Vol. 3, pp. 26, 191.

24. *ibid*. Vol. 3, p. 408.

25. G. Ó Tuathaigh, *Ireland Before the Famine*. p. 204.

26. Séan O'Donnell, Famous Irish Scientists — Robert Kane. *Technology Ireland*. September 1976.

27. Graves, *Life*. Vol. 2, p. 398.

28. *ibid*. Vol. 2, p. 528.

29. *ibid*. Vol. 1, p. 25. Uncle James' son to R. P. Graves: "My dear father was not systematic or careful of his papers."

30. WRH to J. Graves, October 11, 1833. TCD Ms. 1493/92.

31. The archives contain many references going back to early days about pet animals.

32. Graves, *Life*. Vol. 3, p. 236.

33. *ibid*. Vol. 2, p. 648.

34. *ibid*. Vol. 3, p. 236.

35. De Morgan correspondence. TCD Ms. 1493/573, 719, etc.

36. Graves, *Life*. Vol. 2, p. 247.

CHAPTER 12

1. WRH to Helen, September 27, 1854. TCD Ms. 5123/33-1282.

2. Graves, *Life*. Vol. 2, p. 675.

3. WRH to de Morgan, May 9, 1855. TCD Ms. 1493/ 825.

4. Hankins, p. 56.

5. TCD Ms. 1492, Notebook 123.5, p. 139 *et seq*.

6. Graves, *Life*. Vol. 3, p. 85.

7. *ibid*. Vol. 3, p. 99; TCD Ms. 1492, Notebook 140.7, p. 163.

8. Graves, *Life*. Vol. 3, p. 160.

9. DNB. Vol. 8, p. 431.

10. Hankins, pp. 326-344.

11. John Graves was a jurist of great distinction as well as a mathematician, being professor of jurisprudence at London University College. His unique collection of 15,000 books and pamphlets concerning mathematics was left to the College in his will.

12. Correspondence with Mr. Jacques, January 1859. TCD Ms. 1493-1034, -1036, -1046.

13. Graves, *Life*. Vol. 3, p. 55.

14. E. T. Bell, *Men of Mathematics*. p. 396.

15. TCD Ms. 1493/195; Graves, *Life*, Vol. 3, p. 245.

16. The extracts given by Graves run to ca. one hundred and fifty thousand words.

17. There are many examples of Hamilton's habit of writing inside the flap just before an envelope was sealed. De Morgan often cut out these flaps for preservation while discarding the rest of the envelope. Cf. TCD Ms. 1493/1120, etc.

18. De Morgan correspondence. TCD Ms. 1493-474, -568, -719, etc.

19. WRH to de Morgan, July 26, 1852. TCD Ms. 1493/ 626.

20. Draft of Bill to Legalise Decimal Currency, May 12, 1857. TCD Ms. 1493/928. See also TCD Ms. 1493/874.

21. Salmon on Quaternions, May 6, 1892. TCD Ms. 4015/122.

22. TCD Ms. 1493/1299.

23. Hankins, p. 321.

24. Graves, *Life*. Vol. 3, pp. 140, 202.

25. Hankins, pp. 382-383.

26. Hamilton was loaning his son Archibald sums like £5 and £20 as late as the start of 1865! Cf. TCD Ms. 5123/33-1640, -1645.

27. Press clipping of Ball's account. TCD Ms. 5123/33-2294.

28. Patrick Wayman in a private communication to author.

29. Notes by WRH. TCD Ms. 5123/33-1551.

30. TCD Ms. 1493/1158.

31. Graves, *Life*. Vol. 3, p. 239.

32. Testimony of Dr. Wyse to R. P. Graves, October 27, 1884. TCD Ms. 7762/72-197.

33. Graves, *Life*. Vol. 3, pp. 180, 610.

34. *ibid*. Vol. 3, pp. 205-208.

35. W. E. Hamilton to John O'Regan. TCD Ms. 7773/76-1655, -1657.

36. Graves, *Life*. Vol. 3, p. 211.

37. *ibid*. Vol. 3, p. 202.

38. New York: Arno Publishers, 1975.

39. Hankins, pp. 380–382.

40. Cf. explanatory notes at start of these references.

41. Letter from W. E. Hamilton, January 29, 1883. TCD Ms. 4015/117.

42. TCD Ms. 7773/76-13.

43. Hankins, pp. 379-383.

44. Graves, *Life*. Vol. 3, p. 148.

45. Sir George Grey (1812-1898) was a cultivated colonial administrator of many interests and founded Auckland Public Library in 1880.

46. Auckland Public Library. GL. G26, 1,2.

47. Public Report to New Zealand House of Representatives, 1875, Sir George Grey Collection, Auckland Library, HZ, p. 2.

48. Sir George Grey Collection, GL. 42, H5.

49. Sydney's tombstone records her connection with the discoverer of quaternions. Cf. *New Zealand Herald*, March 4, 1889.

CHAPTER 13

1. Susan McKenna, *Vistas in Astronomy*. Pergamon, 1968, Vol. 9, pp. 283-296.

2. DNB. Vol. 15, p. 425.

3. Patrick Moore, *Armagh Observatory*, 1967, p. 14. Cf. TCD Ms. 5123/33-632, -703, -2021, etc. These are letters about the rocket experiment.

4. DNB. Vol. 4, p. 1066.

5. *ibid*. Vol. 2, p. 1255.

6. Graves, *Life*. Vol. 2, p. 485.

7. J. L. Synge, *Scripta Mathematica*, Vol. 2. 1945, p. 22.

8. E. Schrödinger, *ibid*, p. 82.

9. M. J. Crowe, *Science*, May 1981, p. 212.

10. C. Lanczos, *University Review of N.U.I.*, 1967, IV, 2, pp. 151-166.

11. Hankins, p. 325.

12. Graves, *Life*. Vol. 3, p. 239.

13. J. L. Synge, *op. cit.*, p. 18.

14. Séan O'Donnell, The Science of Time. *Technology Ireland*, February 1975.

15. J. L. Synge, *New Scientist*, Vol. 5, 1959, p. 410.

16. TCD Ms. 3558.

16a. Graves, *Life*. Vol. 1, p. 415.

17. *ibid*. Vol. 3, p. 188.

17a. *ibid*. Vol. 2, p. 525.

18. *ibid*. Vol. 3, p. 8.

19. WRH to de Morgan, May 26, 1851. TCD Ms. 5123/33-2184.

20. Graves, *Life*. Vol. 3, pp. 142-145.

21. Liam Hudson, *Frames of Mind*, London: Methuen, 1968.

22. DNB. Vol. 13, p. 1240.

INDEX

(WRH refers to William Rowan Hamilton; his relations with individuals appear in brackets after their names. Bold italic numerals refer to illustrations.)